THE RESPONSA LITERATURE

The
RESPONSA
Literature

BY

SOLOMON B. FREEHOF

THE JEWISH PUBLICATION SOCIETY OF AMERICA

PHILADELPHIA, 1959-5719

Copyright, 1955, by The Jewish Publication Society of America

All Rights Reserved

Library of Congress Catalog Card No.: 55-6706

Printed in the United States of America
By American Book-Stratford Press, Inc., New York

Second Printing, 1959

To my honored father

ISAAC FREEHOF

With a prayer for his health and happiness
This book is lovingly dedicated

PREFACE

Whoever writes a book in the field of Rabbinics is bound to think of the teacher who first taught him to swim in the "Sea of the Talmud." Whatever I have learned of talmudic ideas and reasoning and the development of the *Halakha* came from my unforgettable teacher, Jacob Z. Lauterbach, Professor of Rabbinics at the Hebrew Union College. I cannot know whether he would have approved of this book, but I hope that it is not entirely unworthy of his teachings.

There cannot be many scholars as thoroughly at home in the field of responsa as Rabbi Wolf Leiter of Pittsburgh. I am deeply grateful for having been the beneficiary of his prodigious memory of the contents of the responsa and his wide knowledge of the history involved.

My dear wife, Lillian Freehof, gave me constant encouragement and so much help that it would seem impossible to have undertaken the task without her assistance.

Dr. Solomon Grayzel, editor of the Jewish Publication Society of America, has been especially helpful, not only in technical matters but with his valuable judgment as to the nature and the coherence of the material. I welcome this opportunity to express my thanks to him.

SOLOMON B. FREEHOF

CONTENTS

THE RESPONSA LITERATURE

INTRODUCTION

If the greatness of a book may be judged by the amount of literature it has inspired, then there can be no question that the Bible is the greatest of books. The number of books which the Bible has evoked in almost every field of human thought, from the niceties of grammar to the wide sweep of philosophy, is far beyond computation. By the same test, the Talmud deserves the reverent attention of students of world literature. It, too, has inspired a vast number of books written by its devoted disciples. No other book of antiquity readily comes to mind—except, of course, for the Bible itself, which is incomparable—whose literary offspring is so numerous and so perennially vital. To be sure, it has happened, occasionally, that one book or another, in a certain era or in a certain environment, has spurred its readers to literary activity; but where can one find a parallel to the fact that, in almost every great country in the world where Jews have lived, books inspired by the Talmud were continually produced and, after fourteen hundred years, are still being written?

This post-talmudic, or rabbinic, literature is extraordinary in many ways beyond the fact that one book has inspired them all. Besides the objective value of the contents of the rabbinic books, the psychological and the social aspects of their production are quite extraordinary. For such books could not be dashed off in one quick burst of inspiration. They were usually the work of a lifetime of careful and laborious study, since the Talmud itself which inspired them is a difficult book, containing the subtle rea-

soning and the sharp debates which led to the development of
Jewish law. The study of the Talmud taxes the mental capacity
of its readers; even so the vast rabbinic literature born of the
Talmud is Talmud-like in keen reasoning and close-knit argu-
mentation. It is doubtful, therefore, whether any other historic
literature has ever called forth so much mental energy in as large
a percentage of its people as the talmudic literature has produced
in this small fragment of humanity.

Besides this psychological phenomenon, the rabbinic literature has had an immense sociological effect. Wherever it was
produced, this literature attained a remarkable consistency of
ideas, of logical method and of literary style. The Talmud so
deeply impressed itself upon its offspring that all rabbinic books
closely resembled one another. A book produced in Germany
could and would be read in Spain, and one produced in Turkey
would be debated in Poland. Hence it was possible for a talmudic author to leave the Rhineland in the thirteenth century
and settle in Spain; and learned correspondence could weave a
bond of unity among all the lands of Jewish dispersion. The creative comradeship of contributing to the rabbinic literature has
bound together the settlements of the people of Israel and helped
them to remain united despite repeated exile and fragmentation.

Yet this highly effective literary activity is very little known.
The post-talmudic or rabbinic books may well be called a hidden
literature. The fact that these books were produced by a small
and often persecuted people, and also that they are extremely
difficult for the uninitiated to read, has confined the rabbinic literature to the circle of those who have created it. If it had been
written in one of the widely known languages, or if its contents
were less abstruse, it would by now have been analyzed and discussed and admired in hundreds of essays, for its contents, its
keenness and its social influence, since it offers a magnificent opportunity for the study of one of the closest interrelationships
between literature and life.

Rabbinic literature has developed simultaneously along three
main lines. There were, first of all, the commentaries on the
Talmud. Since the Talmud was difficult in language and thought,

the explanation of what it says was a necessary first step. When a number of commentaries had been written, especially the great commentary of Rashi in the eleventh century, the newer rabbinic writers sought to do more than merely understand the text and the argument. Led chiefly by Rashi's grandson, Rabbenu Tam, they went far beyond the explanatory commentary which now lay before them. They questioned its explanations. They also questioned the apparent meaning of the Talmud itself, citing passages from some other tractate of the Talmud which seemed to contradict the passage under discussion. After they had brought various apparent contradictions together, they re-explained and harmonized them.

Actually this type of harmonizing commentary was not new. It was in effect a continuation of the work and the method of the Talmud itself. The Talmud, in discussing the Mishna, the earlier legal work on which it is based, proceeds by citing passages apparently contradictory to the passage under discussion. The two or three contradictory passages are then re-analyzed and wherever possible finally harmonized. The commentators on the talmudic text, who lived in France and in Germany in the twelfth and thirteenth centuries, were known as Tosafists, that is, "writers of additional notes." The basic motivation of this sort of commentary is, of course, the faith that the Talmud, being the repository of God-given laws, must and can be proved to be consistent and harmonious throughout. The work of the Tosafists, the *Tosafot*, is printed opposite Rashi's commentary in every edition of the Talmud. The *Tosafot* is thus a special kind of talmudic commentary and has served in turn as the model for thousands of books of a type still being written, namely, the *hiddushim*, novellae, that is, "new notes" on the Talmud. These usually consist of pointing out new apparent contradictions and inconsistencies and providing new harmonizations. Thus, while the old explanatory commentary of the type of Rashi's is hardly ever written any more, the harmonizing novellae of the type of the *Tosafot* is a permanent part of and a continually growing section in rabbinic literature.

The second major grouping of rabbinic literature is made up

of the Codes. The need for codifying the law grew out of another difficulty of the talmudic text. The specific laws to be observed and practiced are not always clearly stated in the Talmud, which seems to be more concerned with the debate leading to the law than with the law itself. Sometimes, too, laws that should be grouped together are scattered over a wide area in the Talmud. Codes of the talmudic law therefore arose very early. This type of literature continued to develop as the years went on, for when further interpretations and more customs came into being, it was necessary to systematize and arrange them anew. Besides, commentaries on the codes came into being which subjected them to the same sort of rabbinic analysis used on the Talmud, comparing one code with another, discovering apparent contradictions and harmonizing them. The various codes with their commentaries have grown into a large subdivision of the rabbinic literature.

The third great division of the rabbinic-talmudic literature are the responsa, the published answers to questions asked of various rabbinic authorities. The formal answering of legal questions is known to many legal systems—the Roman and the Arabic as well as the American Law (the opinions of the Attorney General). But the legal responsa in rabbinic literature are far different from the legal responsa in other systems of law. They share the long history of all rabbinic literature, having been written over the span of at least fourteen centuries and in various lands. Because they cover so vast a range of time and space, they are necessarily a reflection of the history and life of many countries. The questions asked are generally specific questions of perhaps passing significance: about the ritual suitability of certain new foods; or involving a dispute between merchants in certain goods. But the incidental information they offer is often of social and historical importance. For example, in a question asked of Isaac ben Meshullam of Barcelona (twelfth century), mention is made casually of two merchants who were travelling to Armenia![1] From a study of these responsa, useful contributions could be made to the history of world trade and commerce and to our knowledge of the changing social conditions during the Middle

Ages. The responsa thus could throw unique light upon day-by-day Jewish life.

As early as the year 1865, Zachariah Fraenkel of Breslau outlined a plan for a scientific study of the entire responsa literature;[2] and since his time a fair amount of work has been done. Benzion Katz wrote a small booklet on the history of the Jews of Poland as reflected in the responsa.[3] Both Assaf and Zimmels have written on the history of the Marranos (the crypto-Jews of Spain and Portugal) as revealed in the responsa.[4] There is an essay on wills and bequests in favor of the settlement of Palestine as reflected in the responsa,[5] and another on the editing of certain responsa volumes.[6] Also a number of recent books in the field of Jewish history lean heavily on responsa material (thus, L. Finkelstein, *Jewish Self-Government in the Middle Ages*; A. A. Neuman, *The History of the Jews in Spain*).[7] Moreover, a number of books have been devoted to the life and work of one or another of the great respondents (Epstein on Solomon ben Adret,[8] Agus on Meir of Rothenburg,[9] Hershman on Isaac ben Sheshet[10] and Hurwitz on Solomon Luria).[11] Boaz Cohen, in his indispensible *Kuntres ha-Teshubot*,[12] a bibliography listing all the responsa printed up to 1930, enumerates articles in encyclopedias, magazines and booklets which deal with phases of the responsa literature. It is evident, however, that there is need for a great deal of modern study in this field. For, while the responsa have been used constantly and extensively for their primary purpose, namely, as a guide in determining the law in certain cases, nevertheless, in spite of the fact that Zachariah Fraenkel's suggestion was made almost a hundred years ago, comparatively little use has been made of the responsa for the scientific study of history and of sociology.

There have been no books at all charting the entire field of the responsa as a section of rabbinic literature, and only a few encyclopedia articles on the subject as a whole. Before such a general work on the responsa can be written, there is need for much preliminary study. Subject indices to the contents of the literature must be worked out; such indices have been attempted but never completed or at least never published. There must be separate

studies of the history of every Jewry as reflected in their responsa. A literary history is needed on the development of the
style and content of the responsa from age to age. It will be
years before an adequate amount of preliminary study is available—too many years, since the number of students in this field
is unfortunately very small.

The present book, written as it is before such scientific preparation is available, must necessarily be inadequate, and scholars
will undoubtedly find many weaknesses in it. Even so, it will
perhaps have some value. For the responsa are of interest, not
only to scholars who would use them as a mine from which to
dig material for their special studies, but to all who read Jewish
literature and history. This book should also have some value for
students of the history of the Law. There is, after all, no adequate parallel to this literature. The responsa in Roman Law and
in Arabic Law were more or less ephemeral. They may have left
their impress upon legal codes, but they were not themselves preserved. Nowhere else in the history of Law is there so large and
widely-ranging a literature, developed from actual cases and discussed by correspondence.

The purpose of this book is to give a general description of
the responsa literature: its development, the great contributors
to it, how it reflects Jewish history, the stirring controversies
which it records, and even some of the strange and curious items
which it contains and which serve to illustrate the spiritual depth
and geographical extent of its influence. The book is addressed,
not to the scholar—although it is hoped that scholars may find
some interest in it—but rather to the general reader. Terms are
therefore explained, literatures characterized and historical back-
grounds described which the scholar would not need but which
the general reader may find helpful. In brief, this book has been
written in the hope that its readers will gain some understanding
of the creative part which Jewish Law has played in Jewish life,
and that younger scholars may, perhaps, be moved to devote
their energies to pioneer in this unplowed field.

1

ORIGINS
AND
DEVELOPMENT
OF THE
RESPONSA

WHEN A LEGAL SYSTEM has not
yet been clearly codified, but is still to a large extent a mass of
unorganized tradition, then those who are the carriers of the
tradition attain a special status. The average man is, under the
circumstances, unable to learn the law independently, as he could
if it were codified. He has to turn to those who are the reposi-
tories of the tradition. "The priest's lips should keep knowledge,
and they shall seek the law at his mouth" (Malachi 2:7). The
priest was the transmitter of the old traditions and, since there
was no clear code, the only way for a person to know the law
was to ask him.

Such personal inquiries were the rule in many legal systems at
the stage when they carried a body of unorganized or half-
organized traditions. Besides, the greater the reliance upon a non-
professional judge—so that the judgment of the average person,
sitting as a member of a jury, was the source of decision—the
greater was the need for special legal guidance. The amateur
judge needed someone to whom to turn with an inquiry in cases
of special difficulty.

These personal inquiries inevitably take the form of correspondence when the people under the legal system involved live
scattered over a large area or in various countries. There is almost certain to develop some system of asking and receiving
opinions from an expert who dwells in the metropolis or in the
mother country from which the colonists had spread. Such were

the circumstances which prevailed in earlier Roman history. The Law itself, originally in the keeping of the priest, was imperfectly codified. Also, the judge, the *iudex*, was not generally a professionally trained lawyer. Thus there emerged a group of people who specialized in the knowledge of the traditions and forms of the Law. These were known as "Consultants in the Law" (*iuris consulti*), or the "Wise Men of the Law" (*iuris prudentes*). The answers which they gave to the questions asked of them were known therefore as *responsa prudentium*, "the answers of the learned." In later Roman Law these responsa attained considerable authority. The Emperor Augustus, for example, gave certain jurists the right to issue responsa which carried the emperor's authority. The right to answer legal questions officially fell into disuse by the end of the third century of the present era, but in the meantime a body of responsa had accumulated which had considerable legal authority.[1]

Similar conditions prevailed in Mohammedan Law. The Mohammedan world was widespread and the Law was still largely in the form of unorganized tradition. Hence there developed the Moslem *fatwa* as an important element in Moslem Law. The bases of Islamic Law, in addition to that found in the Koran, are the decisions and statements made by Mohammed himself. These were handed down by tradition. These traditions were variously collected and organized into different systems of law. Moreover, since the judge, the *cadi*, was not a professionally trained lawyer, there was constant need for experts who could be approached for opinions. Thus there was a *mufti* in every community who gave *fatwas*, or responsa, as to what the law was. These *fatwas* were generally not discussions, but merely brief answers to the questions before him, sometimes merely "yes" or "no." The sultan in Constantinople appointed a supreme *mufti* who answered questions which the Palace presented to him.

In the American legal system, there is also some need for what might be described as responsa, or law set forth in correspondence. This is chiefly due to the fact that the amount of new legislation is always large; and it is frequently important, before undertaking certain business enterprises, to know what the implication of the relevant laws may be. Hence the attorney general of most states, and also the attorney general of the United States with regard to Federal laws, will issue opinions which constitute a definition of the meaning of a law. While they do not always have the effect of law itself or that of a case decided in the courts, these "responsa" of the attorneys general have great weight in the development of law. This parallels exactly the place and influence of responsa in Jewish Law.

The factors mentioned above—the inchoate nature of the tradition, resort to non-professional judges, distance from a central authority, risk involved in relying on unofficial interpretation— operated toward the development of the responsa in Jewish Law. The Law was largely a tradition. That which was written in Scripture had been amplified and explained by the Oral Law taught in the schools in Palestine and later in the schools of Babylonia. There was constant need for the opinion of experts as to what the Law implied or intended. Furthermore, in Jewish Law the judges were often laymen selected as arbitrators by the parties to the dispute and therefore they frequently needed guidance and advice. Perhaps the most important factor was the fact that Jewry was widely scattered almost from the very beginning of the development of the post-biblical Law. The amplifications of Scripture which gradually found their way into the Mishna had to be made known to the populous Jewry which remained in Babylonia. Hence we find already in the talmudic literature evidences of the development of law by correspondence, through messages sent from Palestine to Babylonia.

There was, however, a special difficulty which hindered the development of Jewish Law by correspondence. This lay in the fact that it was forbidden to put the Oral Law into written form. The part of the Law which was written, namely, the Bible, could always be copied; but that which was oral had to remain oral, to be taught by word of mouth and not be recorded. How then was it ever possible to send legal advice by correspondence? This problem is taken up in the Talmud.[2] The question arises incidentally in a discussion about the sacrifices offered in the Temple, specifically as to whether the libations could be offered at night as well as by day. "When Rav Dimi went up (that is, came to Palestine from Babylonia), he found Rabbi Jeremiah lecturing in the name of Rabbi Joshua ben Levi as follows: 'Whence do we derive the fact that the libations which accompany a sacrifice can be offered only by day?' " Rav Dimi heard Rabbi Jeremiah prove this law on the basis of an interpretation of a biblical verse. The discussion then continues as follows: "He (Rav Dimi) said: 'If I could have found a messenger, I would have written a letter and sent it to Rabbi Joseph in Babylonia (telling him of what Jeremiah here in Palestine had said).' "

The Talmud then continues to discuss the statement of Rav Dimi that he would have sent a letter to Babylonia if he had found a messenger. It says: "If he *had* found a messenger, could he have written such a letter at all? Did not Rabbi Abba in the name of Rabbi Johanan say that those who write down the traditional (the oral) teachings are like those who actually burn the Torah and that he who learns the Oral Law from such writings receives no reward?" (In other words, how could he write a letter on a question of Oral Law when the Oral Law may not be written down?)

The answer which the Talmud gives is that perhaps the case is different in regard to *new* interpretations (that is, new ideas may perhaps be written down). Furthermore, it is better that one letter of the Torah should be uprooted than that the whole Torah should be forgotten. In other words, it is better occasionally to give up the old prohibitions against writing down the Oral Law than to run the risk that the expanding Law, growing through the accumulation of new ideas, should become too vast for the memory to hold and thus be forgotten.

Because the Oral Law could not possibly be remembered as it expanded and developed, the old prohibition against writing down the Oral Law lapsed and soon much of it to that date was written down in the Mishna. From then on there was less objection to new questions in the Law being dealt with by correspondence. Thus, for example, Rabbi Johanan in Palestine wrote to Rab and Samuel in Babylonia; while at another time Samuel

sent to Rab Johanan thirteen scrolls full of questions and discussions as to the ritual unfitness of certain animals or birds.[3]
Once, when Judah ben Ezekiel in Babylonia was discussing a
matter of trespassing, Rab Kahana said to him: "I will bring a
letter from the west (that is, from Palestine) that the law is not
according to Rabbi Simon (whom you are following)." Clearly
these letters from Palestine were considered authoritative.[4] There
are frequent references in various tractates of the Talmud to Rab
Abin, a Babylonian who went to Palestine and sent letters from
there giving the opinion of the Palestinian authorities. Thus, in a
discussion as to the rights of a widow to be sustained by the
estate of her late husband, Rab Pappa says, "If it were not for
the fact that Rab Abin had spoken of it in the letter that he sent,
I would not know the law, etc." [5]

These letters continued to come from Palestine to Babylonia.
When the two Talmuds, the Palestinian and the Babylonian,
were finally completed, the authority of the Palestinian center
began to fade, with the weakening of that community, and
Babylonia became the dominant authority. From then on, for
five centuries, from the sixth to the eleventh, letters streamed
from Babylonia to every part of the Jewish world. These letters,
the responsa from Babylonia, constitute a great mass of legal
material and are the chief foundation of the responsa literature.

The authority of the Babylonian teachers became as great as
that of the Palestinian teachers had been in the earlier centuries.
It is true that the Palestinian teachers had had a unique basis for
their authority. The old ordination by actual laying on of hands
began with Moses himself, who ordained Joshua, and continued
from Joshua to his disciples. This traditional ordination was
transmitted uninterruptedly in Palestine and, while any one who
had been thus ordained could ordain his own disciples, the right
of ordination could be exercised only in Palestine. There were,
of course, duly ordained teachers in Babylonia; but they had
moved to Babylonia after having been ordained in Palestine.
They in turn could not ordain their pupils outside of Palestine.
In actual practice, the descendants of Hillel, the patriarchal
house in Palestine, the religious heads of the Palestinian com-

munity, were the source of ordination; and when, in the time of Patriarch Hillel the Second (fourth century), ordination lapsed, the old authoritative Mosaic succession ceased. But up to the middle of the fourth century Palestine enjoyed an authority in the Law which no other country could share.

Babylonia too had a special status, but on a somewhat different basis. While Babylonia lacked the patriarchal family, the descendants of Hillel, it had the House of David, whose descendants were the exilarchs. Under these exilarchs the Jews of Babylonia enjoyed a large measure of self-government. While the exilarch could not give the traditional ordination, *semikha*, he could give an official appointment, *minui*, which accorded the judge thus appointed the right to summon people to judgment before him; and if he erred in his judgment, such a judge was not liable to make good the loss from his personal funds.

In addition to the exilarch, who was virtually a king over the Babylonian community, and his officially appointed judges, there were the great Babylonian schools, those of Sura and Pumpeditha, whose chief teachers had the title of "Gaon" (Eminence). These teachers were the direct successors of the teachers who had developed the Babylonian Talmud. As a result of this unbroken tradition, transmitted from generation to generation of permanent disciples, and through the great biennial assemblies (*kallah*) they were undisputed authorities on the Talmud. Hence, when the Palestinian influence waned, Babylonia with its exilarchs and gaonim, guardians and masters of the Talmud, became the absolute source of authority in Jewish life whose adherents by now were scattered to the east and far to the west.

To the gaonim questions began to come from every land where Jews were settled. The gaonim encouraged the sending of these questions for a number of reasons: their sense of duty to Judaism, a consciousness of their own authority in Jewish life and, no doubt also, because each inquiry was generally accompanied by a contribution for the maintenance of their schools. As the Jews of the diaspora in the earlier centuries had maintained the Temple, so from the sixth to the eleventh centuries they maintained the schools of Babylonia by means of these and other contributions.

The answers, the responsa, of the gaonim accumulated in the course of those centuries. While, presumably, tens of thousands of them have been lost, many hundreds remain and form the first great body of Jewish laws-by-correspondence. Cairo in Egypt was the natural distribution point for the answers sent to the western lands—to northwest Africa, Spain and elsewhere— and these answers were often copied in Cairo and a copy kept there. Hence, when the great *Geniza* ("the lumber room") in Cairo was uncovered by Solomon Schechter a generation ago, perhaps the greatest treasure discovered there was the hoard of gaonic responsa. The Cairo *Geniza* gave a new impetus to the study of these early legal letters.

The gaonic responsa were generally brief and direct. We wish they were a little more elaborate. It would have been better if they began, as in later responsa, with more (there are some) honorific salutations to the writer and to the people of his community. Perhaps, then, the addressee and the address would have been preserved. Mostly, however, they are not preserved, and the only introduction we have in most of the responsa is, "as for your question, etc." Had they been preserved we would know the names and the status of many Jewish communities and have a far clearer idea than we now have of the distribution of the Jews in those days. The answers were rarely long. Sometimes the questioner asked for an interpretation of a difficult passage in the Talmud and the answer had to be somewhat elaborate; but generally it was a direct, concise response to a specific question.

A large proportion of the questions dealt with the procedure and customs of worship. With the Jews scattered far and wide, different synagogue customs quickly developed and the gaonim felt the necessity of bringing order into this situation. Thus, the following question and answer reveal the situation and also the regulative influence of the gaonim. The question came from Spain and concerned the regulation that the Scriptural portion of the week be read twice in Hebrew and once in Aramaic. In Spain, the Aramaic translation was beginning to fall into disuse and the Gaon Hai (tenth to eleventh century; the last of the great gaonim) was asked whether it was permissible to omit it altogether. His answer was forthright and clear.[6]

> This was asked of our teacher, Hai Gaon: The people of Spain are accustomed to abandon the Aramaic translation altogether; yet we find in many places in the Talmud that the use of the Aramaic is mandatory.
>
> And he answered: The matter is clear. Not in the Talmud alone do we find the mandate to use the Aramaic, but even in the Mishna:—"He who reads in the Torah shall not read less than three verses nor shall he read to the translator (into Aramaic) more than one verse (at a time), and in the prophet three verses" (m. Megilla IV, 4). Furthermore, the Mishna contains an explanation of the many passages which are read and translated (into Aramaic) and the passages which are read and not translated, and also discusses the matter of a minor reading in the Torah and translating (into Aramaic) (ibid., IV, 6). There are many such cases in our Mishna which are explained in the Talmud. Are we to say that all these matters are no longer of any account? God forbid! For behold, all the prophets ordained these things for Israel. We did not know until now that in Spain they have neglected the Aramaic translation.

Another question concerned the custom of scholars to study early in the morning, while the introductory Psalms were being read in the synagogue, and then later joining the congregation in its prayers. Is it a proper custom for the scholars to study before they recite the Shema' in the morning? Gaon Natronai (ninth century) answers: [7]

> Thus has it been shown us from Heaven, that, when the people of Israel come early into the synagogue, on Sabbaths and holidays, and study, they follow a worthy custom; for this has been the custom in Babylonia from the very beginning of the first Exile. When they were exiled to Babylonia and the knowledge of Scriptures diminished and pupils ceased to exist because of the sorrows of exile, the Children of Israel gathered around the prophets and the scholars and said to them, "We do not possess either Mishna or Talmud to study at night (in our

homes) and we have the burden of earning our livelihood (during the week). But on Sabbaths and holidays when we have time, shall we sit idle and sleep all through the night?" Therefore they established the custom of going early to the synagogue and studying until the morning (dawn), relying on the custom of King David, of blessed memory, who said (Psalm 119.62):—At midnight I rise to praise the Lord.

A gaonic responsum will often simplify a rather complex law in a terse, almost epigrammatic way. For example, the question of the status of apostate Jews is quite complicated. A Jew who violates the Sabbath in public is not considered a Jew. On the other hand, if such an apostate Jew marries a Jewess, the marriage is considered religiously valid. The Gaon Saadia (tenth century) clarifies the situation. The man who violates the laws, especially the Sabbath law, in public is not a Jew insofar as being acceptable in religious matters: for example, he cannot be counted among the three for grace after meals; his testimony generally is not valid. Yet, when it comes to marriage and divorce, his status as a Jew remains unchanged. Saadia ends his responsum, putting the matter very clearly. He says: [8]

> In summary, the matter stands thus. With regard to the commandments (as to whether a man may participate in the rituals), we judge by whether he observes the Sabbath. But with regard to marriage laws, we judge by his birth. This matter is beyond doubt. This is the law and it is not to be changed.

A large number of the gaonic responsa answer questions which ask for the meaning of talmudic passages. Some of the questions are rather simple, such as a student might ask of his teacher. But in the days of the gaonim many of the communities were just beginning to become acquainted with the Talmud and there were no available commentaries.

The following question was asked of Hai Gaon, or of his father, Sherira Gaon:

> As for your question: Wherever the Talmud speaks of "that old man," to whom does the Talmud refer? Answer:— Thus it seems to us that "that old man" was not a well-known, identi-

fiable person (as your question implies), but any old man that happened to be present at the time, for we find the expression "that old man" used by rabbis in different generations. (The gaon cites a number of cases of rabbis of various generations who referred to "that old man," thus proving that it could not be the same person.) And let it not enter your mind that "that old man" was Elijah (who, of course, could, according to legend, appear in many generations), because it says in the tractate Sabbath (page 34a):— "That old man said to them, 'Ben Yohai purified the graves,'" and at the end of the passage it says, "Ben Yohai turned his eye upon him and he died." So it could not be Elijah and must have been some chance old man in each case.[9]

The gaonim, thus, regulated synagogue customs, clarified complicated questions in the Law and interpreted and explained the Talmud to inquirers in many lands. Their interpretations of the laws became the basis of later codes and later responsa, and their explanatory comments on talmudic passages the basis of later talmudic commentaries.

Although one of the later gaonim might refer in a responsum to responsa of his predecessors, there is no evidence that the gaonim themselves collected their responsa or considered them as a separate branch of Jewish literature that would need to be preserved as such. To the gaonim, their decisions were simply decisions. Sometimes the decision required some elaboration; sometimes they gave expository commentaries on a portion of a talmudic text. But these were not preserved any more than most people preserve a copy of their correspondence. The recipients, however, did preserve them. Collections of gaonic responsa have therefore come down to us; and in the age of printing many of them were published. To the gaonim themselves, their responsa thus represented their legal correspondence; but to the scholars of the diaspora, the responsa were the source and the foundation for their own study of the Talmud and for their own commentaries as well as compendia of law.

The knowledge of the Talmud, helped and fostered by the activity and guidance of the gaonim, eventually began to flourish in the western lands. Soon competent local authorities emerged in western North Africa (in what is now Tunis and Algiers), in Spain, in France and in the Rhineland. Since it was always difficult and expensive to send inquiries by land and sea all the way to Babylonia, it was natural that more and more questions, which might earlier have been addressed to the gaonim, would now be directed to the local scholars. These scholars answered as they had been taught to answer in the responsa of the gaonim—briefly, directly and with a minimum of explanation. The responsa of the early diaspora scholars were also to a large extent in Arabic (the universal language of the Islamic lands), as were many of the responsa of the gaonim. Since they were not yet considered an independent branch of Jewish legal literature, but merely answers to inquiries or decisions on problems, they were not preserved by their writers but by others. In fact, many of the decisions of those scholars who lived at the time of the later gaonim were often preserved amid collections of gaonic responsa. Thus, the responsa of Kalonymus of Lucca and of his son, Meshullam in Germany, and the responsa of Rabbenu Hananel of Kairouan in North Africa, were preserved in other books. For a century or so after the gaonim, the western scholars felt no need to preserve their own responses. Isaac Alfasi, the great authority of the eleventh century in Spain, and Maimonides, in the following century, wrote their responsa mostly in Arabic. Their brief, unelaborated decisions were not made available as separate collections for many centuries after their death, and certainly many hundreds of their responsa have been lost. So, too, in northern France, Rashi, the chief authority of his day, did not gather or preserve his responsa. All we have are scattered references to his decisions in the books of his disciples.

Not until the respondents began to write elaborate responsa, each responsum being virtually an essay, not until the responsa were in Hebrew or in the Aramaic-Hebrew of the Talmud, not until the author himself began to feel the necessity of preserving his responsa, can the responsa be said to have arrived at the status where they constituted a separate branch of rabbinic literature. This status was arrived at in northern France in the responsa of

Rabbenu Tam (1100–1171), Rashi's grandson; and in Spain in the responsa of Solomon ben Adret (1235–1310).

The reason for this elevation of responsa to a separate branch in Jewish literature at this period can be explained chiefly by the changing status of talmudic knowledge. In the time of the gaonim, the knowledge of the Talmud was well established and widespread only in Babylonia. The great semi-annual assemblies and the permanent schools kept the tradition unbroken from the days of the Talmud itself. In the diaspora, this huge and difficult work was largely unknown. But through the influence of the gaonim, the knowledge of the Talmud spread first among their correspondents, and later, through the efforts of these scattered scholars who established schools. In time there were thousands of students competent in Talmudic Law. When that stage was attained, the answer to a legal inquiry assumed an entirely different character.

In the earlier period, inquiries had dealt in large measure with the meaning of talmudic passages. Such inquiries were no longer needed. The meaning of the text was taught directly in the Talmud schools. In the earlier period, inquirers had been after decisions in the specific disputes in which they were involved, and the decisions were given. Now that the inquirers were likely to be talmudic scholars themselves, a mere "yes" or "no," or "permitted" or "prohibited," no longer served as an answer. Now the questions and answers took on the nature of correspondence between approximate equals, and a respondent had to give an elaborate talmudic justification for his answer, the questioner being in a position to evaluate the reply. Even in the responsa of Alfasi and Maimonides this distinction is to be noticed. When the inquirer was a scholar, the answer was elaborate; while the answer to most inquirers was brief, sometimes only one word.

In northern France, where the analytical study of the Talmud flourished first and developed the *Tosafot*, we find that Rabbenu Tam, the greatest of the Tosafists, gave virtually every responsum the form of a well-rounded rabbinic essay. Solomon ben Adret's responsa, in Spain, a century later, were generally likewise full rabbinic essays. From then on, responsa were nearly all written in Hebrew, preserved by their authors and copied and made available to a larger group of students. There was now a widespread talmudic world. The average questioner was himself a scholar. The responsa were no longer, as in the time of the gaonim and the earliest respondents, merely decisions, but full discussions of the law. Thus the responsa came into their own as a specific type of literature, with fixed characteristics destined to be maintained in all the centuries that followed.

The only differences between the later responsa and those of the twelfth and thirteenth centuries were incidental. Though their content and background may differ, the proportion of subject-matter varying from time to time and place to place, their style and structure have remained essentially the same. First comes a statement of the case, usually in the question, which was generally printed together with the responsum. Then the responsum begins by indicating what at first appearance would seem to be the law as recorded in one or the other of the codes. Then follows a discussion of difficulties, due to contradictory opinions in the codes on this or on related questions, which compel the respondent to go back to the basic talmudic discussion from which the law in question ultimately derives. This in turn is followed by an analysis of passages in the Talmud that may possibly yield a principle relevant to the case at hand. The principle is tested by being subjected to real or apparently contradictory opinions in the Talmud; and, having withstood the test, it is applied to the case in hand. In some countries there was more and in some countries there was less of such internal talmudic discussion. In some centuries one code was referred to, in other centuries another. But the responsa have retained essentially this classic form.

As Jewish life developed in the various countries, historical, political and economic changes raised new questions. As the number of talmudic scholars, teachers of *yeshibot*, communal rabbis, increased, so did the number of responsa writers. There are by now about fifteen hundred books dealing with responsa alone and perhaps five hundred more which deal primarily with other branches of rabbinic literature but also contain a number of responsa.

To obtain a bird's-eye-view of this vast literature, it is necessary to deal with historical circumstances as well as the literary products of certain types of personality. There were some famous Jewish communities which contributed greatly to this literature, and others, equally famous, which produced very little. So, too, there were renowned scholars who became respondents of world-wide fame, and others, equally great, who wrote almost no responsa at all.

The personality and motivation of the most famous respondents will be discussed in the next chapter. In the rest of the present chapter we shall deal with the classic lands of responsa writing, while making only passing reference to the scholars who were representative of these various literary centers.

The geographical and chronological distribution of responsa writing is rather remarkable. One country suddenly emerges as a center of responsa literature, only to fade out even though its Jewish population may still be large and its Talmud students still numerous. As suddenly, another country arises as a center, remains the premier land for responsa for a century or two, and then in its turn sinks into obscurity. Often there are two great centers simultaneously, as North Africa and Germany in the fourteenth to the fifteenth centuries, and Turkey and Poland in the sixteenth to the early seventeenth centuries. In order to present a broad view of the important lands of responsa writing, only those respondents will be mentioned who have become sufficiently well known to be read beyond the land of their origin and whose decisions form the basis of later responsa and may even be embodied in the codes which summarized Jewish law from time to time.

Germany and Spain to the Fifteenth Century

Jacob ben Meir (Rabbenu Tam, 1100–1171), the grandson of Rashi, was, next to his grandfather, the greatest master of the

Franco-German school. He organized his learned correspondence in what is the second volume of his *Sefer ha-Yashar* ("The
Book of the Upright"). He was the greatest among the tosafists
(the writers of additional notes to the Talmud). The tosafists
noted the difficulties in every part of the Talmud and then explained them brilliantly away. It was these deeper analyses, the
discovering of difficulties and the harmonizing of them, that
Rabbenu Tam brought into the responses in his *Sefer ha-Yashar*,
so that this procedure became thereafter a part of every classic
responsum. Up to now, as has been pointed out, the responsa of
the gaonim, of Maimonides, of Alfasi, had been primarily decisions. These newer responsa were debates, discussions, learned
conversations.

Rabbenu Tam was followed in Germany by Meir of Rothenburg (1215–1293),[10] whose many responsa, extant in numerous collections and quoted in other works, are a permanent part
of the structure of the legal tradition. In the next generation in
Germany, at the end of the fourteenth and the beginning of the
fifteenth centuries, there were Jacob Moellin (Maharil) and
Israel Isserlein of Neustadt, Vienna,[11] and somewhat later, their
disciples, Jacob Weil and Israel Bruna.

In the same period there flourished in Italy the prime respondent in all the history of Italian Jewry, Joseph Colon
(1420–1480).[12] His responsa are likewise among the classic
works in the field. He was influenced largely by the German
school of Talmud study, but was a bridge with the Jewry of the
Mediterranean.

Incidentally, Jacob Moellin, who was as famous for his notes
on customs and ceremonies (*minhagim*) as for his responsa, indicates how vitally important he considered this type of legal
decision to be as a source of authority. He says to a correspondent: [13] "As for your statement that one should not rely
upon responsa; on the contrary, I say, they are practical law and
we should learn from them more than from the codifiers who,
after all, were not present at the time when the decision was
made." In other words, whereas the codes may summarize the
decisions of various responsa or of the talmudic debates, a re-

sponsum, which arose from an actual case submitted, should be the prime source of authority. Jewish Law is in this regard like the Anglo-Saxon Law, more emphatically case-law than code-law.

While these authorities flourished in France and Germany, a great light in the field of responsa arose in Spain, Solomon ben Adret (1235–1310).[14] He wrote, according to some reports, seven thousand responsa, of which three thousand are extant. His works are authoritative throughout the Jewish world down to our day.

Soon after his time, Jewish life in Spain began to break up under the blows of persecution. Spanish Jewry scattered from the Iberian peninsula and during the next three centuries established new and creative communities. Their first place of creative resettlement was northern Africa, chiefly in the areas which today are Tunis and Algiers, where the earliest talmudic schools in the diaspora had developed to which the gaonic responsa had first been sent in the west.

It was almost inevitable that the responsa literature should have flourished in the new North African-Spanish Jewish communities. The native Jews differed greatly from the new immigrants. Their learning, Jewish and secular, was far inferior to that of the newcomers; their economic development was backward; and many of their religious customs were peculiar to themselves. The misunderstandings and communal disputes between the native African Jews ("the wearers of the turban") and the Spanish newcomers ("the wearers of the biretta") required adjudicament and harmonization. Furthermore, many of the Jews who had remained in Spain had been forcibly converted to Christianity and, during the next century or so, numbers of them escaped to the African communities. Their status presented immediate problems. Many of them had married in the church. Was their marriage valid as Jewish marriage? And what of their children? Did they need to be reconverted? These vexing problems of the escaped converts, added to the tensions due to the differing customs and manners of the communities themselves, required immediate solution. This was no time for leisurely theoretic studies. The immigrant Spanish scholars were besieged with urgent questions, and so the responsa literature achieved a rapid development through their efforts.

Thus, three and a half centuries after Rabbenu Hananel, the correspondent of the gaonim, had flourished in Kairouan, North Africa, from which scholars like Alfasi had moved to Spain, the reverse current began. It was led chiefly by Isaac bar Sheshet,[15] (Ribash; 1326–1408), whose great volume of responsa soon became a classic. His younger colleague and sometime rival, Simon ben Zemach Duran (*Tashbetz*),[16] likewise was the author of a great volume of responsa. Simon's son, Solomon ben Simon (Rashbash), who succeeded him as rabbi of Algiers, and two of his grandsons published jointly a work of responsa that won a permanent place in this literature. Its curious title, *Yakhin u-Boaz*, borrows for these two sons of Rabbi Solomon the names of the two columns beside the bronze "sea" in the Temple built by King Solomon. With these two scholars in the early part of the sixteenth century, the fame of the North African community as a source of decision came to an end; and, although the study of the Talmud continued in North Africa, it produced in later times only one more writer of responsa whose works were known beyond the confines of his own country, namely, Judah Ayyas (1690–1760). The contemporary school in Germany likewise lost its creativity, although it experienced a revival some generations later.

Turkey and Poland, Sixteenth and Seventeenth Centuries

Although Algerian primacy in the responsa literature had ceased, the ex-Spanish Jews were destined to write a new chapter in the history of responsa. But another century was to elapse. From about 1400 C.E. to 1500, the two great centers were virtually silent: Germany, because the effects of the persecutions resulting from the Black Plague broke up communities and crushed the creative spirit; Spain, because the persecutions rising toward the climax of the expulsion in 1492 left no energy for cultural discussion. While German Jewry would wait for at least two centuries before reviving sufficiently to produce world-famous respondents, Spanish Jewry would, after somewhat less than a century, begin once more to produce responsa which became a permanent part of the literature. Spanish Jewry, especially after the expulsion in 1492, moved eastward. It was at the eastern end of the Mediterranean—in Egypt, in Palestine and in Turkey—that it began to flourish anew. As with German Jewry and Spanish-Algerian Jewry in the earlier period, this efflorescence in the Turkish Empire was one of a pair of two great centers. Almost exactly at the same time, Polish Jewry achieved its greatest development. As Spanish Jewry, exiled to the east, revived in Turkey, so German Jewry, exiled to the east, came to a new flowering in Poland.

As with Algerian-Spanish Jewry a century or so earlier, the needs of time and place almost compelled the scholars to undertake the practical task of responsa writing. In the Turkish Empire, as had been the case previously in North Africa, there was an urgent communal problem. The Spanish exiles found Greek-Jewish congregations already established in the cities and towns to which they came. To complicate matters, the exiles themselves established a number of separate congregations, the immigrants grouping themselves according to their home cities or districts in Spain. There immediately arose questions of jurisdiction. Bans were frequently proclaimed forbidding members to leave their present congregation in order to join another congregation. How valid were these bans? What was the "Jewish community"? Was it the entire Jewry of the city, or was it each separate congregation? Many questions were asked and responsa written on these difficult and often acrimonious questions of communal organization. These were the first questions which arose; then other questions were added, and soon a flourishing responsa literature developed.

In Poland the problems were somewhat different, but they were analogous. Poland was a new and undeveloped country. There were no pre-existing communities. The Jews immigrating westward from Germany and Bohemia had to build their life upon new foundations. They soon developed talmudic schools, regulated problems of trade and taxation and planned nation-wide councils. The rabbis were required to lay down the legal basis for a network of new communities whose individuals were working out their careers in a new environment. The practical problems required specific answers to specific questions. Responsa literature inevitably expanded in this new home.

In Palestine, in Salonika and Constantinople, and also in Cairo, Egypt, the Spanish exiles produced at least a dozen great respondents whose works are still in use, besides a host of lesser lights who likewise wrote responses. Most, though not all of these, were exiles from Spain. Some of them had been brought out of Spain as children by their parents. Some had been born in exile. The most famous of these was Joseph Caro, the great codifier, the author of the *Shulhan Arukh*. His immense commentary on the *Tur*, a legal code compiled in Spain in the 14th century, *Bet Joseph* ("The House of Joseph"), is a veritable treasure-house of the responsa of all the past ages, Spanish and German. While his own books of responsa, the collection of *Abkat Rokhel*, and his responsa on marriage laws were not outstanding, his *Bet Joseph* made the responsa a permanent and determining factor in the codes of Jewish law. One might well say that the responsa of the past became part of the intellectual apparatus of all succeeding decisors by virtue of their decisions being cited in Caro's great commentary.

His contemporary, David ben Solomon ibn Zimra (Radbaz, 1479–1589), passed most of his life as rabbi of Cairo. His responsa are in the first rank of this literature. Elijah Mizrahi (1455–1525), rabbi of Constantinople, was somewhat older. He was not of Spanish, but of Italian origin. David Cohen (Radak) was rabbi of the island of Corfu in the early sixteenth century. Samuel ben Moses Medina (Rashdam, 1505–1589), was rabbi in Salonika. Moses of Trani, Joseph Trani and Joseph ibn Labi (Leb), rabbi in Salonika and Constantinople; Jacob Berab, likewise an exile from Spain, famous for having made the attempt to revive the old form of Mosaic ordination, and his great opponent, Levi ibn Habib (1480–1555), rabbi of Jerusalem, both of them exiles from Spain—all these men transcended the region of their activity. Their books are quoted by scholars of Jewish Law in every land.

Simultaneously with the Turkish productivity, Polish Jewry had its time of greatness. The chief respondents were Moses Isserles of Cracow (Rama),[17] his kinsman, Solomon Luria of Lublin, and, somewhat later, Meir of Lublin (Maharam).

The Polish and the Turkish schools did not need to wait for future generations to unite them in the common treasury of Jewish legal literature. The two luminaries, Joseph Caro of the Turkish group, and Moses Isserles of the Polish, moved together and, as twin stars, shone upon Jewish legal literature. Joseph Caro had written his great code, the *Shulḥan Arukh* ("The Set Table"). This work, for all its clarity and succinctness, would never have been accepted by German and Polish Jewry had Moses Isserles not written his notes to it, embodying the customs of the north European Jews. Together the book and the notes became one work, and the one work has ever since been the predominant governing code in Jewish religious life.

After this high tide of responsa writing, there was again a subsidence; and while, of course, some responsa were always being written, no great respondent arose for almost a century. The next writer destined to make a permanent contribution was the German, Yair Hayyim Bacharach (1639–1702),[18] the rabbi of Worms. His somewhat later contemporary was Z'vi Ashkenazi (Hakham Z'vi, 1660–1718), rabbi of Amsterdam and Altona; and then Ashkenazi's son, the famous Jacob Emden (1697–1776). It was almost a century thereafter that two great centers once more arose to exist side by side. The forerunner of this new time of creativity was Ezekiel Landau (1713–1793), rabbi of Prague, a many-sided talmudist, famous chiefly as author of the responsa, *Noda bi-Yehudah*. He was followed in Prague by Elazar Fleckeles (1754–1826), and in Nickolsburg, Moravia, by Mordecai Benet (1753–1829). It seems strange that these three men constitute almost the only responsa writers in the great Bohemian-Moravian community. There were many great and creative rabbis of Prague before them, but not one became widely known as a writer of responsa.[19] Somewhat older than Ezekiel Landau was the well-known Jacob Reisher (*Shebut Ya'acob*), rabbi of Metz, who died in 1733. A contemporary of Ezekiel Landau, but not comparable to him in greatness or fame, was Joseph Steinhart (*Zikhron Joseph*, 1720–1776), rabbi of Fuerth. Of this group in Bohemia and in Germany, only Ezekiel Landau and perhaps Jacob Reisher were of first rank. However, they were soon followed by the great development of responsa in Hungary and in Galicia in the early nineteenth century.

Hungary and Galicia, the Nineteenth Century

Jewish life remained fairly static for another century. Very few new religio-legal problems arose. The great responsa collections of the Turkish and Polish rabbis of the sixteenth and early seventeenth centuries contained the answers to most questions that would arise. But in the beginning of the nineteenth century, vast and rapid changes took place. The modern era was dawning over the mass settlements of eastern Europe. New modes of business developed. New and closer relationship with the Gentile world grew up. New inventions brought new questions. New ideas of worship were advocated. The old communities of Galicia and Hungary, being west of the Czarist "iron curtain," came face to face with modernity. The new adjustment, the resistance to or compromises with modernity, brought a renewed flowering to the historic responsa literature.

Both these centers produced, at the same time, a galaxy of famous respondents. First and foremost in Hungary was Moses Sofer of Frankfort-on-the-Main, who spent most of his career as head of the *yeshiba* in Pressburg, Hungary (now Slovakia). Before his day there had been only one well-known respondent in Hungary, Meir Eisenstadt (*Panim Meirot*, 1670–1744). Moses Sofer [20] (1763–1839), an indefatigable respondent and brilliant talmudist, inspired his contemporaries and a host of successors. A somewhat older contemporary was his second father-in-law, Akiba Eger (1761–1837), of Posen. Among his younger contemporaries was Judah Assad (*Yehuda Ya'aleh*, 1794–1866);

Meir Ash (*Imre Esh*, died 1861); Moses Schick (1807–1879); Abraham Samuel Sofer (*K'tab Sofer*, 1815–1872), the son of Moses Sofer; Eliezer Deutsch of Bonyhad (1850–1916), and many others.

Equal creativity occurred simultaneously in Galicia. Ephraim Zalman Margolis of Brody (*Bet Ephraim*, 1762–1828), was followed by Solomon Kluger, one of the most prolific of rabbinic authors (1783–1869); his great contemporary, Joseph Saul Nathanson of Lemberg (1808–1875); Chaim Halberstam (1793–1876), who represented a fine combination of hasidic mysticism and legal learning; Isaac Aaron Ettinger of Lemberg (1827–1891); and, later, Isaac Schmelkes of Lemberg, whose *Bet Yitzhak* contains a veritable mountain of responsa.

While this great creativity took place in Hungary and in Galicia, the part of Poland which was within the Russian Empire, the other lands in Russia and Lithuania produced very few respondents. Mention might be made of the famous head of the *yeshiba* in Volozhin, Naftali Z'vi Berlin (*Meshib Dabar*, 1817–1893), and Menachem Mendel of Lubovitch (*Zemah Zedek*). But, considering the vast population of Jews in the Russian Empire and the tremendous amount of Talmud study which went on there, one would expect a much greater activity in this field. This strange paucity of responsa in Russia, when the two adjoining lands were so active, is partially explained [21] by the fact that in Hungary and in Galicia most rabbis had small *yeshibot* in their own communities; and their disciples, when they later came to congregations of their own, would each send questions to his teacher. In Russia, great nation-wide *yeshibot* were established whose scholars were not in contact with the active problems of the rabbinate.

Another explanation may be the different degree of westernization in Russia and the other two lands. Russia was, even in those days, behind an "iron curtain" of isolation; whereas Galicia and Hungary were both part of the Austro-Hungarian Empire and therefore in the main stream of western life. The great changes which modernity brought—new ideas, reforms, new inventions—had to be faced by every rabbi in Hungary and

Galicia. Therefore there were innumerable new, practical problems to cope with. Whereas in Russia, new invention was slow to penetrate and the new ideas in those days, while they manifested themselves in the writings and in the lives of a few, never resulted, as in Hungary and Galicia, in attempts to capture the old communities. Thus the vast learning in Russia and Russian-Poland continued to confine itself to theoretical discussions of talmudic problems. Many of the books published as responsa were really not responsa at all, but an exchange of *hiddushim*, talmudic analyses, between learned scholars. A large volume of responsa by a Russian scholar might contain ten or fifteen questions, each exhaustively dealt with, generally on a theoretical basis; whereas a volume of the same size by a Hungarian or Galician contemporary might have three to four hundred responsa, the overwhelming percentage of which dealt with practical, urgent matters.

The old and largely isolated life of Jewry in the Russian Empire suddenly broke up, not because of the impact of outer forces as in the Austro-Hungarian Empire, but due to the inner desire of millions of Jews to leave Russian oppression and run away to the New World. In the latter half of the nineteenth century, a large proportion of Russian Jewry moved westward. Thus inevitably the honored rabbis of the old homeland became part of the memory and a source of religious authority for Jews scattered all over the world. By the centrifugal force of immigration, certain great Russian rabbis became world figures. Naftali Z'vi Berlin, in his *Meshib Dabar*, already indicated how many questions had been sent to him from America. Isaac Elhanan Spektor (1817–1896), rabbi of Kovno, quickly became known all over the vastly expanded Jewish diaspora. Within Russia, too, Jewish life was affected by the changes now attempted by the Russian government. It interfered with the old type of Jewish education and the training for the rabbinate; also the emigration of millions created a problem for many wives whose husbands disappeared without a trace (*agunot*). Isaac Elhanan Spektor suddenly was confronted with a host of urgent, practical problems. He had the ability and the will to cope with them, and his responsa, *En Yitzhak* and *Be'er Yitzhak,* came to be among the best-known books in this field.

Simultaneously with the rise of Isaac Elhanan Spektor, and to some extent for similar reasons, Galicia developed a great authority, in the latter half of the nineteenth century, in the person of Sholom Mordecai Shwadron of Berzun.[22] Six volumes of his responsa have been published and many other responsa still await publication. He and Isaac Elhanan Spektor were by far the greatest respondents at the close of the last century.

In the early part of the twentieth century, there were no respondents who attained world-wide fame. Perhaps one of the best known is David Hoffmann (1843–1921). He represents a rather unusual type of respondent. Born in Hungary, a pupil of Moses Schick, he became rector of the great Rabbinical Seminary for Orthodox Judaism in Berlin. Thoroughly trained in modern scientific method, he nevertheless was an active and widely-sought respondent. His book of responsa, *Melamed le-Ho'il* ("Teaching to Benefit," based upon the verse in Isaiah 48.17, "Who teacheth thee for thy profit"), shows a new style in the long history of responsa writing. Although he cites past authorities and analyzes the Talmud, which is the classic procedure in responsa, his style is exact and his responsa read like scientific essays. A similar change in style is found in the responsa of the contemporary chief Sephardi rabbi of Palestine, Benzion Uziel (*Mishp'te Uziel*). His responsa are a model of system and clarity. After stating the subject, he lists all the subproblems involved and takes them up one by one, dealing with them in unadorned and lucid style. Perhaps the fact that Hebrew had become a living language in Israel converted his, as it has done with other responsa, from the old, rather difficult, rabbinic style to readable modern writing.

The history of the responsa literature reveals a steady development from the terse decisions of the gaonim through the complicated talmudic analysis of Rabbenu Tam. There was shifting of dominant themes, revealing changes in history and in social living. It flourished in certain countries, generally in two countries simultaneously, fading away into generations of sterility and rising again to periods of creative splendor. It is, of course, not possible to explain completely the ups and downs of this development. Sometimes a new efflorescence was due to the personality and authority of some individual, and sometimes even where there was a need for practical decisions, responsa writing nevertheless did not develop for want of adequate, authoritative scholars. In such circumstances, the most urgent questions were sent to rabbis in distant lands. Thus, Joseph Hayyim ben Elijah, rabbi of Bagdad in the nineteenth century (*Rab Pe'alim*, Jerusalem, 1901), responded to questions from Singapore, Bombay and Calcutta.

But, generally, the circumstances evoked the needed scholarly labors and the literature developed when there was special need for it. Wherever a new community was being built, as in Algiers, Turkey and sixteenth-century Poland, or wherever new influences created new situations and where these requirements were able to call upon a broad, Jewish, scholarly competence, there the responsa literature awoke to a new springtime. So, too, as the problems of the modern day impinge upon the historic Jewish faith, there will be need for more and more responsa writing. This unique type of Jewish legal literature may well be at the beginning of a new development, especially in Israel where a Jewish society must seek to achieve a harmony with a long Jewish tradition.[23]

2

THE
LEADING
RESPONDENTS

THE STAMP OF the Talmud is recognized in every branch of rabbinic literature. The novellae, the sermons, the commentaries, the codes, the responsa—all use the talmudic vocabulary and follow its mode of reasoning. Therefore any competent rabbinic author can write with equal facility in all these branches.

Of all the types of rabbinic writing, the one that we would expect to be the largest is the responsa, since they represent the primary function of the rabbi. The talmudic formula for the ordination of rabbis [1] contains the words, "He shall teach; he shall judge," and this formula is still used in ordination documents (*semikhot*). The rabbi is expected to be above all a decisor and a judge. Questions in law are constantly brought before him and it is his duty to give answer. Of course, many of the questions which come to him are simple and can be answered adequately by reference to the codes of law. But many of them are far from simple and require research and analysis and the careful drawing of conclusion. Every rabbi in his day-by-day functioning piles up, as the years go on, responsa to legal questions. It might, therefore, be expected that of all the types of rabbinic writing in which most rabbis are competent, the responsa should by now be the largest in size.

Yet this is not the case. *Hiddushim*, new interpretations as to the meaning of the Talmud, and the like, are much more numerous than responsa. Boaz Cohen, in his valuable handbook, *Contres ha-Teshubot,* which attempted to provide a complete listing of all the responsa up to 1930, listed only twelve hundred and fifty books devoted solely to responsa. As one wonders why the responsa literature is so much smaller than some other branches of rabbinic literature, there immediately comes to mind the realization that some of the greatest of the rabbis of the past, though creative writers and, many of them, serving great communities where they certainly had many questions to answer, left us no books of responsa. A partial listing of some famous rabbis who never published responsa is both impressive and surprising.

The outstanding rabbinic authority of the fourteenth century was Jacob ben Asher, the author of the famous code *Arba Turim,* known as "The *Tur.*" This code inspired learned commentation on the part of the greatest scholars of later centuries. Indeed, it served as the foundation of the *Shulhan Arukh.* Hardly anyone was more actively concerned with the entire scope of Jewish Law than Jacob ben Asher. True, he was not the rabbi of a famous congregation and was rather neglected during his lifetime, but surely he was not so neglected or ill-regarded as not to have received inquiries on legal matters. On the contrary, many questions must have been directed to him. Yet Jacob ben Asher, the great legal authority, left no responsa. His father, Asher ben Yehiel, on the other hand, in addition to his legal compendium-commentary on the Talmud, left us a magnificently organized volume of responsa. Jacob's brother, Judah, left responsa. But from Jacob ben Asher, the great authority himself, there are no responsa. What may explain this strange situation?

Mordecai Jaffe was one of the greatest Jewish legalists of the sixteenth century. His famous code, *Lebush,* seriously threatened the supremacy of the *Shulhan Arukh.* Yet even this great authority, whose chief interest was the practical explanation of the Law and its clarification and who was rabbi in the great community of Prague where many questions of Jewish Law must have been asked of him, left no volume of responsa. There is but one responsum of his in the collection of Meir of Lublin (no. 125).

Rabbi Loew ben Bezalel was one of the most famous of all

European rabbis. He had been rabbi in Poland, but for most of his career he was connected with the community of Prague. He was one of the most creative personalities of the sixteenth century. He wrote many different types of works—commentaries, kabbala, philosophy—conducted disputations defending Judaism against Christianity and was deeply interested in the moral problems of the community. He was also a great educational reformer and advocated a complete revolution in Jewish education. He certainly must have dealt with many religio-legal problems as rabbi in one of the great communities of the Jewish world. It is hard to imagine that many questions of law were not directed at him. How can one explain the fact that this master of the Law, this man so intensely aware of the problem of the changing times, left no books of legal responsa?

One of the greatest disciples of Rabbi Loew ben Bezalel was the famous commentator on the Mishna, Yomtov-Lipman Heller. He, too, was one of the great legal authorities, but he left only a few scattered responsa. All that are left of Heller's responsa are one or two scattered ones in the collection *Gaonim Batrai*, and in *Zemah Zedek* and in *Etan ha-Ezrahi*. Is it not strange that three great rabbis of Prague, creative literary men, masters of the Law, guides of great communities, should not have left a volume of published responsa?

Joshua ben Alexander Falk was the pupil of Moses Isserles and Solomon Luria, both of whom left volumes of responsa. He was the head of the *yeshiba* in Lemberg and had many disciples who must have addressed questions to him. He was active in public affairs, being a leader in the Council of the Four Lands, and vital problems must have come up before him for solution. He was a prolific rabbinic author. He wrote *hiddushim* to the Talmud and a large, analytical and explanatory double commentary to Jacob ben Asher's code, the *Tur*. He wrote a commentary on a section of Joseph Caro's code. Yet, strangely enough, he left not a single volume of responsa.

Isaiah Pick Berlin, in the eighteenth century, was for a long time rabbi of the great community of Breslau. Hundreds of practical questions must have been brought to him. He wrote many works in talmudic literature and did indeed write responsa; but they have not been preserved. How could it happen that this author, rabbi of a great community, in the age of printing, did not have his responsa in shape for preservation? Was it mere accident?

Of the two classic commentators on the *Shulhan Arukh*, one, Sabbatai Cohen (*ShaKh*), left a volume of responsa (*G'vurat Anashim*); the other, David ben Samuel Halevi (TaZ) left only a handful of responsa. Yet David ben Samuel Halevi (1586–1667) was rabbi of Ostrog and the head of a large *yeshiba*.

The great community of Altona-Hamburg was a metropolis of Jewish life in north-central Europe. It was led by famous rabbis. One of its most famous rabbinical leaders was Jonathan Eibeschuetz. His sermons were widely read. He wrote a great deal on Jewish Law. He was the author of a famous commentary on the *Shulhan Arukh*. Yet the only responsa which he left are a handful published in the back of his book, *B'nei Ahuva* ("The Children of the Beloved"). At the same time, his famous opponent, Jacob Emden, in Altona, who never actually served as rabbi of the community, received and answered many legal inquiries and his volume of responsa is famous in the field (*Sh'elat Ya'abetz*).

The great Gaon of Vilna left no volume of responsa, although he wrote brilliantly in almost every rabbinic field and was the leading talmudist of the eighteenth century. True, he was not a practising rabbi; but neither was Jacob Emden, who *was* a great respondent.

Elijah of Vilna's great pupil, Hayyim of Volozhin, was also not a practising rabbi, but he did leave many responsa, some of which, alas, were lost by fire in 1815, but a considerable number of which were incorporated by his great-grandson in the collection, *Hut ha-Meshullash* ("The Three-Fold Cord").

Abraham ben Yehiel Danzig was one of the most famous rabbinic authors of the late eighteenth century (1747–1820). He wrote two of the most popular legal handbooks, *Hayyei Adam*, and *Hokhmat Adam*. He was rabbinic judge (*dayyan*) in the great Jewish community of Vilna. He certainly dealt with hundreds of important questions of the Law, and yet has left no separate volume of responsa although he does provide some responsa as incidental additions to his two legal codes.

Yehiel M. Epstein, the author of *Arokh ha-Shulhan*, the latest popular and authoritative re-working of the *Shulhan Arukh*, also left no responsa.

Thus there is a large number of rabbinic authors who certainly had to deal with religio-legal problems and gave answers to questions in this field, and yet left no recorded responsa. Whereas others, and some of them not outstanding authors in other rabbinic fields, left large numbers of responsa. It was, therefore, not primarily the question of ability. Most rabbinic authors were able to work in all the rabbinic fields. It well may be that there is not just one simple explanation. Many interlocking factors—personal, historical and social—may be involved.

The only rabbinic field which has had still fewer workers than that of responsa is the preparation of legal codes. There have been very few codifiers. This is easily understood. In the first place, the codifier must know the entire body of the Law. In the second place, it takes much more breadth of mind and self-confidence to simplify the Law into a code than, for example, to expand it by a commentary. The humblest of scholars could add his *hiddushim*, his additional comments on scattered passages of the Talmud, but it took a towering personality like Moses Maimonides or Joseph Caro to presume to say which opinion is essential and which is only secondary. To condense, to clarify and therefore to reject and set aside the nonessential required a sense of authority given only to a few. Hence there are no more than a handful of codes.

If one considers the list of great rabbis who did not write or publish responsa, it is observed that many of them either wrote codes or devoted their energy to commentaries on and explanations of existing codes. Of course, there were some great codifiers who also wrote responsa; but it is nevertheless a fact that a significant proportion of codifiers and commentators on codes did not produce responsa.

There is evidently a difference in mood between writers of

responsa and codifiers. We know that many of the great rabbis who wrote responsa scorned the codes as too simple, as representing an arbitrary choice between opposing opinions on certain points of law. These respondents preferred to skip the codes and go back to the Talmud, which is the original fountain of authority. Each responsum is in a sense an amplification of the Law, while a code is a simplification of it. Thus, Isaac Alfasi who did not leave many responsa, answered in a brief line or two, as if to make certain that the answer should not involve any amplification of the Law, since he was concerned with simplifying it. As a matter of fact, his code was really not a code at all but an abbreviation of the talmudic text and therefore he is not quite a codifier; yet, even so, his responsa are brief and simple.

Maimonides, who was a great codifier and whose *Mishneh Torah*, (The *Yad*) achieved world-wide authority, could not avoid answering innumerable legal inquiries, since he was a rabbi of Cairo, a great and central community. Nevertheless, it is clear that he did not lay too much stock in his legal responsa. As a matter of fact, although he himself was the most systematic of men, he never organized a collection of his responsa. It was not until the eighteenth century that the first collection of Maimonides' responsa was published, and another and more complete collection finally was published in our day, most of which are translated out of the Arabic. It is clear that the great codifier and philosopher did not put too much emphasis upon his own responsa as a separate branch of literature.

Jacob ben Asher, the great author of the *Tur* left no responsa at all. Joseph Caro, the great author of the *Shulhan Arukh*, left only comparatively few responsa in the field of marriage law and a collection of his own and other respondents in a miscellany (*Abkat Rokhel*), and yet Joseph Caro was clearly better acquainted with the entire responsa literature up to his day than perhaps anyone else. His masterpiece, his commentary, *Bet Joseph*, on the *Tur*, is a mine of information on the responsa up to his time; and yet, considering his knowledge of the responsa, the number of his own responsa is small indeed.

Mordecai Jaffe, the author of the code *Lebush*, left very few responsa.

David Halevi, the great commentator on the code *Shulhan Arukh*, left no responsa.

Joshua Falk, the commentator on the *Tur*, and the *Shulhan Arukh*, left no responsa.

Abraham Danzig, the author of the code *Hayyei Adam*, left only a few responsa.

In our day, Yehiel Michel Epstein, author of the compendium code, *Arokh ha-Shulhan*, left no responsa.

The rule indicated is, of course, not iron-clad, since it deals with a large variety of personalities and circumstances. Thus, for example, Moses Isserles, the commentator on both the *Tur* and the *Shulhan Arukh*, left considerable responsa. And Joel Sirkes, the great commentator on the *Tur* ("BaKh"), left two volumes of responsa; and so did Sabbatai Cohen ("ShaKh"), the commentator on the *Shulhan Arukh*, leave responsa. Yet, in spite of these exceptions, it is nevertheless a noteworthy fact that there is a strong tendency on the part of those engaged in writing or developing or commenting on the codes, to avoid recording responsa. They may have answered many inquiries; but either they answered them briefly, as Alfasi or Maimonides did, or they did not bother to keep their answers and systematize them as a separate literature. They clearly felt that the code was all-important and that all questions could be answered from it, and that it was not necessary or helpful to amplify the Law further by excessive, detailed discussion in an elaborate responsum. Generally, codifiers were not respondents.

Many questions asked of a rabbi do not need a formal responsum. The question is, often, relatively simple. It is clearly dealt with in one or another of the codes, nowadays generally in the *Shulhan Arukh*. The rabbi either answers it *viva voce* or looks it up in the code and gives the answer that he finds there.

The only type of question which needs an elaborate responsum is one that is not clearly dealt with in the codes. Either it is a new detail for which no provision is made in the codes, or it deals with some new article of diet—a fish or poultry—as to whether it is kasher or not, or it is based on the effect of new inventions, such as a steam-driven machine for the making of matzot, or electricity for heat and power (as to whether and how it may be used on the Sabbath). Such questions as are not dealt with in the codes require study on the basis of certain legal principles elicited from the Talmud itself and applied in a new way. It is such new questions that require the detailed working out of a new responsum.

In a small town, the questions which usually come up are simple questions. Most of them come from housewives and deal with problems involved in cookery, the accidental mixture, for example, of meat or milk dishes, or a foreign body found in the poultry when it is being prepared for food. Or there will be disputes between businessmen with regard to contracts, sales and debts. Most questions of this type have already been dealt with in the codes. But in a large city, in addition to these everyday questions which are already covered by the Law—of which, of course, there are many—there is a much greater likelihood that unusual questions will come up which require special analysis.

Furthermore, the rabbi of a large city is more likely to be a well-known man whose reputation extends beyond the confines of his own community. Visitors to the community may bring questions to him and people of other communities send their inquiries. A rabbi in Prague might get inquiries from Italy, from Hungary, from Poland and even from the Balkans. Thus it will be noticed, as might have been anticipated, that most of the famous respondents were rabbis in large cities. Of course, not all the great Jewish communities have produced great respondents. There was, for example, no famous respondent from the great community of Vilna (until Chaim Ozer Grodzinski in our day), or from the still greater community of Warsaw, or, for that matter, from the community of Vienna (unless we count Elazar Horwitz, *Yad Elazar*, who was not in the first rank). No famous respondent came from Rome or from London. Nevertheless, the greatest respondents *were* from the large cities, from Barcelona, from Algiers, from Salonika, from Constantinople, from Prague, from Frankfort-on-the-Main, from Hamburg-Altona, from

Posen, from Pressburg, from Lemberg, from Cracow, from Brody and from Kovno.

To this fact, that it was usually the rabbi of a great city who was more likely to become a famous authority because so many questions were sent to him, there must be added another element. In the larger cities, all through the Middle Ages, wherever the community was large enough to attract a famous scholar, it was also considered a communal duty to maintain a talmudical college, a *yeshiba*. The community was often large enough to maintain a school of hundreds of pupils who would come from far distances to study with the great teacher. The situation was much the same as in the Christian world during the heyday of scholastic philosophy; thousands of disciples would follow the great scholastic philosophers from place to place and listen to their discussions and their debates. Similarly, every rabbi of any consequence would consider it an essential part of his rabbinical function "to raise up many disciples," to conduct a *yeshiba* and spread the knowledge of rabbinic lore.

This conjunction of a famous rabbi in a large community, with a large *yeshiba*, had a natural effect on the growth of the responsa literature. When these students would complete their studies and, having been ordained, would become rabbis in their own communities, they would naturally send to their teachers the difficult questions which came their way. Thus it happens that a considerable proportion of the responsa in the responsa collections are answers sent by a famous teacher to inquiring former students.

Not only did the questions from rabbinical disciples increase the number of questions which a teacher-rabbi had to answer, but the disciples who were still studying with him would often be responsible for gathering and organizing the scattered responsa and their ultimate publication. A great many of the books of responsa were published and preserved in this fashion.

This was true even in the earlier centuries, before responsa ceased to be a separate and important branch of rabbinic literature; that is, before the time when the teacher himself would take the trouble to preserve or to systematize or to spread abroad collections of his own responsa. The reason, for example, why the responsa of the great French authority, Rashi, have come down to us is not that Rashi himself collected them, but that his various disciples possessed collections, which they themselves must have made in classroom notebooks, and embodied them, in the name of their teacher, of course, in their own books. Thus, most of Rashi's responsa are in *Sefer ha-Ora*, *Siddur Rashi* and *Mahsor Vitry*, collected and written by Rashi's pupils. A large proportion of the responsa of Meir of Rothenburg are in the *Mordecai*, by his disciple Mordecai ben Hillel, and in the *Maimuni*, by his disciple Meir ha-Cohen. A large number of the responsa of Israel Isserlein are in *Lekket Yosher*, by his disciple Joseph ben Moses. Even in the later centuries and in more modern times, many of the responsa collections of famous rabbis were collected, organized and published by their pupils.

This may explain a strange difference in the responsa output between Russia and Hungary during the last century and a half. In this period, very few volumes of actual responsa were published in the Russian Empire, while, at the same time, scores of volumes dealing with practical and important questions were published in Hungary. Isaac Hirsch Weiss, in his reminiscences (*Zikhronotai*), describes his student years in Hungary after leaving his native Moravia. He speaks with surprise and admiration of the fact that almost every rabbi of any consequence in Hungary conducted a *yeshiba* of his own. This was a continuation, of course, of the older system of instruction. During the last century or so in Russia, however, the organization of the *yeshibot* had changed. Instead of separate *yeshibot* maintained by each rabbi in each town, great, nationwide *yeshibot* were established—in Volozhin, Slobodka, Mir, and elsewhere. Thus, while the rabbi in every Russian town may well have had a few disciples, and while there always were scholars studying at home and in the *Bet ha-Midrash*, nevertheless, the old medieval bond between hundreds of disciples and their teacher-rabbi, who was also the head of a large community, had ceased to exist in Russia, but continued unchanged in Hungary. Hence, there were comparatively few volumes of responsa published in Russia, considering the huge size of the Jewish community in Czarist days. What responsa were published were generally pilpulistic, keen analyses of talmudic and codal difficulties, rather than usable solutions of practical problems. We must, of course, always except the great Isaac Elhanan Spektor of Kovno, to whom questions were sent from all over the world because of his personal status and fame. In Hungary, on the other hand, where all the disciples sent questions to their respective teachers and rabbis, very many volumes of responsa were published. The attachment of disciple to teacher is, therefore, a crucial element in the development of the responsa literature.

During the last two centuries a sense of inadequacy, or at least of humility, has overtaken many of the respondents. They have felt that, compared with their great predecessors, they really had no right to lay down the law. Many of the respondents say that they are too shy to make a decision. They frequently use a phrase which plays upon the usual phrase for a "decisor": instead of saying that they are *Morei Ho-ra-ah*, they say that they are *M'yorei (Mi-yere'ei) Ho-ra-ah*, in other words, instead of "teachers of the decision," or "guides to decision," they are afraid or they "shy away from making decisions." Often, at the end of a long and learned responsum, the author will say, "This is for the teaching of the Law, but not for actual practice" (*l'halakha v'lo l'ma'aseh*). In recent years, for example, Simon Schreiber (of Eger), in his *Hit'orerot Teshubah*,[2] heads every single page with the statement, "One must not rely upon this teaching of mine."

Such hesitation was more frequently applied to responsa than to any other part of rabbinic literature even when these contained decisions. It was, in fact, considered a legal maxim with regard to the decisions of the great Asher ben Yehiel. Asher's son, Jacob, the author of the *Tur*, excerpted his father's commentary on the Talmud, selecting the practical law which his father derived from the study of the Talmud (*Piskei ha-Rosh*). In addition, Asher ben Yehiel left a volume of responsa. It is a legal rule that, whenever the talmudic derivations of Asher disagree with his responsa,[3] the talmudic derivations must be preferred.

This general diffidence about laying down the law in re-

sponsa and the maxim in the case of Asher ben Yehiel that his
talmudic excerpts (*P'sokim*) are more valid than his responsa
where they disagree, were used by the famous nineteenth century German Orthodox rabbi, Isaac Dov (Seligmann Baer) Bamberger, as an argument to his sons why they must never print his
responsa. After Seligmann Baer Bamberger died, his grandson,
Seckel Bamberger, rabbi of Kissingen, Germany, wrote to the
two great rabbinic authorities of his time, Naphtali Z. J. Berlin,
the head of the Volozhin *yeshiba*, and to Isaac Elhanan Spektor
of Kovno, to ask whether he may or may not publish his grandfather's responsa.

The responsum of Berlin [4] discusses the entire matter. First
he says that the reason for the maxim of the law that Asher's
talmudic excerpts are to be followed rather than his responsa, is
no reflection on the authority of responsa. There was another
reason entirely for this attitude. Asher's son knew that the talmudic excerpts were made *after* the responsa and, wherever they
differ from the responsa, it was because Asher had changed his
mind on the matter at issue. In general, he says, responsa are of
greater importance precisely because they are practical, and God
helps us make them correct. So Berlin concludes that Law
(Torah) which develops from arriving at a practical decision is
much closer to the truth than that which is derived from theoretical study. But, he adds—and this is of direct relevance to our
theme—many scholars (Gaonim) did not desire to have their responsa published. This was precisely because responsa *are* more
authoritative and they did not want people to rely upon their
opinions. But as for their *hiddushim* (their analytical studies of
the Talmud), they did not hesitate to have them printed because
they knew that they had no direct bearing on practical decisions.

In the collection of Seligmann Baer Bamberger's *Teshubot*,
which were finally published by his grandson in Frankfort-on-
the-Main in 1925, he refers to the permission given by N. Z. J.
Berlin to have them published and adds the letter that he had
received from Isaac Elhanan Spektor of Kovno, who suggested
that they be printed but that his grandfather's hesitations should
be honored to this extent:—In the Introduction to the edition it

should be stated that it was not his desire that people should act upon the decisions in his responsa until the reader had gone thoroughly and independently into the matter with which the relevant responsum deals.[5]

The same hesitation is found in the greatest of the respondents of the nineteenth century, Moses Sofer of Pressburg. He had refused to allow any of his writings to be published. His son, who did publish Rabbi Moses' responsa, quotes a letter from his great father: [6]

> I never thought of printing a book; for the majority of the (scholarly) world who are greater than I, or at least equal to me, do not need me; and as for the small minority who are lesser than I, why should I toil in behalf of a small minority? If, indeed, God forbid, it were the fact that most of the (scholarly) world need me, I do not know of any obligation to print and scatter my words abroad. As long as God keeps me alive and gives me strength, I am ready to teach whomever comes and to answer questions as far as I am able, without pay. I write in a book with ink whatever God had vouchsafed to me, and whoever wishes to copy may do so. Thus did our predecessors do before the time of printing. More than that I am not in duty bound to do. God forbid that I should earn money (from printing a book). Therefore it never entered my mind to do so.

But his son said that before his death, he and his father's disciples pleaded with him and overcame his objections and he gave them permission to print.

Moses Sofer, although averse to publishing his responsa, was quite willing to collect them in manuscript. But there were other great scholars who were unwilling even to collect and preserve them. Jacob Pollak (1460–1541), rabbi of Prague and founder of talmudical studies in Poland, was opposed to keeping a copy of the responses which he gave to inquiries sent him. His famous disciple, Shakhna of Lublin, followed the custom of his teacher.

Shakhna's son, Jacob, in a responsum written just after his father's death says: [7]

> Many times did I and his other pupils ask him to compile a book of decisions; but he answered that he did not wish that

later scholars should rely upon him for their decisions, but, that they should decide each case as it comes before them. For this reason, his teacher, Jacob Pollak, had not written any book, nor had these scholars (Shakhna and Jacob Pollak) allowed that any responsum which they sent abroad should be copied in their house.

Other scholars, while they were not as strongly opposed as Jacob Pollak and Schakhna to recording their responsa, nevertheless were not especially interested in doing so. Fortunately, their students wanted copies. Many of the responsa collections which we have were either copied down by pupils with whom the teacher discussed the responsum while he was writing it, and thus many manuscripts were preserved, or else, after the age of printing, many of the collections were printed by the descendants of the author.

To all these considerations, there must be added the fact that the personality and the intellectual interests of the scholar also played an important part in determining whether he was likely to compile and publish a volume of responsa. Each important question as it came to the scholar involved a great deal of study, often in a field of the Talmud far removed from the one in which he happened to be immersed at the time. Frequently, too, the scholar in his large and busy community was deeply involved with public responsibilities which generally included the supervision of a large *yeshiba*. Thus, every question of any importance was definitely an intrusion into a busy life. The opening sentences of many responsa speak of the author's preoccupation with community affairs or with his school; sometimes, his health is mentioned as not good at the time when the question came.

We must, therefore, assume that many famous scholars in great cities resented the intrusion of these problems from distant points and would answer either briefly or not at all. Others, on the other hand, although busy, welcomed the new problem, discussed it fully and sent a complete reply to the questioner. One can easily understand that those who brushed questions aside would soon cease to get other questions, while those who took the trouble to give a full and complete answer would soon receive more. Therefore, in addition to the other elements mentioned, it often depended on the man himself whether he chose to become a respondent or not.

In the time of the Mishna there was a graded system of judiciary: lower courts, higher courts and the supreme Sanhedrin. Such an organized system did not long continue after the destruction of the Jewish state. Moreover, the regular ordination which fitted a man for membership in the Sanhedrin then ceased to exist and Jewish legal authority lost its formal basis. After the close of the Talmud, the heads of the academy in Babylonia, the Gaonim, were accepted as final authority. But they were effective only when questions were directed to them, which could not have been often, since the road to Babylonia was hard and long. Thus there was no graded legal system left for day-by-day opportunity for appeal from a decision deemed unjust. Such an authority had to be re-created, and this is exactly what happened in time. To begin with, any scholar had at least the authority which was granted to him by the litigants themselves, as well as that of his learning which guaranteed that he spoke in the name of the Law of God. Besides, the Jewish communities in the Middle Ages achieved the power to discipline and to tax. Before long, a sort of a super-authority developed for an entire region, the local communities forming themselves into a larger community, as in the Council of the Four Lands in Poland in the sixteenth, seventeenth and eighteenth centuries. At times, a book became the authority, as the *Shulhan Arukh* did when certain communities decided that no one shall be elected rabbi who does not decide according to its precepts.

On the whole, however, it was the responsa that provided a rule-of-thumb substitute for and a concomitant with a system of graded courts. Men could write to a well-known rabbi for his opinion on a question at issue. Certain questions were even sent to scores of famous rabbis, who often ranged themselves in opposing groups and the case became the theme of a heated continent-wide controversy. Usually, in each generation there were two or three respondents who, informally but effectively, were looked upon as the courts of last resort. In some generations there was only one. He had, to be sure, no such official position and need not necessarily have been the greatest scholar of his age. Other scholars of the time also wrote responses; but somehow one of them became the *posek aharon*, the final decisor. Mordecai ben Hillel (Germany, thirteenth century), at the end of chapter 3 of Sanhedrin, discusses demands made for changes of venue when one litigant says, "Let us go to the *Bet Din Gadol* (that is, to the Supreme Court)." Mordecai comments as follows: "Nowadays, when there is no longer any Nasi (an official Patriarch) in Israel, it appears that the great rabbi of the generation must be considered as tantamount to the ancient Supreme Court (*Bet Din Gadol*)."

For example, Meir of Rothenburg, in the thirteenth century in Germany, was said to be the chief rabbi of Germany. There was, of course, no such position under Jewish Law. Every congregation, with its rabbi, was independent of every other. It used to be believed that Emperor Rudolph I appointed him to this position for the purpose of facilitating the taxation of the Jews of the Empire. This is now doubted by most scholars. Yet there can be no doubt of the fact that, in questions of Jewish Law, Meir of Rothenburg was in a definite sense, if informally, deferred to as a chief rabbi. From his responses it is clear that he rarely, if ever, answered questions from the litigants themselves, but always answered those which the communities referred to him after the case appeared beyond the powers of the local authorities. His responsa constitute, therefore, in effect, the decisions, or the proceedings, of the "higher court" of the Jews of Germany in the thirteenth century.

Many hundreds of rabbinic authors have written volumes of responsa, and it would be an almost hopeless task to attempt to give the life story of them all. There is special interest, however, in the careers and personalities of these "respondents of the last resort," the great respondents, who received questions from many lands and whose works, therefore, were carefully preserved and remain the classics of the responsa literature. With some of these, as has already been indicated, their work as respondents was only incidental to their major work as commentators (Rashi), or as codifiers and philosophers (Maimonides), or as epitomizers of the Talmud (Alfasi). These men were almost forced to be respondents because of their great authority in *other* fields; they, therefore, do not interest us here. But most of the great respondents were well aware of the importance of their responses. They did not give the brief, one-line answer which frequently Rashi, Maimonides and Alfasi gave. The responsum was to them an essay, a work of rabbinic literature. It is the life of these especially devoted respondents, who were also the leading decisors of their time, which merits special attention.

Solomon ben Adret

Solomon ben Adret of Barcelona was one of the most prolific of all the respondents. The chronicler, David Conforte,[8] reports about a certain scholar who had told him that he possessed manuscript-responsa of Solomon ben Adret numbered up to six thousand. Whether such a manuscript really existed, or whether, if it did, it still is in existence, the fact remains that Solomon ben Adret is the author of at least three thousand extant responsa and that these responsa, although written in the thirteenth century, are still frequently quoted and are still authoritative. This Spanish rabbi has exerted perhaps the widest and most enduring responsa influence.

He was born in Barcelona in the year 1235 and died in 1310. Three centuries later, Samuel di Medina, rabbi in Salonika, said [9] that Solomon ben Adret is to be preferred over all other scholars in specific cases of financial law:

I have frequently testified in the name of my teacher, Joseph Taitazak, that he relied on Solomon ben Adret's decisions in civil matters against all the other authorities (that is, even if all other authorities disagreed with him).

Indeed, he was known as *el Rab d'España, "The* Rabbi of Spain." He had been a pupil of the great Moses ben Nahman, Nahmanides (RaMbaN), and of the famous Spanish rabbi, Jonah Gerondi.

He lived in the time before the great persecutions, which did not begin until the end of the fourteenth century when the Church was feeling more powerful and secure in Spain. But it was already the time of the great disputations. Rabbis and priests were summoned to debate their respective faiths before kings and nobles. Famous rabbinical leaders were required to develop polemical skill. They had to learn the favorite arguments of the Church and its special interpretation of Scriptural verses. Thus, while Solomon ben Adret did not, as far as we know, personally engage in a public disputation, as did his great teacher Nahmanides, he nevertheless wrote the book against the notorious anti-Jewish treatise by Raimond Martinez, *Pugio Fidei* ("The Dagger of Faith").

But another great disputation also occupied his time. A full century had passed since Maimonides had completed his works. They seemed to have started a slow fuse in the Jewish world and set off a series of minor flares which by now mounted up into a great explosion. The great center of opposition to Maimonides' works came from southern France, the Provence, which had been closely related to Spanish Jewry for centuries. Southern French Jewry constituted a bridge between the pious, Talmud-absorbed Jewry of the school of Rashi and his followers in northern France, and the science-studying Jewry of Spain. Therefore it was in southern France that attempts had to be made to find, if possible, the harmony between the two spirits, the Talmud-centered minutiae-discovering spirit of northern France and Germany, and the calm, logical, systematic spirit characteristic of Spain, preoccupied with the study of Jewish law as well as science. It was from the Provence that the great translators of Maimonides had come: the illustrious family of the Ibn Tibbons, who had rendered his works from Arabic into Hebrew and made them accessible to all of Jewry. From southern France had come also Abraham ben David, commentator and critic of Maimonides' great legal code, *Mishneh Torah*. And it was in southern France that the great controversy developed against his philosophic book *Moreh Nebukhim* ("The Guide to the Perplexed"). The effort to ban the writings of Maimonides as non-religious would never be successful unless the Provençal controversialists could draw in on their side the great Spanish authority, Solomon ben Adret. After a great deal of correspondence with Abba Mari ben Yarhi,[10] ben Adret finally pronounced a ban against the study of philosophy; but it was a compromise, a conciliatory ban. Those who were students of medicine were permitted to study philosophy (because philosophy and science were one, science being natural philosophy); but all others might not study philosophy until after they have passed the age of thirty. Thus ben Adret hoped that the average student would be well grounded in Jewish lore and could then, without harm, study the opinions of Aristotle and others.[11]

All these concerns with Christianity and with philosophy were incidental to his main interest, his rabbinical studies. As did nearly all great rabbinical scholars, he wrote *hiddushim*, explanatory analyses of the Talmud. He wrote a book trying to clarify the Law as it was observed in the home: *Torat ha-Bayyith*, ("The Law of the House"); but his prime work was his responsa. Questions came to him from all over the Jewish world— from Spain, from Portugal, from France, from Italy and from Germany. Throngs of students flocked from distant places to listen to his lectures, and he was constantly working with his disciples. He must have received many inquiries from them after they left him to serve in various communities. It is they who, in their reverent loyalty, must have preserved his works. The great Spanish respondent of the next century, Isaac bar Sheshet, said of him,[12] "Who is greater for us among all the later scholars than he?" He was, indeed, among the very greatest.

The long centuries which have passed have dimmed the memory of his personal life, his joys and his sorrows, his family, his companions. Only his works remain and whatever personal hints might by chance be found within them. By this time, the person has become a monument, but a monument on a high pedestal, and a symbol of deep knowledge, the courage to decide and the ability to transplant Jewish life into thousands of lives and to many communities. Seven centuries have not diminished the popularity of his thousands of responsa, nor shrivelled his authority.

Isaac bar Sheshet ("Perfet")

Isaac bar Sheshet was born in Valencia, Spain, in 1326, and died in Algiers, in 1408, a century after Solomon ben Adret. That century marked a tragic decline in the fortunes of the great Jewish community of Spain. In 1375, the plague struck in Spain and decimated the population. Following this widespread calamity, in Spain as elsewhere in Europe, mob passion, expressed in violent rioting, swept the country. These storms of popular fury came to a climax with the murderous anti-Jewish persecutions of 1391. Led by the fanatical monk, Fernando Martinez, the mobs turned against the Jews. It was in this period that hundreds of thousands of Jews were swept into the Church and thus the first marranos appeared in Spanish history. But other Jews, unwilling to save their life by conversion, fled from Spain. This period, therefore, started the first wave of that emigration of Spanish Jews which revived and transformed Jewish life in other lands. The emigration to North Africa was the first of successive waves of Spanish Jews which were to sweep eastward across Africa to Egypt, to the Turkish Empire and to the Near East, then eventually also northward to London, Amsterdam and Hamburg, and ultimately to the New World. The career of Isaac bar Sheshet was lived amid all these storms and, because his experiences are reflected in his responsa, we know much more about his personal life than we do about his great predecessor, Solomon ben Adret.

When the plague struck Barcelona in 1375, he lost four of his relatives: his mother, his brother Judah, his son and his son-in-law. According to the account given in the *Chronicle of Sambari*,[13] two of his sons (Sheshet and Shealtiel) were burned at the stake on the island of Majorca. Rabbi Isaac himself fled Spain at the age of sixty-five and had to begin a new career in North Africa. His life was full of tribulation and sorrow, but none of the miseries of existence availed to keep him from his studies and from answering inquiries that reached him from many lands. He was one of the greatest of the respondents, not only in his day, but even to our own.

Though Valencia was his birthplace, he spent his early years in Barcelona and was a pupil of Nissim Gerondi. He was a businessman up to the age of fifty; but when business reverses left him poor, he entered the rabbinate, becoming rabbi of Saragossa. Devoted to the strict requirements of the Law, he did not hesitate to oppose certain customs in Saragossa which he considered unwarranted. For example, he opposed the old local custom of reading the *Megilla* (Scroll of Esther) on Purim in Spanish; he objected to proclaiming on the Sabbath an impending sale of land so as to forewarn any who had demands against the former owners. (He held that such a proclamation was in effect the obtaining of consent to a sale and therefore an unwarranted business transaction on the Sabbath.) [14] These, and possibly other insistences on his part, created bitter dissension against him and he accepted the rabbinate of the city of Calatayud. However, the Saragossa community persuaded him to stay. It was there that the plague struck, so that he suffered such wholesale bereavement. Also, false charges were levelled against him and he was imprisoned. After his release, he became rabbi of Valencia and conducted a rabbinical school there. In Valencia he became famous as a respondent.[15] He said to one of his correspondents,

> If I have delayed answering your question, it was because questions on important matters from distant places have surrounded and besieged me; while my colleagues and students are busy copying comments on the tractate of the Talmud which we are currently studying.

In 1391, King Juan I died. His son and successor, Henry VII, was a boy of eleven. In this period, when the hand of government was weak, the fanatical, bigoted priest, Fernando Martinez, roused the populace, and bloody riots took place against the Jews in Seville, Toledo, Cordova and other cities. It was then, in his sixty-fifth year, that this rabbi fled Spain and began his life of exile. If the account in the *Chronicle of Sambari* is correct, that his two sons were martyred on the island of Majorca, he must have first fled there, although the Balearic Islands belonged to the kingdom of Aragon and therefore were affected by events on the mainland. If he went by way of Majorca, he did not stay there long, for he was soon in northern Africa, first settling in Miliana, in Tunis, and then in Algiers where he spent the rest of his life.

The original Jewish inhabitants of North Africa were Arabic-speaking Jews ("the wearers of the turban") whose life was about to be transformed by the arrival of Spanish Jews ("the wearers of the biretta"). The Spaniards brought new business, general culture and, above all, great knowledge of Jewish Law. There were already two Spanish rabbis in Algiers when Bar Sheshet came there: Isaac Bonastruc and Simon ben Zemach Duran. Simon Duran, although much younger than the famous Bar Sheshet, was his rival and opponent for the rest of Bar Sheshet's life.

The occasion for the rivalry was the fact that a famous Spanish physician and talmudist, a great admirer of Bar Sheshet, Saul ha-Cohen Astruc, persuaded the king to appoint Bar Sheshet chief rabbi of Algiers. This was, of course, Bar Sheshet's right by virtue of great knowledge and high standing; but it was wrong to accept an appointment by a secular authority except as a confirmation of a previous appointment by the Jewish community. This led to controversy and, although Simon Duran was frequently invited by Bar Sheshet to cooperate in many communal activities, he never ceased to express his opposition to his older colleague. Thus, even in his old age, in his new home, Isaac bar Sheshet did not have peace. But he was never embittered. He was blessed with a quiet, gentle, forgiving nature and he continued to serve the Jews of many lands through the responsa which he sent to their inquirers. Joseph Caro, author of the *Shulḥan Arukh*, fully two centuries after Bar Sheshet, said of him that his own great teacher, Jacob Berab, had relied on Isaac bar Sheshet more than on any of the other decisors.[16]

This storm-tossed life was a magnificent symbol of the life of many great Jewish scholars who, in the midst of storm and suffering, found their strength in the study of God's Law and were able through their influence to give direction and guidance to their brethren all over the world and to later generations.

Simon ben Zemach Duran

His younger adversary, Simon ben Zemach Duran, was born in 1361 on the island of Majorca and died in Algiers in 1444. He represented a more secular side of Spanish-Jewish life than that typified by Bar Sheshet. A student of mathematics, philosophy and astronomy, he was also a practicing physician in the city of Palma, the capital of Majorca. Since these islands were part of the Spanish kingdom of Aragon, the anti-Jewish riots of 1391 soon spread there, and Simon Duran fled from Majorca and settled in Algiers, arriving there, as has been mentioned, ahead of Isaac bar Sheshet.

Just as Isaac bar Sheshet was forced to become professionally a rabbi when his business affairs failed, so Simon Duran likewise became a rabbi under the difficulties of exile. In a number of places in his writings he explains and apologizes at great length for accepting pay while performing the functions of teacher and judge.[17] He served as co-rabbi under Isaac bar Sheshet and, after the latter retired because of old age, he succeeded him. He had the good fortune to have his son and his grandson succeed him in the rabbinate, and he and these descendants all achieved fame as respondents, their books of responsa being frequently referred to centuries later.

Meir ben Baruch of Rothenburg

This great German rabbi was a somewhat earlier contemporary of the Spanish respondent, Solomon ben Adret. Adret was born in 1235 and died in 1310. Meir of Rothenburg was born in Worms-on-the-Rhine in 1215 and died in the fortress prison of Ensisheim in 1293. His life and the character of his responsa throw a clear light on the harsh realities of Jewish life in the Middle Ages, particularly in northern Europe, in the German and French lands.

Rabbi Meir of Rothenburg's life and his responsa stand out against the drab background of the life of the Jews of the time. The last seven years of his own life were passed in prison, where he was held for ransom, and the overwhelming bulk of his responsa concerned the painful, difficult problems of assessing the confiscatory taxes upon the tiny Jewish communities so that this unfair burden should at least be shared fairly.

For a number of centuries, up to the end of the thirteenth, the Jewry of the Rhineland, the champagne country, and that of northern France, were virtually one. The same type of scholarship prevailed in both; the schools in the one land and in the other attracted students from either. Meir ben Baruch studied in France and, while there, saw the burning of the twenty cartloads of Talmud manuscripts in Paris in the year 1242. He wrote an elegy on that tragic event. He wrote a good deal of other synagogue poetry, much of which has been preserved.[18] In Germany he served as rabbi in many communities: Augsburg, Rothenburg, Worms, Mainz and Nuremberg.

His literary activity was many-sided. Besides liturgical poems, he wrote *Tosafot*, additional notes to the Talmud, special ritual compendia for funerals, and the like. But, above all, he wrote responsa.

Questions came to him constantly. Even the great Solomon ben Adret sent him a question from Spain—and a tragic question it was. It concerned a man who slandered the Jewish community and thereby greatly endangered it. The question was whether the community had the right to punish him with the extreme penalty.[19] Rabbi Meir's influence was spread far and wide by his many disciples, as was the case with all the great respondents. One of his disciples, Mordecai ben Hillel, embodied many of his decisions in his work, *The Mordecai*, and another, Meir ha-Cohen, in his work *Hagahot Maimuni*. His disciple, Samson ben Zadok, in his work *Tashbetz*, records the many ritual observances and personal pieties of his saintly teacher. Rabbi Meir's famous pupil, Asher ben Yehiel, migrated to Spain and thus carried the influence of his teacher to Spanish Jewry where his son, Jacob ben Asher, wrote the monumental code, the *Tur*.

Besides the many responsa of Meir of Rothenburg which were embodied by his disciples in their works—as Rashi's responsa had been embodied by his disciples in their works—there are three great collections of Meir of Rothenberg's decisions. They have been published in Cremona, in Prague, in Berlin, in Budapest (a re-print of the Prague) and in Lemberg, respectively.

There is a striking difference between the general content of the responsa of Rashi, insofar as they have been preserved, and those of Meir of Rothenburg. Rashi's responsa deal almost entirely with ritual matters. Meir of Rothenburg's responsa discuss mostly fiscal matters.[20] This was not due to any lack of concern with ritual matters, but rather to the fact that the tragic financial problems of the Jewish communities of Germany imposed special tasks upon him. The German emperor was imposing new financial burdens on the Jews in addition to those placed on them by the local authorities. The tiny Jewish communities were beside themselves to determine how to bear the burden. There were innumerable questions about the right to settle in a community, problems of the sale of property, and many similar problems.

He is spoken of as the Chief Rabbi of Germany; but whether or not that was true in any official sense, he was certainly the most important rabbi in Germany. He, therefore, had no time to answer questions of individual litigants; but he would deal with such questions only, as it were, on appeal or, rather, when they were referred to him by the community.[21] But all the questions which puzzled the communities ultimately came to him. It was he, for example, who made the final decisions on the fiscal matters which were the inescapable burden of the Jewish communities.

In the year 1286, when he was seventy-one years of age, he was travelling in northern Italy. It may be that he was on the way to Palestine. A Jewish apostate recognized him and informed the bishop of Basle. The bishop arrested him and turned him over to the Emperor who imprisoned him. Meir refused to allow himself to be ransomed, lest this ransoming of leading Jews become an additional form of blackmail. He spent the rest of his life in the fortress of Ensisheim, that is, the seven last years of his life, until 1293 when he died. While in the fortress, he continued to teach and to answer questions. His life, with its wanderings, its sufferings, its awesome responsibility and its many sorrows, was like that of Isaac bar Sheshet, the Spaniard, a type of great Jewish scholar of by-gone days in whom culture was wedded to courage and whose suffering could not wean him away from the study and the teaching of the Divine Law.

His body was ransomed. Alexander Wimpfen of Frankfort-on-the-Main paid the Emperor for the privilege of removing the great rabbi's body from the fortress, that he might be buried in the Jewish cemetery of Worms. He asked only for the privilege that, when he died, he be honored by being buried beside the great teacher.

Israel ben Petachiah Isserlein

Just as the influence of the Jews of Spain extended eastward across Africa into the Balkans and the Near East, so did the spiritual realm of the northern French and Rhineland Jewry extend eastward into Slavic Europe. The chief stop between the Rhineland and the communities farther east was at Vienna. Vienna and its suburb, Neustadt, had survived persecutions and expulsions and, in the early fifteenth century, became a center of Jewish learning and authority both for the German and the Slavic lands. This authority was embodied in Israel Isserlein who is among the first of the respondents known much better by the title of his book of responses than by his own name. The title of his famous book is *Terumat ha-Deshen*, ("Heave-Offering of the Ashes"), based upon the verse in Leviticus 6.3. Many more of his responsa were preserved by his pupil, Joseph ben Moses, who embodied them in his book *Leket Yosher* (Berlin, 1904). Isserlein may have selected the title for his book in order to indicate that, although the persecutions had left only a remnant—as burnt-offerings leave only ashes—even the ashes have some sacredness and must be reverently handled. It was a humble title and characteristic of him; he signed his responsa "The Small and

Immature in Israel" (a reminiscence of Judges 6.15) which made use of his name Israel. Also, the family name, Isserlein, means "Little Israel." He never permitted himself to be called up to the Torah by any title, not even the title *Morenu*, "Our Teacher." At all events, he is rarely referred to by his own name. He is the *Terumat ha-Deshen*.

Israel Isserlein lived in the second half of the fifteenth century and thus was an almost exact contemporary of Isaac bar Sheshet's younger colleague, Simon ben Zemach Duran. He was born in Ratisbon, from where he and his mother emigrated to Neustadt after his father's death. There his maternal uncle, Aaron Blumlein, was his teacher. After his uncle and mother were martyred in Neustadt during the persecution of March 1421, Israel left for Italy, later returning to Neustadt where he stayed until his death in 1460. He built up a large *yeshiba* there, which attracted hundreds of students. His efforts were directed to reviving the study of the Talmud in German lands. In those days, people were turning more and more to the existing codes for quick and easy reference, whereas he wished to bring the students back to the basic source, the Talmud, and to the responsa of the Gaonim, and away from the easy decisions based upon the codes. Thus he was responsible for a considerable revival of the study of the Talmud, as, indeed, Meir of Rothenburg had been two centuries before him.

A scholar like Isserlein, who preferred the study and analyses of the basic sources, naturally would develop responsa, settling questions through a creative re-study of the ancient talmudic texts rather than giving a brief answer based upon a quick reference in the codes. He, therefore, preserved his responsa, which were in answer to questions sent to him from many lands. Although many of his responsa are still in manuscript, two volumes of them have been published (now generally bound together). His *Terumat ha-Deshen* (Venice, 1519), containing three hundred and fifty-four responsa, the numerical equivalent of the word *deshen* ("Ashes"), and his *P'sakim u-Ketabim* ("Decisions and Writings"), containing two hundred and sixty-seven.

Isserlein's book of responsa was perhaps the first to receive a fanciful name, selected by the author and based upon Scripture. All the previous collections of responsa are merely described by the name of the author, without any special title. Thus, Solomon ben Adret's responsa are known merely as *The Responsa of Rashbo*. Isaac bar Sheshet's responsa are known merely as *The Responsa of Ribash*, which are the initials of his name. His young contemporary's responsa are known as *Tashbetz*, again the initials of his name, the T being the initial of the word *Teshubot*, ("Responsa"). His two grandsons, however, would have had to use two sets of initials since they were co-authors; hence they selected the title, *Yakhin u-Boaz*, the two columns in Solomon's Temple.

As for Isserlein's standing in the legal tradition, Samuel di Medina of Salonika [22] says, "We rely on him, that is, on Israel Isserlein, as much as on Isaac bar Sheshet," which is rather an unusual opinion from one of the leading Sephardic scholars of Salonika.

Isserlein's influence was especially strong in the Slavic lands. Within a century after his time, the great *yeshibot* in Poland began to flourish and, since almost the entire Polish-Jewish population came from Germany and Austria, it was only to be expected that the overwhelming influence in the Law in Poland would be German and Austrian. Solomon Luria, the sixteenth-century talmudic authority, said of Israel Isserlein,[23] "Do not deviate from his works because he was great and eminent." Solomon Luria's contemporary, Moses Isserles, whose additional notes to the *Shulhan Arukh* made that Sephardic work authoritative for German-Polish Jews by giving status to the customs and decisions of northern Europe, cites Israel Isserlein constantly in his notes. Isserlein was the bridge between East and West, as a great scholar is sometimes privileged to be, a bond of unity between communities and eras.

Joseph ben Solomon Colon (Maharik)

Each of the historic Jewries had its distinguishing cultural characteristics. The philosophic, scientific mood of Spanish

Jewry contrasted sharply with the talmudic, mystical Jewry of northern France and Germany. The Italian Jewry, unique in its frequent and friendly contact between Jewish and Christian scholars during the Renaissance, was outstanding in literary elegance, in clarity of expression, which revealed itself in its Hebraic writings. The Jewry of the Spanish exiles, in the sixteenth century in Palestine and in the surrounding lands, developed a mixture of talmudic knowledge and kabbalistic vision. Yet, though each of the great Jewries embodied individual lines of development under differing environments, there was always the integrating influence of the common study of talmudic Law which gradually elicited the basic unity beneath the various diversities.

This unifying force was brought to bear upon the separate Jewish cultures first by immigration and secondly by the far-ranging and alert minds of individual scholars. The Jewries of the Rhineland and of northern France achieved a unitary culture through the fact that students from France studied in Germany, and students from Germany—as, for example, Meir of Rothenburg—studied in France. Between northern France, with its Talmud-immersed culture, and Spain, scientific and philosophic, the Jewry of southern France, the Provence, served as an intermediary. The check on the Spanish over-absorption with philosophic studies originated in southern France; and, as though to balance, it was the southern French family of Ibn Tibbon whose translations from Arabic into Hebrew made the great Spanish philosophic works the property of the Jews throughout the world. Also, Moses ben Nahman helped bring the northern French talmudic analyses into Spanish-Jewish studies. More directly, Asher ben Yehiel, emigrating from the Rhineland to Spain, brought the French-German influence to bear on the Iberian peninsula.

Italian Jewry was outstanding as an example of a Jewish culture which influenced and was influenced by other Jewries. Jewish students from northern Europe, even from far away Poland, came to the Italian universities to study medicine, and students from Italy must have gone to Poland to the talmudic academies which developed there. Italy received waves of immigrant Jews from other lands. There was a constant settling of German Jews in Italy, and there were ancient German congregations there. Spanish Jews came in large numbers after the persecutions of the fourteenth and fifteenth centuries, while southern Italy was from ancient times in contact with African and Babylonian Jewry.

Italian Jewry, never large in numbers, was always, as it were, a metropolis of cosmopolitan Jewry under many influences and, in turn, it was widely influential. One of the leading authors in the field of responsa literature was the fifteenth-century Italian rabbi, Joseph ben Solomon Colon (1420–1480). His origin, his career and his type of writing constitute a symbol of the Jewry of Italy. He was born in Chambéry, in the province of Savoy, the borderland between Italy and France. He was under the influence of German-Jewish studies and combined their painstaking thoroughness with Italian-Jewish clarity. His family had migrated in the early fifteenth century from France to Italy. He left home early in his life and was a wandering instructor in Hebrew in many Italian towns. He was successively rabbi in Pieve de Sacco near Venice and also in near-by Mestre, then in Bologna, Mantua and, finally, for the bulk of his career, in Pavia.

Early in his life he met a pupil of Israel Isserlein of Austria and was converted by him to that great teacher's deep talmudic analysis. As a result, he became the center and inspiration of new talmudic studies in Italy. When he was rabbi in Pavia, pupils flocked to him from all over Italy and, as happened with many of the great teachers of talmudic students, he became a famous respondent. Questions came to him from former pupils and also from all those Italian towns whose small communities lacked a rabbi of their own. Later, as his fame grew, questions came from northern Europe and from the Balkans. His answers show a clear, systematic mind, striving to connect the questions asked with basic principles derived from the Talmudic text. He paid little attention to most legal codes or to local customs,[24] but went directly to the original talmudic source and used the principles logically derivable from it.

His clear mind traveled in uneasy harness with what must have been a fiery temperament. Early in his career, in Mantua, he got into a quarrel with Messer Leon, a quarrel so bitter that both of them were banished from the city. He had heard that Moses Capsali, the Chief Rabbi of Turkey (the *Haham Bashi*) was rather liberal in his interpretations of certain marriage laws, among which was the case of a widowed, childless woman, whose husband had been a non-repentant Christian Marrano. Moses Capsali was reported to have permitted her to remarry without her having previously obtained permission *(halitza)* from her deceased husband's brother.[25] Colon indignantly denounced the Chief Rabbi of Turkey and threatened to put him under the ban. Towards the end of his life, Joseph Colon discovered that he had been misled about Moses Capsali, that local quarrels had caused certain persons to spread slander about their Chief Rabbi. He was deeply repentant and on his deathbed directed his son, Peretz, to go to Constantinople and ask pardon of the *Haham Bashi*.

His volume of responsa is the book by which he is best known in the world of Jewish literature. He had written a commentary on the Torah and other works, but only his responsa were published. They were collected, as often happened with these works, after his death, by his son-in-law and his pupils. The book is known simply as *The Responsa of Maharik*, which are the initials of his title and name, Morenu ha-Rav Rabbi Joseph Colon. It became a classic in the responsa literature and has appeared in many editions. The first edition was published in Venice in 1519, the second edition soon afterwards in Constantinople, the third edition in Cremona, 1557, and in comparatively modern times there have been four more editions. While other works of responsa were published in Italy, it is the responsa of Maharik which constitute the Italian contribution to the first rank of works in this literature. It is the symbol of a man who was moved by a combination of moods, and represents a country which itself was the product of a combination of influences. Cool logic and fiery zeal, southern France and Germany and

Italy, combined their influences to produce one of the monuments of the responsa literature.

David ben Solomon ibn Zimra (Radbaz)

The test of the basic health of a human body is its power to resist destructive infection when illness strikes, and the power to fight back and re-establish health; this "healing power of nature" is equally a symbol of healthy societies. It is doubtful whether any social group has sustained so many grievous blows as has world Jewry and yet found the power so often to throw off the mortal illness and to regain creative health.

One of the outstanding examples in the long series of Jewish recoveries is the cultural achievement of ex-Spanish Jewry. The last century of Jewish life in Spain had been a hideous succession of persecution, massacre and forced conversion, culminating in complete and absolute expulsion. If history did not tell us that it was true, it would be hard to believe that this Jewry, dragged down from its high eminence, pursued to the death and then strewn like dust to the winds of the earth, should ever again become a living and creative force. But the fact is that the ex-Spanish Jews revived old Jewries, built new ones, and wrote great literature almost wherever they came. Though their influence was felt wherever they settled in any considerable numbers—as far north as Hamburg and London, as far west as the New World—their greatest achievement was in the Near East, the Levant. Under Isaac bar Sheshet and Simon ben Zemach Duran, they had given new life to the Jewries of northwest Africa. Then under a whole galaxy of scholars, they brought a new religious and cultural flowering to Egypt, Palestine, Asia Minor and Turkey.

Long and illustrious is the list of scholars, exiles from Spain or children of exiles, who contributed to the new life of the Jews in the Near East: Jacob Berab of Safed, Levi ben Habib of Jerusalem, Joseph ibn Lev of Salonika, Joseph Caro of Safed, and, high on this list, David ben Solomon ibn Zimra. All of the men mentioned wrote books of responsa and most of the books have remained important in the field. David ibn Zimra is not necessarily the greatest of these legal scholars, but he is a dramatic example of courage, of recovery in exile and of endurance.

He was born in Spain in 1479 and died in Safed, Palestine, in 1589. He lived to the age of one hundred and ten active years! He was thirteen years of age when the great Expulsion from Spain occurred in 1492. He first settled in Safed, Palestine, where he studied under Joseph Saragosa. He moved to Cairo in Egypt and in his thirties was a member of the rabbinical court there. In 1517, when he was thirty-eight, he became Chief Rabbi of Egypt, a position which he retained for over forty years. He conducted a large *yeshiba* and many famous scholars were his pupils. The great talmudic author, Bezalel Ashkenazi, was one of them; and Isaac Luria, the world-famous kabbalist, was another. He had an ample fortune of his own and therefore was prominent not only as scholar but also in the social life of the community. It was he who abolished in Egypt the old dating of documents according to the Seleucidean era, which went back to the time of the successors of Alexander the Great in the third pre-Christian century, and introduced the dating from creation followed by the rest of Jewry.

At the age of ninety he resigned his position as Chief Rabbi of Egypt, distributed his large fortune among poor scholars and emigrated to Jerusalem. There the Turkish authorities, knowing of his former wealth, tried to extort money from him; whereupon he left Jerusalem and moved to Safed, the city of the mystic scholars in Galilee. Joseph Caro, who was the head of the Safed rabbinical court, was proud to include David ibn Zimra in this tribunal and we have documents which he signed along with Joseph Caro.[26] He wrote many works, commentaries on Maimonides, rules of talmudic interpretation, kabbalistic commentaries; but, above all, he was a great respondent. Questions came to him from all over the world. He has left about three thousand responsa and these are still studied as authoritative.

David ibn Zimra, by his long life and unflagging energy and his great achievements, must have left a deep impression upon his generation. Hayyim Joseph Azulai, the eighteenth-century

chronicler and rabbinic author, quotes the impression of Isaac
Akreesh, who himself was an exile from Spain and who lived for
ten years in Egypt in the house of David ibn Zimra. Azulai
quotes Isaac Akreesh substantially as follows:

> He (David ibn Zimra) had the diadem of the Torah. In the
> light of his keen reasoning walked those who had wandered
> in darkness; and his responsa went forth to every questioner
> from all over the world. And in his house there were thrones
> of judgment like the thrones of the House of David. There was
> the wealth of treasures, of pearls and sapphires. But the crown
> of his good name outshone them all. He judged Israel in Egypt
> for forty years and in Jerusalem and in Safed for twenty years.
> His countenance was heroic as a lion and no evil or favoritism
> nor taking of bribes could stand in his presence. Before him
> bowed princes, and nobles prostrated themselves.

Even allowing for the florid style of his day, one can see how
one Spanish exile was moved at the greatness achieved by a fel-
low-exile. David ibn Zimra's life was an evidence of the powers
latent in the broken Jewries to find new health, new strength,
and to give continuity to the word of God which speaks through
Jewish Law.

Meir ben Gedaliah of Lublin (Maharam Lublin)

The Jewish cultural center in Poland reached its highest point
of development in the sixteenth and the early seventeenth centuries. In 1648, it received a wound from which it never recovered: the Chmielnitzki revolt, when the Cossacks and their
Tartar allies, in rebellion against their Polish overlords, inundated
scores of Jewish communities in a tide of blood. Before that
tragedy, the various communities met during the great fairs at
Lublin and Yaroslav, and all of Polish Jewry was organized in a
council of nation-wide Jewish self-government, the Council of
the Four Lands. Great *yeshibot* graduated hundreds of students.
Great scholars flourished in those days, teachers whose fame
during their lifetime spread over many lands. Many of their
works remain as a permanent part of Jewish legal literature.

Three and a half centuries later, they still are studied and are still authoritative.

Since many of these scholars in the heyday of Polish-Jewish glory wrote responsa which are used to this day, it is difficult to decide who among them was the leading respondent. Moses Isserles (1520–1572) and his kinsman, Solomon Luria (1510–1573), were both famous respondents whose decisions have survived. Yet the fame of these great lights of learning does not rest primarily on their responsa, but upon their other works. Isserles, famous for his notes to the *Tur* and the *Shulhan Arukh*, is a code authority for the Jews of northern Europe. Solomon Luria is famous for his textual notes on the Talmud, *Hokhmat Shelomo* ("The Wisdom of Solomon"), and for his great legal appendix to the Talmud, *Yam shel Shelomo* ("The Sea of Solomon"). A younger contemporary of theirs, Meir ben Gedaliah of Lublin, is famous almost exclusively as a respondent. Into his responsa he poured his learning, along with the story of his struggles with his contemporaries. His opponent in controversy, the equally famous Joshua Falk, presents an interesting contrast to him. Falk's main career was passed in the city of Lemberg, where Meir of Lublin likewise served as rabbi for a time. Both men engaged in a bitter dispute over a divorce which Joshua Falk wrote in Vienna.[27] Joshua Falk wrote a famous commentary on the "Hoshen Mishpat" section of the *Shulhan Arukh* (*Meirat Enayyim*, "Enlightening the Eyes") and a widely used double-commentary ("Derisha" and "Perisha") on the *Tur*. Of these two great contemporaries whose controversy involved many others, Joshua Falk, who wrote chiefly commentaries on codes, left no book of responsa; whereas Meir Lublin's chief work (and except for some *novellae* on the Talmud, his only other published work) is his famous book of responsa.

What is known of his life is gleaned chiefly from passing references and comments in his responsa. Thus, in his responsum no. 138, he is asked concerning a murder case and states at the very beginning, "Since I am not as yet settled and my tools (that is, my library) are not in my hands, but are still in the congregation of Lublin, I will answer briefly." From similar personal notes we know where he journeyed and the congregations he served.

He was born at Lublin in 1558 and died there in 1616. His principal teacher was his father-in-law, Isaac Cohen Shapiro, rabbi of Cracow. He signed many of the responsa, "Meir, the son of Gedaliah, the son-in-law of the great scholar, Isaac Cohen." While still in his twenties, he was called to the rabbinate of Cracow and then for a while was rabbi of Lemberg. It was while he was in Lemberg that he engaged in the controversy with Joshua Falk. Then he returned to Lublin as rabbi, and he remained there for the rest of his life. In Lublin, he conducted a *yeshiba* and many famous scholars were his disciples. Among them were Joshua Heschel of Cracow and Isaiah Horowitz, author of *Sh'nei Luhot ha-Berit* ("Two Tables of the Covenant") which exerted so profound a kabbalistic influence on the ritual and life of north European Jewry. In fact, a large proportion of the rabbis of Poland were his pupils. He himself, in a responsum addressed to the city of Worms,[28] refers to some scholar who presumed to criticize a decision of his and, in defending his status and his right to make the decision, says, "I do not say this by way of boasting, but it is a well-known fact that, thank God, I have established as many worthy disciples as all my great predecessors, and many of my pupils are today chiefs of *yeshibot* and rabbis in Israel." He was a great influence on the rabbinic life of Poland, and questions reached him from many other lands. Thus responsa nos. 12 and 13 came to him from Italy, no. 21 from Germany, and no. 89 from Constantinople. His responsa are still cited frequently. Meir of Lublin was not of as great stature as his older contemporaries, Isserles and Luria; but because he was devoted entirely to the training of rabbis and answering questions addressed to him, he attained an honored place among the great respondents.

Jair Hayyim Bacharach (Havot Ya'ir)

Bohemia and Moravia, the westernmost of the Slavic lands, constituted a bridge between eastern and western Jewries. In the seventeenth century, when Polish Jewry received its mortal blow through the Cossack rebellion, Moravia and Bohemia enjoyed a century of leadership in the world of Jewish rabbinic learning. Many of the exiles from Poland settled there and many of the original Bohemian and Moravian families produced famous scholars. In the seventeenth and early eighteenth centuries, some of the greatest respondents either came from Bohemia and Moravia or had settled there.

Jair Hayyim Bacharach was born in Leipnik, Moravia, in the year 1639, and died as rabbi of Worms-on-the-Rhine in 1702. Unlike many of the leading respondents, he was not famous as rabbi of a great Jewish community. He had been rabbi of Mainz possibly for a year or two; of Coblenz for three years; and rabbi of Worms for a similarly short period. When he was its rabbi, Worms was a broken community, having just reestablished itself after the French had burned it in 1689. He, therefore, did not have the advantages or the fame of the rabbi of a Jewish metropolis. Yet he became one of the best-known of the respondents of his day. None of his contemporaries had produced a book of responsa as widely read and as frequently cited as his.

His eagerness to become a rabbinic scholar and his ability to develop as a respondent in the Law were perhaps motivated by family tradition. His father, Samson Bacharach, had been rabbi of Worms, and his grandfather, Abraham Samuel Bacharach, had been rabbi of Worms before him. His book of responsa is named in reference to his grandmother, Eva Bacharach, who, interestingly enough, was herself famous as a rabbinic scholar. The title, *Havot Ya'ir*, means "The Tents of Jair" (son of Menasseh) and comes from Deuteronomy 3.14; but the first word *havot* sounds like his grandmother's name, "Hava," or "Eva"; hence the title. She was the granddaughter of Reb Loew ben Bezalel of Prague, famous as the maker of the *Golem*. His family name, as well as his own reputation, brought questions to Jair Hayyim Bacharach which otherwise would have gone to some more widely-known rabbi in a great community.

When Bacharach's father, Samson, was called to the rabbinate of Worms, Jair Hayyim was only twelve years of age. At the age of fourteen, he was married to the daughter of Sussman Brilin, who was also rabbi in Worms. He studied in his father-in-law's house and under his guidance for seven years. At the age of twenty-one, he received his rabbinical license from the rabbi of Frankfort. After a brief rabbinate in Mainz and in Coblenz, he returned to Worms where he lectured on talmudic law. His father hoped to see him elected as his successor as rabbi of Worms, but the congregation elected someone else. Bitterly disappointed though he was, he continued creative study. He wrote a large compendium on the Jewish religion, *Etz Hayyim* ("The Tree of Life"), and then published a collection of his grandfather's, his father's and his own responsa in one volume under the title, *Hut ha-Shani* ("The Scarlet Thread").

In 1699, a decade after the city of Worms had been burned by the French army, the scattered members of the community came together again, obtained an imperial charter and re-established their congregation. It was then that they finally elected Bacharach as their rabbi. He was now sixty years of age, broken in health, crippled and with scarcely any hearing left; but he had the satisfaction of being elected by this historic congregation to succeed his father and his grandfather. He held the position for a few years and died at the age of sixty-four.

In him independence of mind and pride of ancestry were combined with personal humility. Although his book was published during his lifetime, he did not title it with his own name, as was the case with most books of responsa. From his time on, books of responsa were called less frequently after the name of the author, but more and more with a reference to some biblical or talmudic phrase.

His book of responsa, *Havot Ya'ir*, was printed in Frankfort in the year 1699, the year when he finally became rabbi of Worms, and has been reprinted twice. While strictly traditional in its decisions, it is a model of clear thinking. Avoiding the painfully minute analysis *(pilpul)* of many of his contemporary writers, he was clear in style, logical in thought and independent in judgment. One of the especially interesting responsa is no.

124 (in the Lemberg edition) in which, in answer to the request
of a father whose son had just become *bar mitzvah*, he draws up
a curriculum for the Jewish youth of his day, working out a
logical sequence of studies for the rational acquisition of rabbinic
knowledge. This man of remarkably independent mind, who
never had any long periods of assured status nor strong health
but was sustained by the memory of honored ancestry and
strengthened by the love of study, produced one of the classic
works of the responsa literature.

Ezekiel Landau (Noda bi-Yehudah)

The religious bonds between the Jewries of Germany and
Poland were intimate and unbroken for centuries. Rabbis from
Germany would settle in Poland and rabbis from Poland in Germany. The westward current grew strong after the Chmielnitzki
revolt of 1648. Beginning then and continuing for two generations, many Polish rabbis emigrated to western Europe and occupied pulpits in Bohemia and in Germany. Many of the famous
rabbis of western Europe were thus of Polish origin. Perhaps the
greatest among these was Ezekiel Landau.

The biography of Ezekiel Landau is easily accessible. It is not
necessary to search through his responsa for stray hints as to the
cities in which he lived and the activities of his life. The second
of the two introductions to the second part of *Noda bi-Yehudah*
is a complete biographic sketch of the author. This second part
of the responsa was edited by Ezekiel's younger son, Samuel, at
whose request the older brother, Jacob (Yacobke), provided the
biography of their illustrious father.

Ezekiel Landau was born in Opatow, Poland, in 1713, although the name of his family indicates that it hailed from the
western German town of Landau. He was educated in Vladimir
and in Brody and already in his youth was a famous and brilliant
student. He married at the age of nineteen and, as was the custom, lived for a number of years with his parents-in-law in
Dubno. In the city of Brody he was one of the rabbis of the
Klaus, the permanently organized study circle, and rose to be a

member of the rabbinical court of the community. In 1745 he became rabbi in Yampol.

About this time, European Jewry was convulsed by the bitter dispute which centered chiefly around Jonathan Eibeschuetz of Hamburg and his resolute opponent, Jacob Emden of Altona. Jacob Emden, who himself is one of the famous respondents, accused Jonathan Eibeschuetz of being a secret adherent of the dangerous Sabbatian heresy. In the attempt to prove his point, Jacob Emden deciphered the mysterious inscriptions on certain amulets which Jonathan Eibeschuetz had given to the sick. He proved that the letters on these amulets were anagrams of the name of Sabbatai Z'vi.[29] These accusations stirred up a storm, both men being famous talmudic scholars. Many of the great rabbis of the time were drawn into the controversy, taking one side or the other. When Ezekiel Landau was consulted—he was then quite a young man—he advanced the suggestion that made possible the achievement of peace. He suggested that the amulets may well have been forged, and thus gave Rabbi Jonathan Eibeschuetz a graceful way out. The young rabbi achieved wide approbation for his letter.

In 1754, at the age of thirty-one, Landau was called to the great Jewish community of Prague, and there he remained as rabbi for thirty-nine years, until his death, in 1793. He was characterized by a great gentleness of character, combined with immense learning, and was respected by the government as much as he was revered by the Prague community. In 1757, during the Seven Years' War, Prague was besieged by the Prussian armies and, although he was urged to leave the city for safety's sake, he elected to stay with his community.

For a strange reason, he, the learned and the gentle, incurred the enduring enmity of the leaders of the other great western Jewish community, Frankfort-on-the-Main. This again was due to a widespread controversy, the famous dispute over the divorce of Cleves.[30] Because Ezekiel Landau came to the support of Rabbi Israel Lipschutz of Cleves who had given the divorce, and thus took the side against the rabbinical court of Frankfort which opposed the giving of the divorce, the Frankfort Jewish authorities decreed that neither he nor any of his sons should ever be elected rabbi of Frankfort-on-the-Main.

In the great conflagration in Prague in 1773, Ezekiel Landau lost most of his manuscripts. Thereupon he decided to prepare what was left for the press. He wrote a commentary on the *Shulhan Arukh*, notes on the Talmud, and other works; but his greatest achievement is his responsa collection. It is only a part of the many responses that he had written. He conducted a great *yeshiba* in Prague and many famous rabbis graduated from his school and later addressed to him their questions. Inquiries came to him from many lands. His collection of responsa was named after his father, Judah, and is called *Noda biYehudah* ("Known in Judah") after the verse in Psalm 76.2. So varied is the field that he covered in answering the multitude of questions addressed to him over the years as rabbi of the great community of Prague, that his responsa can well be studied for the picture that they give of the Jews at the time, in Bohemia and the surrounding lands. A recent writer has gone through his responsa to glean from them the reflections of the economic and social conditions of the time.[31] Although he frequently made decisions which were controverted by other rabbis—such as declaring the sturgeon to be kasher, or permitting the cutting of the hair on the half holidays—his work towers as one of the highest pinnacles in the entire range of the responsa.

Moses Sofer (Hatam Sofer)

Corresponding to the stream of rabbis from the East moving to congregations in western Europe, there was a counter-stream from western Europe to eastern-Jewish communities. Yomtov Lipman Heller, born in Bavaria, and long rabbi in Prague, became, at the end of his career, rabbi in Cracow, Poland. Z'vi Ashkenazi, rabbi in Amsterdam, became rabbi in Lemberg, Poland. Moses Sofer, the leader of Hungarian Orthodoxy, and one of the greatest of all respondents, was born in Frankfort-on-the-Main, and always signed his responsa, "Moses Sofer of Frankfort-on-the-Main."

Moses Sofer was born in 1763 in Frankfort. At the age of nine he was a student at the *yeshiba* in Frankfort under Nathan Adler, talmudist and mystic. In his *bar mitzvah* year, he delivered such learned lectures that Phineas Horwitz, the famous Rabbi of Frankfort, invited him to become his personal pupil; and he did, for one year. Then he went to the *yeshiba* in Mayence, where he studied under Rabbi Tevele Scheuer. There he was a favorite and a protégé of the whole Jewish community. In addition to his rabbinic studies, he studied certain secular sciences: astronomy, geometry and general history. After his ordination, he returned to Frankfort, whence he followed his teacher, Nathan Adler, to Boscowitz and Prosnitz in Moravia. He married and became the head of the *yeshiba* in Prosnitz.

In 1798 he accepted the rabbinate of Mattersdorf in Hungary; it was the beginning of his brilliant career in Hungary and, it may well be said, an epochal event in the history of Hungarian Jewry. In Mattersdorf he fostered the *yeshiba* which grew to large proportions. Then, in 1803, he moved to Pressburg, Hungary, where he remained for thirty-six years, to the end of his life, in 1839. His *yeshiba* in Pressburg quickly became the most famous *yeshiba* of modern times, growing to five hundred pupils and more. Moses Sofer knew almost all of them and considered them the special objects of his consideration and his affection. He became the leader of Hungarian Orthodoxy. A great succession of scholars followed him in his generation and during the next century, and his name was always uttered with profound reverence.

The monument of his scholarship, besides his *yeshiba* which was the fountainhead of rabbinic knowledge for Hungary, were his responsa. He wrote, of course, in many fields other than responsa. His famous *novellae* on the Talmud are still studied. He is said to have left a hundred volumes in manuscript. As a matter of fact, as is clear from the statement of his son in the Introduction to his father's responsa (section "Yoreh Deah"), Moses Sofer never thought of publishing any of his works and had to be persuaded by his son to do so. His work is entitled *Hatam Sofer*, based on Daniel 12.4.

While, of course, his opinions are undeviatingly orthodox, they are characterized by considerable rationalism and a brushing aside of mere folkloristic accretions to Jewish observance. For example, when asked about the direction of the rows in which the graves are dug in the cemetery, he said that the graves are usually laid out in a certain way so that at the resurrection, the revived dead will arise and face Jerusalem for their return; but, he adds, since it is possible to go to Jerusalem from Hungary by two routes, either eastward through Constantinople, or directly south through Trieste, it does not really make any difference in which direction graves are laid out.[32] He was an uncompromising opponent of Reform and one of the leaders in the war against it. The Jewish Reform movement came into Hungary from Germany, and it was chiefly due to Moses Sofer and his influence that it never made headway there. His will, which was edited with commentary (*The Heart of the Hebrew*) was also an influence for strict piety. But, above all, his responsa, clear, brilliant, decisive, rational, uncompromising, gave traditional Judaism a rebirth in Hungary and have kept Moses Sofer as a towering figure on the horizon of Jewish legal literature.

Joseph Saul Nathanson (Sho'el u-Meshib)

As Poland was progressively partitioned among Russia, Germany and Austria, Polish Jewry, broken into segments, began to develop along three different lines. The part that became embodied into the Russian Empire was dragged back into the semi-medieval past in which Russia lived. The part that was taken into Germany was rapidly and purposefully Germanized. Galicia, the part of Poland that was embodied in the Austrian Empire, developed in its own unique way. It turned neither to the East nor to the West, exclusively, nor entirely to the old or the new, but found a middle path. Whereas the responsa of Russian-Poland tended to veer away from modern problems and to confine themselves to discussions of difficult passages and maxims of the Law, and whereas the Jewry of German-Poland tended to grow modern and lose more and more of its rabbinical knowledge, the Jews of Galicia became constantly aware of modern problems and questions, even while retaining deep rabbinical knowledge by which they could cope with them. Hence, it was inevitable that, of the three sections of former Polish Jewry, it was Galician Jewry which produced the most famous respondents who brought the ancient rabbinic knowledge to bear upon modern conditions for the solutions of modern problems. The responsa literature has been permanently enriched by men like Solomon Kluger of Brody, and, at a somewhat later date, Isaac Schmelkes of Lemberg; but perhaps the greatest of them all a century ago was Joseph Saul Nathanson, the rabbi of Lemberg, whose famous responsa collection, *Sho'el u-Meshib,* ("He Who Asks and Answers") based upon *Ethics of the Fathers* V, 10, is one of the grand works in the literature.

His father, Aryeh Lev Nathanson, was rabbi in Berzan, Galicia, where Joseph Saul was born in 1808. He grew up there and married the daughter of Rabbi Isaac Aaron Ettinger of Lemberg, and then, as the custom prescribed, moved to Lemberg to live in his father-in-law's home. While this was the usual procedure with young scholars, a rather unusual development occurred in this case. Joseph Saul Nathanson's brother-in-law, the rabbi's son, Mordecai Zev Ettinger, was likewise a scholarly young man, and both brothers-in-law formed, as it were, a literary partnership. Among the books that they wrote together, whose number was considerable, was *M'forshe ha-Yam* ("Seafarers," but also "Expositors of the Sea"), a commentary on a book, *Yam ha-Talmud* ("The Sea of the Talmud"), by their uncle. At the end of the book, they added a number of responsa which they had already written in correspondence with some of the great rabbis of their day.

After some years, Joseph Saul began to study independently and gradually accumulated a circle of students who came eagerly to listen to his teaching. He continued studying, teaching and writing in Lemberg in almost all branches of rabbinic literature. When Jacob Ornstein, rabbi of Lemberg, died, Rabbi Simcha Ellenberg was given the rabbinate for a while; but old age made it too difficult for him to continue. Then Joseph Saul Nathanson, at the age of forty-nine, was made rabbi of this great community. He served Lemberg for eighteen years, to his death, in 1875.

Solomon Buber who, in his youth, knew Nathanson as an old man,[34] said of him:

> He guided the congregation of Lemberg for eighteen years in righteousness and uprightness. In all the ends of the world his name was great, and all the great men of the generation sent to him their questions as a man would consult the word of God; and he answered every inquirer. He established a house of study in our city and taught many disciples who became great men in Israel. He was invited to the Heavenly Academy after his final sickness, and his soul came to its rest on the 27th day of Adar, 5635 (1875). Throughout the scattered dwellings of Israel, the leaders of the generation mourned for him. And I, when I was young, had the merit of knowing this great eminence.

His many-volumed collection of responsa, by its very size, by the immense variety of the questions dealt with and by the lands from which the questions came, indicates that Joseph Saul Nathanson was for a generation the center for Jewish legal decision for Jews the world over.

Isaac Elhanan Spektor ("En Yitzhak," "Be'er Yitzhak")

The vast Russian Jewry of Czarist days attained widespread rabbinic learning. Its large *yeshibot* graduated thousands of scholars. In every village and town there were men who all through their life devoted much of their time to rabbinic studies. There can be little doubt that in Russian Jewry about the year 1800 there was a larger total number of competent talmudists than in any other two Jewries combined. This was due, of course, to the great size of Russian Jewry, but, more importantly, to the fact that through the great *yeshibot* talmudic knowledge had penetrated this community through and through.

But, in spite of the vast amount of learning, Russian Jewry has produced very few world-wide authorities in the field of responsa. Modernity, with its changes and day-by-day challenges which interpenetrated the life of Hungary and Galicia, was still kept at a distance in the Russian-Jewish villages and towns. Judaism could still be observed just as it had been observed for centuries. Therefore, the problems discussed by the Russian rabbis in their learned correspondence were, generally, not the practical problems that came before the Galician and Hungarian rabbis, but the theoretical, analytical problems as to the meanings of certain texts and apparent contradictions between older authorities. Russian responsa were, on the whole, not meant for the guidance of the average man, but were the exchange of learned opinions between scholars. In later years, of course, particularly after the Russian Revolution, the problems which found their way into Russian responsa, such as those of Yehudah Lev Zirelsohn, became suddenly practical and urgent.

Yet there was one Russian authority who enjoyed a world-wide influence, namely, Isaac Elhanan Spektor of Kovno. It was as if all the Russian scholars, themselves interested only in the abstruse, theoretical problems of the texts, had shunted their practical problems to him. In point of fact, of course, this was the result of his being an indefatigable correspondent, willing to answer all the practical questions sent to him from all over the world. Though there were many great scholars in his day, there was no other Russian authority who even approached his standing as a practical guide whose help was sought from near and far, except, perhaps, the great authority of the HaBaD Hasidim, Menachem Mendel of Lubavitch, whose responsa are collected in *Zemah Zedek*.

Isaac Elhanan Spektor's life was typical of the lives of many of the famous rabbinic authorities: the same boyhood manifestations of intellectual genius, the same early marriage and support in the house of his parents-in-law and the same gradually extending influence over the entire Jewish world. One additional element, however, is found in his life. The deep, tragic poverty of Russian Jewry of a century ago left a record on his personal story. But other than that, it is like the life of Jair Hayyim Bacharach, Ezekiel Landau, Joseph Saul Nathanson and scores of others.

He was born in the little town of Rosh in the government of Grodno, Russia, in 1817. His father, Israel Isser Spektor, was rabbi in Rosh, and Isaac studied with him. Very soon he became known over the entire district as a wonder-child, an *illui*. He married at the age of thirteen and moved to Volkovisk, to live for six years in the home of his parents-in-law. He studied with Benjamin Diskin, the rabbi of Volkovisk, from whom he received his ordination (*semikha*). In 1837, when he was twenty, after the little dowry which he and his wife had been given by his parents-in-law was lost, he was compelled to become self-supporting, and he became rabbi in the little community of Sabelin. He suffered great poverty for six years. Then he went to the city of Karlin and introduced himself to Rabbi Jacob of Karlin, who recommended him to the community of Baresa, where he received a salary of one rouble a week! After five years in Baresa, he went to the somewhat larger community of Nishvez. Finally, after serving for a while in the community of Novorodok, near Kovno, he became, in 1864, rabbi in Kovno, where he served for thirty-two years, until his death, in 1896.

Rabbi Isaac Elhanan Spektor was a man of boundless energy and maintained a correspondence that soon became world-wide. He worked for the support of the great *yeshibot*. He lived at a time when far-flung Jewish philanthropy was in its beginnings, before it became as systematic as it is today, so that the personal authority of a famous leader was indispensable to the raising of funds. Thus, whereas in the past most of the rabbis devoted their philanthropic efforts to the support of *yeshibot*, Isaac Elhanan, besides doing that work, led in the relief of communities ruined by fire and other misfortunes. He went to St. Petersburg for conferences called by the government; and no authority in his time equalled the wide fame and reputation which he enjoyed. Perhaps, as has been mentioned, this was partly due to the fact that, at the time when his reputation was at its height, in the eighties, vast numbers of Russian Jews began to leave the Czarist domain and scatter all over the globe. Naturally, if any thorny questions came before their rabbis, they would refer them to the great authority of their homeland. Isaac Elhanan Spektor was, as far as Jewry was concerned, truly a world figure.

Sholom Mordecai Schwadron (Maharsham)

The scholar who took the place of Isaac Elhanan Spektor as the generally accepted world authority in Jewish Law was the Galician scholar, Sholom Mordecai Schwadron, rabbi of Berzan. He was born in 1835 in the little East-Galician village of Niv. His father, a village businessman, was nevertheless a lover of learning and had by himself studied through the entire Talmud six times. In later years, when his son had become famous, the father found the money for the publication of the first volume of his son's responsa.[35]

Moses Leiter, in *Sinai*,[36] has written the only extensive biographical essay about him. He tells of the various congregations in which he served until he finally became rabbi in Berzan, where his predecessors had been Solomon Kluger and Isaac Schmelkes, both great respondents.

Isaac Herzog, the Chief Rabbi of Israel, wrote a letter of commendation for the sixth volume of his responsa produced by his grandson and namesake in Jerusalem. In it Rabbi Herzog says the following of Sholom Mordecai Schwadron:

> Behold the true eminence, the rabbi of all Israel, Sholom Mordecai Schwadron of Berzan, may the memory of the righteous be a blessing, was long ago accepted as the outstanding decisor in all the scattered dwelling-places of Israel; his words were accepted as law as the words of the Divine oracle.

Allowing for the somewhat florid speech of the old-fashioned rabbinic Hebrew, the Chief Rabbi describes the actual fact which was true of the leading decisors in each generation. Each of them was the *Posek Ahron*, the court of last resort, whose decision was accepted by all. This status had been attained by Isaac Elhanan Spektor a generation before; and it was the status attained by Sholom Mordecai Schwadron in the middle of the nineteenth century.

In the career of Sholom Mordecai Schwadron were manifested the qualities possessed by the men thus accepted by scattered Jewish communities. He had great learning. Joseph Saul Nathanson of Lemberg recognized him early as a scholar with a great future, and in one of his commendations to an early work of Schwadron's, said, "I do not see in this generation his equal as a scholar." His knowledge was especially rich in the field of past responsa: he knew the decisions of his predecessors. But it was more than knowledge which he possessed and which suited him for the role which he came to occupy; he himself was decisive in temperament. He frequently urged his rabbinical correspondents not to hesitate to come to a decision.[37] He answered all inquiries gladly and promptly. He was an able and a willing carrier of the burden of dealing with the problems of the Law.

In the introduction to the sixth volume, his grandson speaks of his brother-in-law, Rabbi Moses Israel Feldman—who therefore was the grandson-in-law of Sholom Mordecai Schwadron, having married his granddaughter. Feldman had edited several of the earlier volumes of his grandfather's-in-law responsa. Sholom Mordecai Schwadron the Second says that his brother-in-law, Feldman, was killed by the Nazis, who had murdered a whole generation of scholars and potential scholars. It is questionable whether, after this immense loss of knowledge embodied in so many human minds, any new scholar great enough to be acceptable to all of Jewry will arise in the near future. That, however, remains to be seen. For the present, at least, Sholom Mordecai Schwadron is in the other sense of the word, the *Posek Ahron*, the last world-wide decisor.

In re-visualizing the careers of the greatest respondents—beginning with Solomon ben Adret of Barcelona, in the thirteenth century, down to Sholom Mordecai Schwadron of Berzan, in the nineteenth—a certain type of personality emerges as characteristic of the rabbi who, in his generation, by an entirely voluntary process, with no official authority, became the accepted supreme court in Jewish Law for his generation. Usually, he was the rabbi of a great community who dealt with a large variety of questions and who became known to litigants in other parts of the country and of the world. Almost invariably he conducted a large *yeshiba* and his students, scattering after their ordination, brought his fame to different regions and began sending him their more difficult questions. Most often he was a man, not too deeply concerned with codifying and simplifying the Law, but with amplifying it and finding new application to new cases as they came up. Above all, there was a personal element involved. The rabbi who became a great respondent had not only to be able to do so, but had to be *willing* to do so. He had to have the temperament to take upon himself the burden and the responsibility of decision and to be willing to answer all sorts of questions even though they were not in the field of his personal study at the time. This, allowing for some exceptions, is the general picture of the type of scholar who became a leader in the field of responsa.

3

A
SELECTION
OF
RESPONSA

ENGLISH AND AMERICAN LAW
develop largely through the day-by-day decisions of the courts. The laws of the continental countries depend to a much greater extent upon a basic code rather than upon individual cases. Since, in English and American Law, case-law is so vital, it is inevitable that certain cases become famous. This occurs when, in deciding a certain case, a crucial interpretation is made of an existing law or a vital principle established for the first time. If this principle is referred to time and again thereafter, then the original case in which it was established becomes a famous case, one of the "leading cases" of the Law.

Jewish Law is predominantly case-law. While the fixed codes, such as the *Yad* [1] and the *Shulhan Arukh*, have broad authority and certain simple matters can be settled merely by reference to the section and sub-section in one or the other of the famous codes, yet even in the codes themselves the decisions are often based on individual cases which had been sent to certain rabbis for decision. As a living practice, Jewish Law is mainly case-law, and the cases upon which the decisions are based are recorded in the individual collection of decided cases (responsa) by the various rabbis.

It was inevitable that certain of the cases in the responsa literature become famous for the same reason that certain cases before the British or the American courts have become famous. In some particular responsum, let us say, a certain new and important interpretation had been given to a talmudic passage, or a certain extension had been permitted in existing law. If this new decision did not become an isolated one, a mere eccentric or exceptional opinion, but was, instead, cited frequently as the years went by and made a precedent for similar decisions or for further development, then it became a "leading case" in Jewish Law.

There were other reasons, besides the fact that it became a precedent, why certain responsa became famous. For example, a question was sent from Kairouan, North Africa, to the schools in Babylonia asking for the correct sequence of the lives of the scholars cited in the Mishna and Talmud. The answer from Babylonia laid the foundation for the history of the development of talmudic literature. In such a case the question asked was not strictly a legal one, but rather a request for information, for guidance in study, which itself is an obligation of Jewish religious life. Or again, a Spanish rabbi was asked by a French rabbi to come to his defense against a third rabbi who, he believed, had been appointed unjustly as his superior. From the answer in this actual dispute we get a picture of the attempt in the Middle Ages to establish system and order in the appointment and ordination of rabbis. Still another example is of a woman who escaped from Spain and appeared with her child in Algiers. A legal question arose as to her marital status, and the decision gives us a clear insight into the condition of the secret Jews, the Marranos, in the early stage of their long history. Thus certain responsa are famous either because they are leading cases in the development of some law, or because they happen to become vital documents in the study of Jewish history and culture.

Such famous responsa are no longer merely a part of responsa literature but a part of Jewish literature in general and belong in any anthology of Jewish writing. The responsa selected below are among the best-known for one reason or another. They are not translated in full. Parts are omitted in order that the modern reader may be spared the difficulty of struggling through the abstruse reasoning which many of them contain. Only enough of each responsum is given, after some background description, to provide the reader with a fair impression of their content and style.

The Letter of the Gaon Amram

When the Babylonian Talmud was completed (about the year five hundred of the present era), the colleges and the teachers and the students in Babylonia, where it had been worked out and compiled, continued to be the central authority in Jewish Law. As long as the two main centers of Jewish life were Babylonia and Palestine, one center tended to balance the other and somewhat to cancel its dominant authority. But when, under the late Roman Empire and in the early Middle Ages, the Palestinian center gradually shriveled up, the Babylonian center grew stronger. It had a special advantage. The Jews in Babylonia had a large measure of self-government under their own "Chief of the Exile," the Exilarch, and under their chief rabbis, who were called the "Gaonim," the "Eminences."

By the time the Jewish communities began to emerge in western Europe and northwestern Africa, and the study of the Babylonian Talmud began to spread, the gaonim of Babylonia rose naturally to supreme authority in Jewish religious life. The questions that were directed to them, and the answers which they gave, constituted an epistolary intellectual blood-circulation in the body Jewish. The earlier legal authorities in Africa, Spain, France and Germany constantly quote the gaonim. While most of the answers of the gaonim were brief responses, some were virtually treatises on some phase of Jewish Law or life.

The Gaon Amram of Mata Mehasia, or Sura, in the ninth century, was asked by a Spanish community to guide them as to the proper order of the prayers. In answer, he gave a full description of the authorized ritual. This description became basic for worship in all the Jewish world, as we can tell from the fact that it is constantly cited by the early authorities. Rabbenu Tam, Rashi's grandson (who died about 1150), one of the founders of Jewish religious life in France and Germany, said to a correspondent: [2] "I am astonished at you that you do not put your reliance upon Rab Amram from whose lips we learn all the blessings and prayers." Yet, in spite of the fact that all the great founders of the Law constantly referred to this answer of Rab Amram, the responsum itself, like many another of the gaonic responsa, disappeared, or at least did not find its way into print. In the middle of the nineteenth century, Nahman Coronel found a manuscript of the entire responsum in the city of Hebron, Palestine. He edited it and published it in Warsaw in 1865. The manuscript had evidently been interpolated in many places and later observances were ascribed to the original author. But the opening part of the responsum makes it clear that Amram is answering a Spanish congregation and refers to an earlier answer on the same question by Gaon Natronai, his predecessor:

Amram, the son of Sheshna, head of the school at Mata Mehasia (that is, Sura), to Rabbi Isaac, the son of the teacher and rabbi, Simon, beloved, dear and honored by us and the entire College. Great peace from the Mercy of Heaven be upon thee and all thy seed and upon all the sages and scholars and our brethren of Israel who dwell there. Accept greetings of peace from me and Rab Zemah, the chief judge of Israel, and from the comrades and sages of the College and the members of our College and of the city of Mehasia, and the sages and the scholars and the children of Israel who dwell here. We are ever seeking your welfare and remembering you in good remembrance, and praying in your behalf and seeking mercy for you, that God may show His many kindnesses to you and protect you and deliver you from all trouble and harm and from all sickness and pain and from evil government and from all types of destruction and punishment which come along in the world. May He in His great mercies fulfill all the desires of your heart. Rabbi Jacob, the son of Isaac, has transmitted to us the ten gold-pieces which you have sent to the *yeshiba*, five for us and five for the treasury of the *yeshiba*, and we have ordained and blessed you with blessings that will be fulfilled for you and your seed for generations.

As for your questions about the order of prayers and blessings for the entire year which you have asked and (the answer to) which they have shown us from Heaven (that is, the answer which God has vouchsafed to us), we have decided to arrange and to give you answer according to the tradition which exists in our possession and as arranged by the Tannaim and Amoraim (that is, the teachers of the Mishna and the Talmud). It is taught: [3] Rabbi Meir said, "Every man is in duty bound to pronounce a hundred blessings every day." . . . and it was King David himself who arranged (these hundred blessings). When they informed him that the inhabitants of Jerusalem were dying at the rate of a hundred a day, he arose and ordained these hundred blessings.

It seems that these blessings were then forgotten and the Tannaim and Amoraim (the teachers of the Mishna and the Talmud) arose and re-established them.

Now as to the order of these hundred blessings; thus has already answered Rav Natronai, the son of Rav Hillai, head of the College of Mata Mehasia, to the congregation of Lucena (Spain) through Rav Joseph, the Light of Our Eyes. It is impossible for a person to pronounce each of the hundred blessings at its appropriate time because of the uncleanness of the hands which are wont to keep busy and touch (unclean) things; but when a person awakens from his sleep, he shall wash thoroughly his face and hands and feet to fulfill the verse:— *Prepare to meet thy God, O Israel* (Amos 4.12). Each and every individual is in duty bound to recite them; and it is the custom of all Israel in Sefarad (Spain) for the cantor to read them aloud in order to discharge the obligation of anyone who cannot say them for himself. Thus answered Rav Natronai bar Hillai.

This ends Amram's quotation from the previous responsum of Natronai and then follows the order of the service for the entire year, interspersed with various comments and explanations by the gaon.

The Ban Against Philosophy

Medieval Jewish philosophy and Christian medieval scholastic philosophy had the same aim—to harmonize the religious tradition with the science and the philosophy which was dominant at the time. It was an attempt to merge reason and faith, or, specifically, Plato and Aristotle with the Bible. The scholastic philosophy, which developed to such a high degree in the Christian Church, led to great disputes among the various philosophers as to which philosophic line to follow. But there was very little record of an opposition to scholastic philosophy as such, that is, to the entire attempt to harmonize philosophy with religion. The scholastic philosophy of Thomas Aquinas, for example, became authoritative and official; but, even before Aquinas's scholasticism became the official philosophy, the whole philosophic or scholastic enterprise had the approval of the Church. There could well be disagreement as to *which* philosophic solutions to follow, but very little disagreement as to whether or not to study philosophy.

In medieval Jewry there was no official body to approve of philosophy or to disapprove of it. It therefore had to stand or fall on its own merits. Furthermore, in Judaism there was a vast area of talmudic learning participated in by a large proportion of the community. Thus there was a widespread traditional culture which already existed as a rival to the new philosophic, Aristotelian culture. In the Christian world, the study of philosophy meant a vast extension of culture in the lives of thousands who had never studied before. But in Judaism the new philosophic studies actually supplanted in many cases the traditional study which had existed until then. A titanic mind like that of Moses Maimonides could master both fields. He wrote the grandest Jewish scholastic work harmonizing philosophy and the Bible, the *Guide to the Perplexed*. He also wrote what is perhaps the greatest Jewish legal code, encompassing the entire Law, the *Mishneh Torah*. But for the average mind it was either one or the other. If a man devoted himself to the difficult and absorbing study of talmudic Law, he had little time left for philosophy; or, if he turned to the charms of the new philosophic and scientific studies, he was likely to neglect the study of the Law. Hence, in Judaism, where there already existed a widespread learning that might be supplanted, there was bound to be a struggle between tradition and philosophy, or, more correctly, between traditional learning and philosophic studies.

Moreover, the rationalist attitude of Aristotle often shook the faith of many Jewish students. The biblical and talmudic accounts, particularly of miracles, would appear to them unbelievable. They either explained the biblical miracles as mere allegories of some hidden philosophic ideas, or they rejected them outright.

The center of Jewish scholastic philosophy was Spain. There, under the influence of Moses Maimonides and his successors, philosophy and science were at home, possessing equal status in the minds of many Spanish students. But the great struggle against philosophy began in the Provence, in southern France, spread across the Pyrenees and engulfed Spanish Jewry in one of the bitterest disputes ever to arise in Jewish history. A Provençal scholar, Abba Mari ben Moses (Astruc), when he moved to the Provençal city of Montpellier, discovered that a large number of people in the city were so enthusiastically devoted to philosophic and scientific studies that they neglected their study of the Torah and the Talmud. He noticed, too, that some of these devotees of philosophy, when they preached in the synagogue, were too eager to explain away the biblical miracles as mere allegories. Astruc then determined to obtain from the leaders of Jewry a ban against philosophic studies. He finally persuaded the great respondent of that day, Solomon ben Adret [4] to enter the lists against philosophy. Though Solomon ben Adret was himself a student of philosophy, and though he deeply revered Moses Maimonides, he saw the harm that this over-enthusiastic devotion to philosophy was causing. He therefore wrote a responsum against it and issued a ban. This responsum, addressed to Astruc in Montpellier, and also the ban, are given in the responsa of Solomon ben Adret: [5]

... Again the sage in Montpellier wrote to me of the fact that men in that land are devoting themselves to the study of the books of the Greeks and are composing books on the Torah and making blasphemous interpretations on it. . . . You say in your letter: "I am not enraged against one who possesses the books of the Greek philosophers; for, if there be found in them something good, it may justify the whole book, and we are confident that even a boorish person will not be misled by them,

since the names of their authors tell us they are gentiles."
But thou, O beloved, lover of the Torah, should you thus con-
ceal their cunning under the wings of a fly? For this is precisely
the ground of our outcry before God, namely, that one who
studies these (Greek books) diligently makes them the essential
of his study and thus uproots the Law of God. This danger is
not ignored in your letter, for you have said that thus it is written in the book, that David, Sweet Singer of Israel, found it
necessary to multiply long and short prayers that his words
might be spoken in the synagogue; yet Aristotle and Plato,
without prayer and supplication, have merited that their books
fill every chamber and room and (these people) rely on their
words as one relies on the statement of the storekeeper or that
of the wholesaler (cf. m. Demai V, 4, 6).

Thus you have written and what you say is true. Who can
say that this is not a bitter evil. For in truth, he who devotes
all his time to them (to the Greek books) does not protect himself from the sword which is in their hands. Such a person
makes the bitter sweet and the sweet bitter; for their words
draw the heart with chords of love (at first), but in the end
they are like a storm raising dissension and dispute against the
Law of Truth. Since all their ideas (of the Greek philosophers)
are derived from Nature, human beings whose origin is dust
draw Nature with a stout cord and the yoke of the Torah is
destroyed within them. . . . In fact, it is impossible for two
opposites to join (that is, tradition and Greek philosophy).
Can a man believe or arrive at a conclusion to consider real the
biblical miracles, while in his heart there remains a conviction
that it is impossible to bring forth water from a rock. . . . As
far as they are concerned, whoever believes in anything which
cannot be deduced from natural syllogisms is to be called a
"simpleton who believes everything" and they alone are wise
in their own eyes and we are considered as cattle . . .

After this responsum follows a ban, signed first by Solomon
ben Adret himself, and then by a whole group of other scholars.
It begins as follows:

Here are the three letters which tell of what was done with
regard to the study of the external wisdoms and with regard to
him who preaches blasphemous sermons. This is done with the

agreement of the entire sacred congregation in Barcelona, and with the agreement of the great teacher, our master, Solomon (may God preserve him) and his court.

After a poetic introduction, the letter continues as follows:

We are servants, servants of God. He has made us, not we ourselves. We have decreed and agreed for ourselves and our seed and all attached to us, by the power of the *herem* (the ban) that for a period of fifty years no member of our congregation shall study the books of the Greeks which were written on the subjects of natural philosophy and metaphysics, whether they be composed in their language or whether translated into another, before he reaches the age of twenty-five; that no member of our community should teach anybody these philosophical studies until he reaches twenty-five; lest they be drawn after these wisdoms and turn aside from the Torah of Israel which is above all of these wisdoms. . . . We exclude from this our decree the study of the science of medicine. Although it too is based upon a study of Nature, nevertheless the Torah itself accords the physician permission to heal. This we have decreed as a ban over the Scroll of the Torah, in the presence of the congregation, on the Sabbath day of the portion, "These are the words," (Deuteronomy 1), in the year sixty-five of the fifth thousand (that is, 1305).

Then follow two other letters and another ban on the same subject also signed by Solomon ben Adret and a group of other scholars.

The Captive Women

In the Mishna (m. Ketuboth II, 9), the law is that if a woman is captured by Gentiles, she is, under certain circumstances, forbidden to live with her husband when she returns, because the life that she would be forced into as a captive would make her unfit for the purity required of a Jewish family. This law is elaborated in the Talmud (b. Ketuboth 26b ff.). The experience reflected in this sad law was unfortunately a frequent one in Jewish life. The *Shulhan Arukh* (sixteenth century), which is meant to be a code for practical use and omits all such laws as are no longer practiced (as, for example, the agricultural laws and the sacrificial laws), has an elaborate section dealing with such tragic situations ("Eben ha-Ezer," Section 7).

Since the capturing of women was a frequent occurrence, the law had need to be specific and precise. As early as the Mishna, a distinction was made between women captured in order to be held for ransom and those captured with the intention of killing or enslaving them. Those captured for ransom were permitted to return to their Jewish family life, because it was presumed that the captors would be careful not to harm their victim so as not to diminish the ransom. If it was in an environment where the Jews were dominant, as in Palestine (and the woman was captured, let us say, in a raid), then, if her capture was merely for ransom, she could return to her husband even if he were a priest (special sanctity was maintained for priestly families since they ate the sacred heave-offering). If, however, it was in an environment where the people of Israel were not dominant, then, even if held for ransom only, she could not return to a priestly husband; but if her husband were an ordinary Israelite, she could return to him. In all cases, witnesses were allowed to testify as to whether she had managed to keep herself in purity; and the usual laws of eligibility of witnesses were greatly relaxed in favor of such unfortunate women.

A vivid responsum by Meir of Rothenburg, which gives a tragically clear picture of the life of the Jews in thirteenth-century Germany, deals with the case of some men and women who were captured in the German city of Dukenhausen.[6]

> The question concerns the *anussim* (literally, "those under duress," a term which is used also for the Spanish-Portuguese marranos), the fugitives of Dukenhausen. I was asked concerning the women, whether they are permitted to return to their husbands. It seems to me that although the Talmud says (b. Ketuboth 26b): "The woman who is captured by Gentiles for the purpose of killing her (that is, not merely for ransoming her) is forbidden to her husband even if he be an Israelite (that is, not a priest). . . ." It says further that if she is captured

merely for ransom, she is permitted to her husband; but that is
so only in an environment where the people of Israel is dominant; but nowadays, where the Gentiles are dominant, even if
she is captured merely for ransom, she is forbidden to a priest-
husband. This is proved there, in the Talmud, and the law is
thus confined by Alfasi.

Nevertheless, in this case, since other Jews were there (fel-
low-captives), she is permitted even to the priesthood; for the
Talmud states (*ibid.*, 276b) that anyone is eligible to testify in
her favor (except her husband and her own slave). Those who
were with her are eligible even if they were not with her
constantly. . . .

One cannot argue that these other captives are ineligible to
testify in favor of such women because they failed in the duty
of preferring death to idolatry. This is not so; for, though the
law is that one should prefer death to idolatry, nevertheless we
follow the opinion of Rava in the Talmud (b. Sanhedrin 61b),
who said that he who worships idols either through love or fear
(of a human being) is free (from punishment); although he has
indeed committed a sin, he is still eligible to give testimony in
this matter, for all are eligible to give such testimony even
though they belong to groups that generally are ineligible.
Certainly in this case they may testify in her favor, since they
said that they never *did* serve the idol, but merely that the
priests uttered their unclean words in the presence of certain
Gentiles and they, the Jews, remained silent. We do not find any
law that a man is in duty bound to sacrifice his life simply because the Gentiles deceive themselves and they, the Jews, do not
utter any contradiction.

Therefore, it seems to me that these women who, even if they
had only one witness, and even if there were only another
woman testifying that she would come and go in their presence
and did not see her (the woman in question) violated, such
women are permitted to their husbands and even to the priesthood. With greetings of peace, Meir, son of Baruch.

The Ordination Dispute in France

During the persecutions in Germany at the end of the fourteenth century, Jewish scholarship declined and there was a lack

of properly trained rabbis. Many individuals began to function as rabbis in spite of their inadequate preparation. To remedy this situation, Meir ben Baruch ha-Levi, who was rabbi in Vienna from 1360 to 1390, introduced into Germany the type of ordination which is virtually the one operative in orthodox Jewry today. He issued an order that no student should ever officiate as a rabbi unless he received a specific permit and title from his teacher.

This ordination, the permission to teach given by one's teacher, is far less than the ancient ordination which prevailed in the days of the Mishna in Palestine, or even the secondary ordination which obtained in Babylonia in the time of the Talmud and later.[7]

The only judicial authority that exists today is in the case of the willing acceptance by the individual litigants of the rabbi as their judge, or the appointment of the rabbi by the community which, being democratically organized, assumes the litigants' willing acceptance of the rabbi as their judge. What then was the meaning of the type of ordination instituted at this time by Meir ha-Levi of Vienna? What authority did it actually bring with it?

The question came up in a bitter dispute which concerned the rabbinate of France. Meir ha-Levi of Vienna had given this new type of ordination to a French rabbi, Isaiah ben Abba Mari (Astruc de Savoie). Armed with this ordination, Isaiah ben Abba Mari came to France and declared that he had been appointed Chief Rabbi of France; and he attempted to depose Rabbi Johanan, the son of Mattathias, who was then Chief Rabbi of France and whose father, Mattathias, had been Chief Rabbi before him. Isaiah ben Abba Mari declared that henceforth all rabbinical functions performed by Rabbi Johanan ben Mattathias were void. Although Johanan's position as Chief Rabbi of France had been confirmed by the King of France, he quite properly refrained from appealing for help to the secular government against this intruder, but wrote to the rabbis of Spain asking them to make the decision.

The answer of Isaac bar Sheshet (Ribash) is found in his collected responsa, no. 271. It is a clear analysis of the whole history of ordination from the very beginning and comes to the conclusion that Isaiah ben Abba Mari had no right to intrude upon the authority of Johanan ben Mattathias, incumbent Chief Rabbi of France. He begins with the honorific, poetic style of address, by then characteristic of many responsa, but soon gets down to his analysis of the case and to a history of ordination.

When the Lord enlarged the borders of the scattered ones of the exile, He, in His great mercies, gave them refuge in the kingdom of France. In order to keep the great people alive, He sent before them a man of God, a shoot from the stock of sages of the Law, a sprout from the roots of humility and sanctity . . . our teacher, Mattathias, may his rest be in Eden. . . . Our teacher, Rabbi Mattathias, set his heart to learn and to teach statutes and ordinances and he founded *yeshibot* and established the Law among the people. . . . There went forth from before him many rabbis who, in turn, established *yeshibot*, for he placed his hand and bestowed of his glory upon them. . . . When all the communities of that kingdom saw his noble works and knowledge (of the Law) and grandeur united in this one personality, they accepted him as their prince and judge and rabbi. Also the King confirmed his standing as ruler over all their laws. Then, when . . . Rabbi Mattathias was called to the Heavenly Academy, the communities appointed in his place his son Johanan; for they saw that he filled the place of his father both in learning and in piety; and, moreover, his father, during his lifetime, had ordained him. . . . Now a lion has come up from his thicket, Isaiah (ben Abba Mari), and, because of a dispute that he had with Rabbi Johanan, went to Germany to that great eagle of the Law, Meir ha-Levi (of Vienna), and obtained from him a decree that he shall rule over all of France and that no rabbi shall establish a *yeshiba* in France without his permission. . . . The earth trembled at this decree. How could such a decision, they asked, come from Meir ha-Levi? How could he issue decrees over a land that is not his? Even though he be distinguished in wisdom and in age, he cannot issue decrees over the kingdom of France without permission of the congregations of that kingdom or the rabbis of that kingdom. . . . Among the rabbis who were asked about this matter, I, the undersigned, also was asked. Although I do not belong among the sages, and I fear to put my head between these two moving mountains lest they crush my skull, yet, at the entreaty of the scholar, Judah ben Eliezer,[8] who comes from a distance, I am unable to turn him back empty-handed. . . .

First of all, it is necessary to explain what is this *semikha* ("ordination"), that the rabbis in France and in Germany are accustomed to give. For, behold, the *semikha* in the days of our rabbis was for the purpose of conferring the right to judge cases of capital punishment and fines which required experts, that is to say, it required ordained men who had been ordained by men who themselves had been ordained, going back to our teacher Moses. . . ."

He proceeds to tell how this original, true ordination had ceased. He then describes the *minui*, authorization, which the exilarch, by virtue of being a descendant of King David, had the right to give. Now that too has ceased. The right to judge today comes only from the consent of the parties; and if a rabbi judges a pair of litigants without their consent and errs, he must make up for the error out of his own purse. What then is the meaning of the ordination which the rabbis now confer in France and Germany? He indicates that it is merely the right to teach and to establish a *yeshiba* during the teacher's lifetime, since no students may teach in the lifetime of his teacher without the teacher's permission. All that the *semikha* given by Meir ha-Levi amounts to is permission for his own disciples to teach during his lifetime. That is all that *semikha* can possibly mean today. Having laid this foundation, he concludes:

The decree that Meir ha-Levi issued is not according to the Law. His own honor is unshaken (that is, we do not deprecate his standing), but no one is bound to pay attention to his decree, except his own pupils who have no right to teach and to establish a *yeshiba* except through his permission (for he is *their* teacher). And it may well be that that is all that Meir ha-Levi intended, for we must presume that a man as great as he would not do that which is wrong.

He then goes into a discussion of the standing of Rabbi Johanan ben Mattathias, discussing the fact that the King confirmed his appointment by the community. He adds that, even if the King's appointment of a rabbi has no validity in Jewish Law, yet, if the congregations have accepted him, Johanan must remain in his position.

Marriages of Marranos

The secret Jews of Spain and Portugal (the marranos) occupy a considerable place in the responsa literature.[9] They kept escaping from Spain and Portugal for centuries and their arrival in a Jewish community would generally give rise to questions about their status under Jewish Law. Sometimes the problems concerned their right to participate in the services. Sometimes the problems dealt with matters of inheritance. Mostly they dealt with questions of marriage. These marranos had all been married in churches in Spain and Portugal. They were not permitted to be married in any other way. Were they married, however, in the eyes of Jewish Law? Can Jewish Law acknowledge the validity of such Christian marriage in the case of Jews? Or was the marriage, perhaps, in a sense, Jewish, Jewish witnesses having been present? Or, as sometimes happened, a preliminary sort of ceremony took place in the home before the couple went for their public marriage to the church. Indeed, are these people to be considered Jews at all?

These problems could not be postponed. A woman appears with her child. Her husband has disappeared, in all likelihood never to return, lost somewhere on a dangerous journey over land or sea. Yet there is no clear evidence brought by witnesses of his death. If the marriage which they went through in Spain is valid, then this poor woman is an *aguna* ("chained") who must wait either for a divorce given by her husband, or for a verifiable report of her husband's death. Otherwise she can never remarry. In these cases it would be merciful to declare that their church marriage was no marriage, as indeed Isaac bar Sheshet (Ribash) did declare it.[10] But such a decision could be tragic if husband

and wife with children arrive together, or when there is a question of inheritance, or the like.

The first marranos appeared at the end of the fourteenth century, after the persecutions of 1391, when Spanish Jews began to settle in North Africa. Therefore the earliest of these questions are found in the responsa of the great rabbis who had settled in Algiers, Isaac bar Sheshet and his younger colleague, Simon ben Zemah Duran.[11] Duran's responsum on the question of the validity of the marrano marriages has become a leading case in the Law, for the marranos continued to emerge from behind the heavy curtain of the lands of persecution and in the succeeding centuries would arrive in Jewish communities all over the world. As the years went by and their Jewish contacts tended to diminish, Jewish Law tended to be stricter in its judgment of them and their status: for, why did they not escape sooner? And perhaps by this time they were of mixed descent. But in all discussions as to their status, those scholars who tended to declare their marriages valid, always referred to the responsum of Simon ben Zemah Duran.[12]

With regard to these *anusim* (marranos) who marry marrano women by *huppah* and *kiddushin* (that is, by private Jewish marriage before going to church): If one of these marrano women comes forth to enter into our covenant and her husband is still alive, is she to be judged as a Gentile or as a war-captive, since Jewish marriage does not apply to Gentiles? Or is this not the case with her? Furthermore, does the law involving her status apply if he, the husband, is uncircumcised, having been born after the persecution (of 1391), or does it apply also to one who married this woman after having become converted to Christianity? The above is thy question.

Answer: There is no distinction at all to be made in this matter between a Jew (that is, an observant Jew) and an apostate; for we hold[13] that, although he has sinned, he is still a Jew, and, as the proverb has it: "A myrtle, standing amid the willows, is still a myrtle and is known as such." Even a proselyte, that is, one who was not born a Jew but was converted to Judaism, who returns to his original beliefs, is still to be considered a Jew with regard to this matter (that is, with regard to marriage), as is stated in the Talmud: [14] If the proselyte had taken the ritual bath, he is now a Jew in every respect. Thus if he reverted to his original faith, he is like an apostate Jew, that is, if he marries a Jewess, his marriage is valid. . . .

All the more then does this apply to these *anusim* (marranos) who are children of Jacob and Judah. Therefore if one of them marries a woman, his marriage is valid, and even as to the child born of them after their conversion, the same law applies to him. Whosoever's mother was a marrano, even if his father was a Gentile, as we know from the Talmud [15] (that is, that the child of a mixed marriage follows the status of the mother . . .) All apostates and children of apostate women are to be considered as full Israelites with regard to marriage. This is derived *a fortiori* from the proselyte who reverted to his original faith, who is then certainly an apostate. So, too, the uncircumcised son of an apostate woman, if he marries a Jewess, his marriage is as valid as that of any full Jew.

He indicates that the only doubt as to the validity of such a marriage arises from the question regarding the witnesses to the marriage, since the law is that marriage without valid witnesses is not valid.[16] One may, therefore, conclude that this marriage is valid only if the marrano man married the marrano woman before Jewish witnesses; because if he married her before marrano witnesses, they, being sinners, are ineligible to testify. He continues:

But even in this matter, as to the ineligibility of marrano witnesses, we would have to consider further. If this (private marriage) is a fixed custom among them, and after that they go to be married in the church, then the very fact that their intention to marry is publicly known has a bearing on the matter. For if there are still Jews in the community even though they were not present at the marriage (this refers to the time between 1390 and 1492 when there were still Jews in Spain), these Jews are eligible to give testimony that the couple lived together as man and wife, and the marriage is valid for that reason.

From all this we conclude that if he married her in the presence of valid witnesses, the marriage is certainly valid. If there were Jews in the community (though not present at the ceremony) the marriage may likewise be deemed valid. If there were no Jews in the community and only marrano witnesses were present at the marriage, then the marriage has no validity.

Rabbinical Competition

When Rabbi Meir haLevi of Vienna gave Isaiah ben Abba Mari the authority to be Chief Rabbi in France in place of Johanan ben Mattathias, the incumbent, the question involved was whether a rabbi of one country may issue decrees and decisions affecting the rabbinate of another country. The Spanish rabbis to whom the question was submitted decided that a rabbi's rights extend only to the control of the activities of his own disciples; he may forbid them to teach in his neighborhood during his lifetime. But the question of one rabbi coming uninvited into the district of another rabbi proved much larger and much more troublesome.

When the one rabbi is not the pupil of the other, what disciplinary relationship can exist between them? May one rabbi come into the city of another, open a *yeshiba* there and practice the various functions of the rabbinate without the permission of the incumbent? Is this not committing the sin of *hasogat-gebul* ("Removing the landmark": Deuteronomy 19.14) which the rabbis in the Talmud[17] extend to include the prohibition of workmen and businessmen, under certain circumstances, from coming into a city and unfairly competing with the resident workmen and storekeepers? Does the right to protest against such competition apply to so sacred a calling as the rabbinate?

The subject receives a great deal of discussion in the responsa literature of recent centuries. It usually comes up in this form: Has a rabbi (or, for that matter, a *shohet*) a *hazaka*, that is, a presumptive right to his position? May he, for example, turn over his position to his son or his son-in-law? One of the leading cases involving this question occurred in the early fifteenth century.

Israel of Bruna (1400 (?) −1480), so named after the Moravian city of Bruenn in which he first served as rabbi, was involved in a famous case of this sort. This tragic figure who, later in his career, was falsely accused (possibly of a blood accusation) and imprisoned, complained about Rabbi Goddell of Orenburg, who came to Bruenn where Israel was rabbi. He brought his complaint to his own teacher, Israel Isserlein [18] of Neustadt, near Vienna. Israel Isserlein told him that a rabbi has no exclusive rights in this matter and that therefore he has no ground for objection. Later, Israel of Bruna himself became responsible for an exactly similar situation. He left Bruenn and moved to the great German community of Regensburg. There he opened a *yeshiba* and served as rabbi. The local rabbi, Amshel, protested bitterly and the community was soon divided in acrimonious quarrel. This spread beyond the confines of the city and Isserlein, who had previously decided that Rabbi Goddell had the right to settle in Bruenn, although Israel of Bruna was already there, decided again in the same way, so that this time the decision was in favor of Israel of Bruna against Rabbi Amshel of Regensburg. Isserlein's responsum is frequently referred to in later discussions on this question. It is in the form of a letter addressed to the community of Regensburg.

May your peace increase, Honored Congregation, Mother in Israel, sacred community of Regensburg. May your power grow and may you enjoy long life. From the above transcript and other letters, I have seen that great bitterness has arisen between the aged Rabbi Amshel and my friend, Rabbi Israel (of Bruna). I am appalled and astonished at the fact that Rabbi Amshel has both decided and acted to humble and demote Rabbi Israel and to make him merely one of the disciples; forbidding him to establish a *yeshiba* and to pass judgment in the Law. How could such a plan come into his (Amshel's) mind; for was he (Israel) not anointed with the oil of the aged Rabbi Zalman Cohen (that is, ordained) and with the fragrant oil of Rabbi Jacob Weil and of David (Schweidnitz)? Also I have poured the oil of anointment upon his head, for I know how worthy he is in his knowledge of the Talmud. Why then should one try to diminish his strength and his reputation?

Is it on the charge of *hasogat gebul* (that is, unfair trespass into the territory of Rabbi Amshel)? If so, I wish to inform you of a tradition which I have from Rabbi Jonah, the son of Rabbi Shalom the Elder, my kinsman, who said in the name of his father: "I and my ancestors have maintained the *yeshiba* and have been judges in the city of Neustadt. Yet if another scholar were to come here to be a leader as I am, I would not hinder him." I wonder, therefore, on what basis the leaders of the community (of Regensburg) argue "trespass" in this case. When I spoke of this matter to Rabbi Amshel of Marburg, he said: "The aged Rabbi Meir ha-Levi said to me as follows: 'Who gave me, or bequeathed to me this territory that another may not enter into it?' " This is the word of the great ones.

Furthermore, whoever looks closely into the *Tosafot* of the chapter, *Lo Yahpor* ("A Man Shall Not Dig")[19] will clearly find plenty of justification for the fact that no scholar has the right to prevent a colleague from establishing his dwelling by his side. In fact, this was my decision to Israel of Bruna himself when he visited me in Neustadt after Rabbi Goddell of Orenburg wanted to establish himself in Bruenn.

Indeed, all the prohibitions that the rabbis have made against one man interfering with the livelihood of another, "removing his boundary" (that is, trespassing on his territory), apply only when there is a diminution of profit and a lessening of his livelihood. But in a case such as this, when one man has rabbinical authority in a city and another comes also, no financial loss is necessarily involved. Each one may benefit from the gifts of the leaders of Israel, for these are gifts which have no fixed measure. It is not similar to a situation where some actually have had presumptive rights (in a certain place) for many years. For it is clear from the language of Meir of Rothenburg, in the *Mordecai* to the third chapter of Baba Bathra, that a rabbi does have presumptive rights, and no one can deprive him of them, only when he formally acquires that right from the community. Only then may he bequeath his rights to his heirs. In any other situation, the crown of the Law and its authority lie there ready for all who wish to take them. As for the income from divorces and *halitzah* and marriages, we are ashamed of the emphasis placed upon these fees and it is very difficult even to justify receiving them; certainly, therefore, we cannot raise them to the status of justified income so that no one else may interfere with them. I will not prolong my discussion. In brief, I hereby confirm, with all emphasis, the decision which Jacob Weil has made in this matter. My mouth is like his mouth, and my hand like his hand . . .

Great is peace. It is the instrument which brings all other blessings. And I have also written to Rabbi Israel (Bruna) that he should respect the honor of the old Rabbi (Amshel) as much as possible. Thus there will be peace upon the judges of Israel. Thus saith the humble one in Israel.

Jacob Weil, to whose responsum Israel Isserlein here refers, adds another element to the discussion.[20] He says:

Since the congregation had not formally selected either Rabbi Amshel or Rabbi Israel, and since both of them have to pay taxes (which indicates neither is officially rabbi, because the rabbi was exempt from taxes) like any other of the householders of the city, neither of them has a presumptive right (hazaka) over the other. Even though Rabbi Amshel was in Regensburg before the arrival of Rabbi Israel, this does not make his rights greater than the latter's, since the congregation had not accepted him to be their head.

A later form of this discussion occurs in the early nineteenth century. Moses Sofer makes a distinction between the modern situation and the older situation. In the older days (that is, in the times mentioned above), the rabbi settled in a community at will; but nowadays he is invited and engaged by the community, and the various perquisites are counted in as part of his income; therefore no other man has the right to interfere with them.[21]

Taxation for Charity

The Jews in central Europe, especially of Germany, could not help acquiring strong community feelings. External forces actually forced them into mutual cooperation. Taxation was continuous, cumulative and merciless. Each community had to tax its members in order to meet these exactions, lest worse evils befall. Hence, Jewish Law in the Middle Ages developed enactments giving power and strength to the community and preventing the individual from evading his duty. There could, of course, be and there were appeals against the quotas imposed by the community; but no one, for example, could make a private arrangement with the secular government and thus avoid paying a proportionate share along with his fellow-Jews.

All this applied to taxation. But what of charity? Suppose it were necessary to rescue another community in trouble? Could a quota of taxes be laid upon communities other than the one directly affected? Logic required that such taxation be permitted because, after all, the so-called regular taxes were not fair taxes either. They were so disproportionate and were imposed so unjustly by the Gentile city council, or by the duke or by the emperor or by all of them together, that they were frequently not really taxes but blackmail. Paying the so-called usual taxes was, therefore, also in a sense participating in an act of rescue from unjust oppression. It is certain that no community would resist being taxed to rescue its leaders when they were held for blackmail by the authorities under some false charge.

Still, the question remained whether one community could be taxed for the deliverance of another community. The historic Jewish community of Regensburg (Ratisbon) in Bavaria was, in the early fifteenth century, subject to such a tragic act of persecution. Its leaders were accused of ritual murder, and a group of rabbis and other leaders gathered in Nuremberg to try to raise the money by imposing a special tax on surrounding communities for the redemption of the imprisoned. They feared that the Jews of the surrounding communities would oppose a tax placed on them for the sake of Regensburg Jewry, and they therefore wrote to the famous Italian rabbi, Joseph Colon (1420–1480).[22] He answered that the danger was a common danger and that all were in duty bound to help. He based his opinion on the talmudic discussion [23] where farmers down-river must help the farmers up-river to clean a channel. The talmudic passage deals with the general question of cooperating for mutual benefit. The responsum is interesting for the picture it gives of the life of Jewry in Germany at the time and of the organization developed, as needed, to spread community cooperation to wider fields.[24]

Since it is well-known that the arrest of our brothers in the congregation of Regensburg will do harm to many places besides Regensburg and her suburbs (since it is a blood accusation and would spread), and since the rabbis who are now gathered in Nuremberg, to deliver those who were innocently carried away to their death, are concerned lest there be some men or women or families or villages who, although they themselves are not free of danger—since the wrath may soon pass over them if they do not find some remedy and deliverance—yet they, nevertheless, say: "The misfortune will not approach us and we will remain at peace 'though we walk in the stubbornness of our heart' " (Deuteronomy 29:18)—therefore, I respond to those who have asked me to see "in which way the light dwelleth," etc. (Job 39.19).

First I will say that it seems to my humble mind that those congregations, concerning which one may assume that it is more probable that the bitter cup will come to them, are by law required to share the burden, since the deliverance of the congregation of Regensburg is their deliverance, and also the reverse, God forbid. Even though at the present moment there are no slanderous accusations of this kind in other places, but only in Regensburg, yet the other towns are to be judged according to the probable future and must help. The proof comes from the Talmud, Baba Metziah, page 108.

Here Joseph Colon analyzes the passage in the Talmud which describes the various modes of group cooperation when a river bed requires cleaning or when excessive rain has to be drawn away from a city, or when the city wall needs repair, and the like. He says further that the rabbis in the Talmud were concerned even with the slightest probability of danger, whereas here we are certainly dealing with a very likely danger. He continues:

It is for the rabbis gathered in Nuremberg today to repair the breach in the wall, and may our Father in heaven confirm their work and may the will of God prosper in their hands. According to the Law shall they teach and according to justice they shall declare, who shall enter under this yoke and who shall not, and on whom it may be made heavy and on whom light. Every individual is in duty bound to observe their decision. But since in Nuremberg, and in many another city in Germany, it is forbidden for the Jews to make their decisions in the form of a decree out of fear of the rulers and the princes, therefore, come what may, I, in all humility, although their words require no fortifying, do decree with a stern decree and with the power of the ban upon all the inhabitants of Germany, man or woman, family or individual or group, that they shall not rebel against the command of the rabbis gathered in Nuremberg as to whatever they shall impose upon each congregation or individual to pay or to help in the matter of the false accusation levelled against our brothers of Regensburg. The Humble One, *Joseph Colon.*

Teaching the Karaites

The Karaites and the Samaritans always considered themselves Jewish and yet remained aloof from the rest of Jewry. Of the two, the Karaite sect was much the more powerful. It was founded by Anan ben David in Babylonia in the eighth century and was based upon a denial of the validity of the Oral Law—that is, the teachings of Mishna, Talmud and the rabbis—but confined itself to a belief in Scripture and what, as they believed, could be logically derived from it. Hence, the name "Karaites," which really means, "Men of the Bible." The Karaites produced many well-known authors of religious works. They gave a strong impulse to the study of Scripture and biblical grammar and engaged in constant controversy with the rest of the Jews, the Rabbanites. They spread from Babylonia. Cairo became their great center; but they grew numerous and powerful in Constantinople and even had a considerable population in parts of Russia and eastern Europe.

While the relations between Rabbanites and Karaites were often acrimonious, especially in literary controversy, there was at least one period of comparative friendship between them, that was in the sixteenth century in Constantinople. The Jewish community there was at the peak of its prosperity. There were more than forty synagogues. The arrival of Spanish and Portuguese Jews and marranos from Spain and Portugal, greatly augmented the prosperity and the culture of the city. The Karaites were also powerful and there were strong intellectual bonds between the two groups. Rabbanite teachers instructed Karaites, not only in Jewish subjects, but also in general culture. It was here, in Constantinople, against the background of these friendly contacts, that one of the bitterest controversies as to the relationship between Rabbanites and Karaites arose.

The subject of the dispute gave the controversy wide reverberation in Jewish legal circles. It concerned education: Are Jews permitted to teach Karaites any subject at all, but especially the Oral Law, that is, the Talmud and its derivatives? This is part of the larger question whether Jews may teach these subjects to Gentiles. This question has been debated all through the history of the Law, from the Talmud itself through all the medieval literature down to our day. At various periods, Jewish scholars taught Christian scholars, particularly in Italy during the Renaissance, and such Jewish scholars had to defend their actions.

One of the key responsa in this long-lasting debate is by one of the greatest of rabbinical scholars, Elijah Mizrahi (circa 1455 to 1525 or 1526). He wrote a super-commentary on Rashi's commentary to Scripture, which has been a widely-read classic down to our day. He is the author of two volumes of responsa. In the last thirty years of his life he served as Chief Rabbi of the entire Turkish Empire (the *Hakham Bashi*). Apparently during his absence from the city a group of men tried to force through an excommunication against all those who were instructing Karaites. Mizrahi denounced the so-called excommunication and declared it to be of no effect, and he then went into the question of teaching the Law to Karaites.

The responsum [25] begins as follows:

> With regard to the ban that came about when some of the men of the congregations in the city of Constantinople, together with some of the leaders of the city, gathered in the Apulia

synagogue to proclaim a ban that no one shall teach the Karaites any subject in the world, neither Scripture, nor Mishna, nor Talmud, nor Halakha, nor Haggadah, nor interpretations of Scripture either following the plain meaning or tradition, nor of any of the sciences which the Greek sages had developed, neither philosophy, nor physics, nor metaphysics, nor arithmetic, nor algebra . . . nor even the alphabet. They sent for the rabbi who leads all the congregations and asked him to proclaim this ban, but he refused to do this, saying that it is not according to law to forbid a man to do such things as are really permitted. It is well known that the (secular) sciences were created by the sages of the Greeks who developed them from their own intelligence and from the searching of their own speculations (that is, they are not a unique revelation to Israel as is the Torah, written and oral). Therefore, any man is within his rights to teach them to Christians, Ishmaelites (Mohammedans), or Karaites, and to anyone else they wish. There is not the slightest prohibition in it. How then can one declare a ban against it? But the rabbi saw that these people paid no attention to his words, so he postponed the matter.

When those who were striving to achieve the ban saw that the rabbi was trying to delay, they arose and made an agreement among themselves that they would gather in the morning to execute their plan and that not one of them should be permitted to change his mind, no matter how many opinions may be voiced to the contrary.

When the pedagogues (who taught the Karaites) heard this thing, they cried out against them and said, "Why do you strive to forbid those things which have been permitted to us from ancient times until today?"

These pedagogues presented their arguments as to why these subjects were permitted to be taught and how they made their living by teaching them. They also called a rival meeting to protest against the proposed ban. But those in favor of the ban broke up the meeting and forced the rabbi to come with them to the Apulian synagogue where three scrolls of the Law were taken out, given to a Kohen, a Levite and an Israelite, respectively, and the ban against teaching the Karaites was solemnly proclaimed.

After giving this description of the events, Elijah Mizrahi takes up the question of the validity of the ban. He begins by saying:

> It seems to me that this ban has no reality, no validity, except for the individuals who proclaimed it. It has no validity for anybody else, for many reasons which I will now, with the help of God, explain.

He enters upon a discussion of the language used in the ban and quotes *in extenso* a responsum of Maimonides which indicates that only those who actually accept such a ban are bound by it. He continues:

> One cannot argue that this ban is necessary in order to guard against forbidden actions, namely, on the ground that the Karaites are heretics and deny the Oral Law and, therefore, belong to the class of those who must be "dragged down and not raised up" by means of teaching them such wisdoms as illumine the mind and may serve to exalt the student. This argument (says Mizrahi) is incorrect, for, if that were the case, we would not be permitted to teach sciences even to Ishmaelites and to Christians. The advocates of the ban themselves admit that we *may* teach these wisdoms to Mohammedans and Christians. Moreover, it is the actual experience of our people, in all places where they dwell, that Jews have taught even Gentiles who were idolators, and not one of our sages who lived in any city prevented this.

He proceeds to quote incidents related in the Talmud which indicate that the rabbis did not hesitate to exchange views and discuss religious matters with pagans, even though by these discussions the rabbis enlightened them and therefore taught them Judaism. He cites a responsum by Maimonides as to whether it is permitted to circumcise the children of Karaites on the Sabbath. Jewish children, of course, may be circumcised on the Sabbath (if it is the eighth day after the child's birth) and no violation of the Sabbath is involved. Maimonides says in this responsum that as long as the Karaites conduct themselves decently and do not mock the rabbis or their teaching, we may circumcise their children on the Sabbath, greet them even in their own homes, bury their dead and comfort their mourners. After quoting this responsum of Maimonides, Mizrahi says that this is how we should conduct ourselves with the Karaites. As long as they do not mock us and do not publicly violate our festivals and the Sabbath, we may teach them and may well hope that through our teaching they will come to repentance. He now reverts to the ban itself and says it is invalid for those who did not participate in it, not only because it is a prohibition of that which is actually permitted, but because a large part of the community has objected to it. Furthermore, the rabbi, whose concurrence in such a ban was needed, strongly opposed it. He ends by explaining the true motives of those who started the bitter agitation against the Karaites. He says:

> And the ban is invalid also for this reason, namely, that it was not imposed in the name of Heaven (that is, not from high motives), as were other bans which had been imposed in the past for the good of the world and the strengthening of the faith. This ban, however, was imposed because of jealousy and hatred which some people felt against the teachers. They were jealous of the honor that the teachers had from the Karaites. Some of them were moved by hatred against the Karaites, because of the interest on loans which the Karaites take from them. All collectors of interest are hated all over the world.

His final argument is that the ban has become obsolete by later events. It is sufficient reason to void a ban if it fails to be accepted and maintained. His statement on this score, incidentally, shows how the Turkish communities grew in that period.

> And (the ban is invalid) also because, after its proclamation, many sages have come from among those who had been exiled from Spain, may God preserve them. They have taught the Karaites in public. Thus the ban is void entirely because it has not spread (that is, been widely and tacitly accepted) and everybody admits that it has no reality. For they (the proclaimers of the ban) are not greater than the disciples of Hillel and Shammai who decreed [26] against the use of oil prepared by pagans, but when investigation proved that the decree (against

pagan oil) had not spread among all Israel, then Rabbi Judah and his court arose and annulled it (the decree had been voided by non-observance). Not only did they void it; behold, it had voided itself; yet they publicly proclaimed that it was void. This is how it seems to my humble mind. *Elijah Mizrahi.*

Wearing the Hat

Solomon Luria (1510–1573) was perhaps the greatest Talmudist in the grandest period of Polish-Jewish culture. His *Yam shel Shlomo* ("Sea of Solomon") is a classic of the Law, brilliantly connecting later enactments with the talmudic source. His responsa are a classical model for clear, logical, yet terse marshalling of all relevant material. He was asked whether a man who was subject to headaches might, in his home, eat his meals without wearing a hat. He answered, in a famous responsum,[27] that there was no prohibition even against praying without a hat; nevertheless, he would not conduct himself in accordance with that permission because it would offend the people who believed that wearing a hat was essential. Luria was a very independent-minded, outspoken man. He did not hesitate to disagree or to rebuke whenever he felt that it was necessary. For this outspoken man to defer to what he considered was merely a popular notion indicates how much the mood of the people was valued in Jewish Law and to what extent their customs (unless they were manifestly erroneous) were respected. This particular responsum has been frequently referred to, especially in modern times when modernist movements in Judaism have raised repeatedly the question of wearing the hat at worship or at home.

> *Question:* For the one whose head is heavy (that is, subject to headaches), is it permitted to sit and to eat with uncovered head?
>
> *Answer:* I do not know of any prohibition against pronouncing blessings without covering the head. It is true that to Israel Isserlein [28] it was an evident fact that it was forbidden to mention God's name with uncovered head. But I do not know

whence he derived this. For, behold, I have found in the tractate Soferim [29] that there is a disagreement on the matter. It says, "One with torn clothes, whose legs are visible, or whose garments are tattered, or whose head is uncovered may publicly recite the *Shema'*; but some say that only he whose legs are visible or he whose garments are tattered may publicly recite the *Shema'*; but he whose head is uncovered is not permitted to utter God's name." And Rabbi Yeruham wrote (end of section 16) that it is forbidden to utter a blessing with uncovered head.

Yet, if it were not for the fact that I am not accustomed to differ with the ancient teachers (the *Kadmonim*), or if there were some great scholar who would stand by my side in this matter, I would be inclined to be lenient and to utter benedictions with an uncovered head, for even to recite the *Shema'* thus is permitted. For, behold, there is a passage in the Midrash: [30] "Said Rabbi Berekhia:— 'A mortal king sends his proclamation to a province and what do the people of the province do? They stand up on their feet, uncover their heads, and read the proclamation with fear and trembling. But God, blessed be He, says to Israel:— "Read ye the *Shema'*, which is My proclamation, and I do not trouble you to read it either standing or with uncovered head, etc.' " It is clear from this that there was no basic prohibition to read the *Shema'* with uncovered head, and that God did not burden them with such a requirement (as the mortal king did).

But what can I do, since other teachers have already taught it as a prohibition (to pray with uncovered head)? It astonishes me (even more) that they are accustomed to prohibit the uncovering of the head even when not at prayer, and I do not know whence this prohibition comes to them. For I do not find any prohibition against uncovering the head except in the case of women, as is said in the Talmud; [31] and it is an act of special piety not to walk four cubits with uncovered head, and this specifically means walking four cubits, as is found in the Talmud: [32] "Said Rabbi Hanina:— 'Count it to my credit that I never walked four cubits with uncovered head.' " But this is merely a mark of special piety, since he says, "Count it to my credit, etc." There is further proof from the first chapter of the Tractate Kiddushin, 31a, where Rabbi Joshua ben Levi says:— "It is forbidden to walk four cubits with proud erect stature, because the whole earth is full of God's glory. And Rab Huna, son of Rabbi Joshua, says that he does not walk four cubits with uncovered head because 'the *Shekhinah* is above my head.' " Evidently it is only the walking with proud erectness that is specifically prohibited. But walking with uncovered head is only a mark of special piety (since the word "prohibited" is not used with regard to it).

But nowadays it is the reverse. People are not careful about the sin of walking with proud erectness. On the contrary, the haughty and the rich walk around with stretched-out necks; but as for the covering of the head, about that they are very careful; not because of modest piety, but because they think that it is (Jewish) law.

He then discusses the question of whether there is a difference between walking outside or being on one's own premises. He continues as follows:

But what can I do if the people consider it prohibited (to be with uncovered head)? I am not permitted to be lenient in this matter in their presence. I have heard of one scholar who studies with uncovered head. He says that the hat is too burdensome. Nevertheless, it seems to me that even if there were no prohibition in the matter, and even if piety were not involved, God's name not being mentioned, nevertheless, a scholar ought to be careful inasmuch as the people consider bareheadedness to be light-minded and frivolous as if one had violated Jewish law. Therefore, even if he studies in his own room, he must not rely upon his privacy. Maybe the people will see and hold him in light esteem. Not in vain do they say [33] that all things are forbidden because they seem wrong (*mar'it ayin:* "how it appears to the eye"), such things are forbidden even in the innermost chamber. . . .

A Charge Against an Anticipated Inheritance

Jewish Law in its present practice covers a much smaller area than it did formerly. Nowadays it is concerned chiefly with matters of worship and observances, ritual laws of food, and laws of marriage and divorce—that is to say, with laws codified in the first three of the four sections of the *Shulhan Arukh* (the "Orah Hayyim," the "Yoreh Deah" and the "Eben ha-Ezer"). But the fourth great section of the Code ("Hoshen Mishpat"), which deals with civil law, has during the past century fallen into disuse. Most Jewish litigants now bring their civil lawsuits to the secular courts. Therefore, except for the oriental lands and occasionally in pre-Revolutionary Eastern Europe, the responsa literature nowadays contains comparatively few decisions in civil matters.

This was not the case in the past. With very few exceptions, all Jews in the Middle Ages brought their monetary disputes before the Jewish courts. They were, in fact, forbidden by Jewish law to bring them to the secular courts. Hence the classic responsa are filled with discussions and decisions in civil law. The decisions cover almost every conceivable subdivision of the law: contracts, partnership sales, taxation, real estate, dower rights, inheritance, and the like.

Many of these subjects have been fully dealt with in books on Jewish history and literature, because the general importance of the responsa on civil law is greater than the specific points of law involved. The question of taxation, for example, was crucial in the development of the self-governing Jewish community in the Middle Ages.[36] Since civil-law questions dominate the responsa of many of the early respondents, they are widely used in monographs dealing with the life and work of these scholars.[35]

The following responsum by Moses Isserles [36] deals with dower rights and with inheritance. It indicates some of the principles of the law in these matters and reveals the method by which the law was derived and applied.

The problem discussed must have created considerable dispute at the time, since it is dealt with by Solomon Luria as well as by Moses Isserles and also by the contemporary Italian authority, Meir of Padua. Specifically, the question involves the rights of a daughter to part of her father's estate. Generally, daughters do not inherit, unless there are no sons. However, a daughter is entitled to support from her father's estate. In the Middle Ages it became customary for a father, at the time of his daughter's marriage, to dower her (that is, to give to his son-in-law), by a special documentary gift, with a portion of his estate—generally a part equal to half the inheritance of a son (*hatzi zakhar*). This was done in form of a note of debt (the father declared that he owed his daughter a certain sum), which debt the sons must repay on their inheriting the estate, or else give her the equivalent of half of a son's inheritance.[37]

In the case at hand there was, however, a serious complication. After the father had executed the "note of debt" for his daughter, he died, but his own father survived him. Then the older man died, and the grandchildren's estate was increased by the amount of the inheritance from their grandfather. Is the daughter (or her husband) entitled to a son's half share of her father's estate or of both estates? That is, does the father's note of debt apply only to the property which he actually bequeathed when he drew the document (*muhzak*), or does it also apply to expected or contingent property which he would have received if his own father had pre-deceased him (*ra'ui*)?

The question, as given in Isserles[38] and in Luria[39] reads as follows:

> *Question:* "Jacob" gave his daughter in marriage while his own father, "Isaac," was still alive. He gave him (that is, to his son-in-law) a document calling for half a son's inheritance (*hatzi zakhar*), as is the custom of the land. This is the form of the note which he wrote as an absolute gift: "that he owes his son-in-law one thousand gold pieces, and that his heirs are in duty bound to pay this debt. But his heirs have an alternative. They may, if they wish, give his son-in-law the equivalent of half of the inheritance of a son either from the property in hand or property in prospect (*ra'ui*). Then they will be free from this debt.

> But behold "Jacob" then died, while his own father, "Isaac," still lived. Then "Isaac," the father, died. Now the son-in-law demands also a part of "Isaac's" (the grandfather's) estate because, he said, this is expected property of "Jacob," his father-in-law, and he is entitled to a part of it since the note referred to property "in possession and expected." But the heirs answer that the son-in-law is not entitled to this, since they are the

direct heirs of their grandfather (that is, inasmuch as their father died while their grandfather still lived, they became the direct heirs of their grandfather. The grandfather's property had never passed into the possession of their father and was not subject to any charge he may have put upon his own property).

Answer: The law in this case needs to be clarified by the passage in the Talmud [40] where we read: They sent (from Palestine to Babylonia) the following statement of law: A son sold some of his father's property during his father's lifetime. Then the son died. *His* son (that is, the grandson of the owner of the property) may take the property back from the purchasers. But cannot the purchasers say (to the grandson): "Your father made a (valid) sale, yet you take it back from us?" This is a difficulty in (understanding the) Civil Law. But why should it be a difficulty? He (the grandson) can say (with justification): "I came (to the property) by my (direct inheritance) rights from my grandfather," for Scripture says (Psalm 45.17): "Instead of thy fathers shall be thy sons" (that is, thy sons shall be the direct heirs of thy father; meaning that a grandson may be a direct heir of his grandfather).

Here Isserles abbreviates the elaborate talmudic discussion wherein is listed a series of analogous cases in which this protest of the purchasers is weighed against the declaration of the grandson that he is the direct heir of his grandfather. He quotes a closing sentence which raises the possibility that the verse from the Psalms is not a legal maxim at all, but only a general description of the blessing which God gives to the families of the righteous. If, then, the verse from Psalms does not prove a grandson's right to inherit his grandfather's property directly, by what right can he annul the sale made by his father? This is the legal difficulty. Thus far, Isserles cites the talmudic debate. Then, in order to clarify the law, he moves on to the post-talmudic commentators and codifiers.

Rashbam (Samuel ben Meir, Rashi's grandson, who is the standard commentator on this portion of the Talmud) says: The son can recover the property from the hands of the purchasers, because the property was only an anticipated possession (of the father: *ra'ui*) which had never come into the actual possession of the seller (*i.e.*, the father), that the purchaser might thus become its legal owner through him; for, just as anticipated (*in spe*) property cannot be mortgaged, so it cannot be sold; and this is the law. . . . It is clear that Rashbam is of the opinion that mortgaging and selling are both of the same status (that is, neither can apply to property which is not completely owned by the mortgager or the seller).

Isserles then marshals the later authorities, in order to set limits to the general principle thus established. For example, he quotes the *Tur* (Asher b. Jehiel, fourteenth century),[41] who declares that, while the principle as stated holds generally, yet, if the father is dying and some of the property has to be sold to pay for the expenses of the funeral, an exception is made and the sale made by the son is valid even though the son has not yet become the actual owner of the property. Nevertheless, even in the case of such a valid sale, if the seller dies before his dying father, *his* son, when he comes into his grandfather's property, can (if he wishes) void the sale.

After marshalling all the relevant authorities on the question of whether such a sale is valid or not, or, should the grandson (if he inherits *directly* from his grandfather) void the sale, whether or not he must return the money to the purchasers, Isserles ends this part of the responsum by returning to the case in hand and says:

Since this matter is a subject of dispute between leading authorities, we follow the rule that, in cases thus disputed, whoever wishes to take property out of the hands of the one who is in possession of it must bear the burden of proof. In all cases the orphans are considered to be in possession. The son-in-law in the case before us comes to take property from the orphans. The burden of proof is on him. In this case, the claim of the son-in-law concerns property which never came into the possession of his father-in-law. While the claim of the orphans rests upon property which they actually inherited directly from their grandfather.

This decision of Isserles is concurred in by Solomon Luria; but Luria disagrees with one phase of Isserles' argument, namely, as to the validity of the opinion of Rashbam (in the commentary to the Talmud). They exchanged letters on the subject, not all of which are extant. At all events, Solomon Luria got tired of the debate and ended one of his letters thus: [42]

> Do not weary me with more quotations from the older authorities unless there is new proof, and even so we will continue our discussion in briefer fashion, for this is burdensome and consumes time.

Aside from this subsidiary disagreement and the touch of impatience, the two authorities (Solomon Luria and Meir of Padua) agreed with Isserles that the grandchildren were not in duty bound to give the son-in-law any part of what they inherited from their grandfather.

Divorce by Post

When a husband divorces his wife according to Jewish Law, the document of divorce, the *Get*, must be placed by him into the hands of his wife. If they live in different cities, he can divorce her through an agent, either his agent or hers. Either he can appoint an agent to bring the divorce to her (*sheliah ho'lakha*, "an agent of transmittal"), or she can appoint an agent to receive the divorce in her name (*sheliah kabbalah*, "an agent for acceptance"). When the husband's agent places the divorce in the wife's hand, she is divorced as if the husband himself had placed the divorce in her hand. Or, if the husband or the husband's agent places the divorce in the hands of her receiving agent, she is divorced as if she had received it.

Divorce through an agent is virtually indispensable when husband and wife live in different countries, unless, of course, the couple meets in one place. As early as the Mishna (second century B.C.E.), it must have been a frequent occurrence for agents to bring divorces from overseas. Thus we read: [43] "He who brings a divorce from overseas must testify as follows:— 'In my presence it was written and in my presence it was signed'." In modern times, with Jews scattered all over the world, and especially under the conditions which brought about the mass migration of the Jews, such divorces became extremely difficult to execute. Often the husband had fled the Russian Empire to avoid military service and had crossed the border illegally. If he wished to divorce his wife, how could he return to the city of her residence to hand the divorce to her? Or, for that matter, how would he find a Jewish agent who would travel into Czarist Russia to bring the divorce to the wife? Because of these difficulties, many tragedies occurred. Husbands neglected to divorce their wives, when it might have been a mercy to divorce them and allow them to remarry; and many thousands of women in their youth became *agunot*, "chained," to an unwanted married state.

There was a crying need of easing the ancient legal requirements for transmitting a divorce. Could not, for example, a way be found for transferring the divorce without a journey by a human agent? Why not, for example, send the divorce-document by mail to the city in which the wife lives? The basic difficulty with this suggestion was that the government which runs the mail was Gentile. Certainly this was true of the European governments in which Church and State were one; and the postal employees were Gentile. Jewish Law does not permit a Gentile to be made an agent in matters of divorce. How then could this tragic problem be solved?

The problem *was* solved; and during the last two generations it has become a general practice to send divorce-documents through the mail. The man who achieved this change was Solomon Kluger, the rabbi of Brody (1783–1869). He was one of the most prolific rabbinic authors and wrote many works of responsa.[44] When he was still a youth, he wrote a responsum justifying the transfer of a divorce by mail. He also wrote a fuller responsum on the same subject. His decision became basic to modern Jewish divorce practice. The two responsa are found in his book *Sh'yarei Taharah*, in the third section called "Tikkun Olam" ("Rectifying," or "Improving the World"). They are the first and second responsa in this book. In his introduction to this part of the book he says:

I have decided to record here matters that deal with the laws of divorce, certain frequent situations which occur and which involve improving present conditions (*tikkun olam*). The first concerns the matter as to whether it is permitted to send a divorce by mail. To settle this question is a great *mitzvah*, especially in our times, when many men, because of the current oppressions, have fled overseas and many have been exiled because of the laws of the government to a very distant place. They have not the means of sending a messenger on a long journey. Their wives, therefore, are living captives. For the last twenty years, I have fixed my mind on this question, as will be explained in this pamphlet.

There follows the first responsum:

This, published first, is what I said in my youth in the first section of my comments to "Eben ha-Ezer," the Laws of Divorce, no. 141.

Question on Section 35: I was asked if a woman can appoint in writing (that is, not by word of mouth, as is usual) her agent to receive her divorce (*sheliah kabbalah*), and (if, moreover,) her letter of appointment goes by the Gentile post; all this because the place is far and it is impossible for the divorce, carried by the (husband's) agent of transmittal, to get there. Is it proper to do so or not? (In other words, the proposal is that the wife should appoint her receiving agent in the city where the divorce is to be written. This agent will be appointed in writing and the note of appointment is to go by mail. When he receives the divorce, he receives it in her name, and she is thus divorced.)

Answer: The *Shulhan Arukh* says, in section 141, paragraph 14, that neither the husband's messenger (of transmittal) nor the wife's (of acceptance) need hear of their appointment directly from the mouths of their respective principals (in other words, they can just as well be appointed agents through other agents). In paragraph 35 of the same section, it is written, "He who sends a divorce through the hand of a Gentile, with the instruction to give it to a certain Jew, and the husband appoints that Jew in writing to be his agent of transmittal, the procedure is legal, because the Gentile is only performing a mechanical act (that is, he is not actually a conscious agent which, of course, he, being a Gentile, could not be in matters of Jewish divorce).

But Isserles writes in his gloss to the above paragraph: 'However, some disagree, arguing that you may not appoint an agent of transmittal in writing (that is, the husband must appoint him by word of mouth).'" Hence (continues Solomon Kluger), it would follow that no one disagrees that the *wife* may appoint *her* agent of acceptance in writing. Yet apparently there is no ground for this distinction on the part of Isserles (between the two agents); moreover, I looked into *Darkei Moshe*, Isserles' notes to the *Tur*, and I find him saying there that some think *no* agent should be appointed in writing. Thus Isserles seems to believe that neither of the two agents can be appointed other than by word of mouth. It is evident, however, that this reference is a printer's error and it is clear that Isserles believed that only the husband's agent of transmittal (and not the wife's agent of acceptance) may never be appointed by writing.

The reason (for this distinction) is that the Gentile (bearing the written appointment) would also be carrying the divorce-document itself (to hand to the intended agent). . . . It might appear (to the public) as if the Gentile were himself the actual agent of transmittal, which by law he may not be. But this objection would not apply if the Gentile carried the wife's note of appointment to her agent of acceptance, for then the Gentile does not carry the divorce document with him at all. We can have no objection to this, since he merely carried the note of appointment. Hence, Asher ben Yehiel decides that we may not appoint an agent of transmittal if the note of appointment is carried by a Gentile, because the Gentile will also carry the divorce-document (to give to the agent of transmittal). But, of course, in the case of the wife's agent of acceptance, where the divorce does not go along with the Gentile, the appointment by writing is permitted.

In accordance with the above, it would appear that it would be permissible to have the letter of appointment carried by post (not only for the wife's agent but also for the agent of transmittal). For, if one sent a letter of appointment by some chance Gentile to the agent of transmittal, it might be possible to say that this Gentile, carrying the divorce document, appears to be himself the agent of transmittal. But since it goes by post, whose regular and public function it is to carry letters, no one will imagine that the post was appointed to be the formal agent of transmittal. It merely carries the letters, just as it carries other letters. (In other words, with regard to the post, there is no doubt that it is merely performing the mechanical task of transportation and is not intended by the husband to be a religious functionary.)

Solomon Kluger again took up the question a number of years later, in answer to an inquiry.

> *Question:* In Paragraph 19 ("Eben ha-Ezer," Section 142, in the gloss of Isserles) we read as follows: "Some say that if the agent brings a divorce attested by its signatories, etc., the divorce is to be accepted in cases of emergency (or in the case where the woman might become an *agunah*) even though we do not recognize the signature. The problem is, however, that this bill of divorcement was sent through the mail, which is Christian (p. 3, column 3)." As to the fact that it was sent by post, I have already written on this matter in my youth and decided to take the lenient view and now I am sending a transcript of that (decision) to you.

Thereupon Kluger proceeds to add other arguments, and concludes this section as follows:

> And now we return to our subject, that we may appoint an agent of transmittal through the agency of a Gentile, specifically by means of the post to which the doubts which applied to a private Gentile do not apply. Indeed, we have acted in accordance with this decision many times here in our community and no one has opened his mouth to object. Therefore, this agent of transmittal (appointed by mail) is an agent as legal as all the agents for divorce which have been appointed in Israel. This in my opinion is quite clear.

The Jew's Oath

Among the many humiliations imposed upon the Jews in medieval Europe was the special oath which Jews were required to take when testifying in non-Jewish courts (oath *more Judaico*). The concept back of this special oath was that Jews and other heretics were not to be trusted when giving testimony in a Gentile court. This libel goes back to the laws of the Byzantine emperor, Justinian, and was carried over to all the countries of Christian Europe. At various times, the laws governing these special Jewish oaths were amplified in order to make them more humiliating. In the *Schwabenspiegel*, a collection of German laws dating from the thirteenth century, it was required that the Jew should stand on a sow's hide and place his hand upon a copy of the Torah. This was a frequent ceremony in Germany; in Silesia it continued until the year 1744. Modern antisemitism, of course, continued the libels which were back of these legal humiliations and pretended to find justification for its doubt of a Jew's testimony in the fact that, on the Day of Atonement, the Jew recites the *Kol Nidrei* formula which, according to the antisemite, frees him from any liability on taking false oaths.[45]

Ezekiel Landau, the great rabbi of Prague (1713–1793) was respected by the Austrian government.[46] Nevertheless, he was officially asked to answer a question concerning the trustworthiness of a Jewish oath in the government courts. The specific form of the question was this: If a Jew takes an oath on a *Sefer Torah* which is *posul* (that is, unfit for public reading due to the falling away of some of the letters in it, or because it was incorrectly written), is the oath taken over such a *Sefer Torah* trustworthy? Does the Jew not feel that he may safely swear falsely? Ezekiel Landau's answer is polite, patient and complete. It is a model of logical development, explaining the significance of an oath in Jewish Law, beginning with the Bible and covering almost the entire relevant literature.[47]

I was asked by the Imperial and Royal Revisor, Translator and Consistorial Censor, Peter Tirsch, by the order of the Consistorium, to give my opinion according to the law of our sacred Torah, whether we Jews, according to our custom, are permitted to swear falsely if the *Sefer Torah*, which we hold in our hands at the time of the oath, is *posul* (unfit for synagogue use).

And this is my answer:

Behold, we Jews are commanded not to swear falsely at all, even if we do not hold a *Sefer Torah* in our hands. The holding of the Book is not the essence of the oath. The essence of the oath consists in the fact that one says, "I swear that I have done this or not done it." That immediately, in itself, is a valid oath. This matter is recorded in the Torah many times and repeated in the Prophets and in the Hagiographa and is explained in the Talmud and in the *Poskim* (decisors) and in Maimonides and in the *Shulḥan Arukh,* as I will now set forth, all proofs, one by one, in detail.

1) It is written in the Ten Commandments (Exodus 20.7): "Thou shalt not take the name of thy Lord in vain." Thus we are warned in this verse against a false oath. Scripture here makes no mention that one should hold any *Sefer Torah* in his hand.

2) In Leviticus 5.4: "If a soul should swear, uttering with the lips for evil or for good, whatever a man shall utter as oath . . ." behold here, in this verse, it is explicit that the essence of the oath is the uttering of the lips, and there is no mention here of holding any book.

3) Leviticus 19.12: "Ye shall not swear in My name falsely and thus profane the name of the Lord thy God." Behold, it is clear that, without holding any book, if one swears falsely, he profanes the great and the awesome Name.

From here on, Ezekiel Landau lists the oaths mentioned in Scripture and the promises made and shows that in no case is there any mention of any book to be held while the oath is taken. Then he goes to the law in the Talmud and the *Poskim* (the decisors). He begins with Maimonides.

And this is the language of Maimonides, in the "Laws of Oaths," Chapter I: "There are four kinds of oath, etc." Whoever studies the words of Maimonides in this chapter will notice that he enumerates here, one by one, the details of all four types of oath and does not mention that it is necessary to grasp a *Sefer Torah* or any book in one's hands at the time of taking the oath. . . . As to one who vows, or swears in a dream, there is a disagreement between Asher ben Yehiel and Solomon ben Adret (see also *Shulḥan Arukh,* "Yore Deah," 210, no. 2) whether such a vow, made in a dream, has any validity. Solomon ben Adret is inclined to believe that one must have regard for such an oath, yet surely such a person had no *Sefer Torah* in his hands. Asher ben Yehiel, who said that an oath in a dream has no validity, says so because there is no real utterance of the lips and conscious agreement of the heart.

So far we have explained with clear proof that the oath is valid without holding any object at all; and now we shall explain the Law in the case of one who desires to take an oath on a book, as to whether in that case we require that he swear specifically on the *Sefer Torah* or whether it is valid with any other books; and also, whether the oath is valid with a *Sefer Torah* which, even if *posul*, is certainly not less sacred than printed Bibles; for, behold, it (such a Torah) still contains many sacred mentions of God, written with the sanctity required of the *Sefer Torah*.

Let us now explain that the custom to place a book in the hands of him who takes an oath, or to have him put his hand upon the book (is not for the purpose of making the oath valid; it is valid without the book, but) is only for the purpose of impressing him and reminding him of the punishments for false oaths written in the Torah. Even so, it is not our custom to use the book except for certain oaths. . . . Now we will explain that even those few oaths which we are accustomed to take while holding some object, the object which we hold is not specifically a *Sefer Torah*, but may be any other book as well. Thus, he may hold the *tefillin* in his hand, if he so desires ("Hoshen Mishpat," 87:15). To this Isserles adds, in his gloss, that any book that has in it the name of God will do. . . .

Now I wish to say that, even if there are some unfitnesses in a *Sefer Torah*, it nevertheless retains its original sanctity. For, behold, we are permitted to correct the imperfection and we may read it again in the congregation and pronounce over it the blessings of the Torah (which shows that it had retained sanctity. . . . There is a further important proof of the fact that the sanctity of the *Sefer Torah* remains upon the rest of the book (the part that has no errors), for, even if all the letters of the entire *Sefer Torah* were erased or worn away, and there were left in the book only enough to add up to eighty-five letters, it would still have the sanctity of a *Sefer Torah* and we would be permitted to violate the Sabbath to rescue it from a fire.[48] As for most of the *Sefer Torahs* which we set aside to prevent reading from them in the congregation, this is not because they are completely unfit, but in order not to delay correcting them. . . .

All that I have written is clear as to law and practice. . . . And truth testifieth unto itself. What appears to me, to my humble opinion, that I have written and sealed."

Church Building Used As Synagogue

Jewish Law considers neither Christians nor Mohammedans to be idolators. Israel Lifschutz of Danzig (1782–1860), in his commentary, *Tiferet Yisrael*,[49] says, speaking of Christians: "Our brethren, the Gentiles, who acknowledge the one God and revere His Law which they deem divine and observe, as is required of them, the seven commandments of Noah . . ." Although this attitude is basic in Jewish Law, there is a great deal of discussion in the Law on the subject of idolatry, and these discussions often come up in the responsa dealing with Christians. The reason is that the various images used in Christian worship and the invocation of saints are abhorrent to Judaism. Jewish Law understands that, in spite of the images and the saints, Christians are monotheists. Rabbenu Tam[50] says: "These days they all swear by their saints, but they do not ascribe divinity to them. Although they do associate God's name with others, the sons of Noah (that is, the Christians) are not forbidden to do so." Nevertheless, the statues and the images remain objectionable to Judaism and questions concerning them come up constantly: whether, for example, a Jewish tailor may sew the garments which a priest uses in Church worship, especially since these garments have a cross on them; whether a Jew may deal in candles used in the churches, either to sell candles or buy the remnants of the candles; whether crucifixes may be taken as pledges for a debt; whether a Jew may worship in an inn where there are crucifixes on the wall, and the like.

A new aspect of the relationship of Judaism to Christian objects of worship has come up in modern times. May a church building be bought by a Jewish congregation and converted into a synagogue? Does not the fact that the building was used for

worship involving images make it, in effect, an idolatrous building and so unfit for Jewish worship? Such questions could not
have come up in medieval times. It was inconceivable that a
church building ever would come into the hands of Jews to be
converted into a synagogue, although, alas, it frequently did
happen that, after persecutions and expulsions, synagogues were
converted to churches, especially in Spain.

A question came from America to Joseph Saul Nathanson
(1808–1875), rabbi of Lemberg.[51] The question concerned a
Protestant church and it is evident from Joseph Saul Nathanson's
discussion that the idea of such a church, without images, was
strange to him. In Galicia, they had either Polish-Roman Catholic churches or Greek-Orthodox churches, both of them with
images or ikons. He, therefore, includes a full description of the
worship in this strange church devoid of images and of its curious, un-Catholic type of service in this far-off country across
the seas from which the question came:

In the year 5618 (1858) a letter came to me from New York
in the land of America, from Rabbi Judah Mittelman, who asks
as follows: "There is (in New York) a house of prayer, a
Lutheran church. At first it was a private house (this is an important detail, because the law might be different if the house
had been built specifically for non-Jewish worship) and afterwards the private owner turned the house over to the Church.
Since the place was too small to hold a large assemblage, they
broke the partitions within the house and increased its size on
the outside along its length. They built a wall at some distance
away and extended the side walls to meet this new front wall,
in order to have room for a large assemblage (that is, they did
do some actual building for the specific purpose of Christian
worship). Over the lintel of the gate of the house, they wrote
in English, 'Welsh-Scotch Methodist Church,' and the interpretation of these words is, 'Lutheran church of the descendants
of the land of Wales and the descendants of Scotland.' They
utter songs and prayers referring to 'that man,' and they dance.
Then one man arises and preaches to them about the greatness
of 'that man,' and they stand and listen. When he finishes, they
sing and dance. These worshippers are Protestants, without any

images or likenesses (in their church)." And now his honor
(that is, the questioner) cites the *Magen Abraham* to "Orah
Hayyim" 154, end of paragraph 17, to the effect that even if
there was fixed worship of idolatry in a house, it is still permitted to pray therein. But he (the questioner) is in doubt as
to what *Magen Abraham* meant, that is, whether worship was
regular in that house, but the house was not specifically set
aside for that purpose; also whether it is permitted for us to
pray in it only occasionally but not regularly; and, above all,
whether we may make of it a house of study for the community. Now it is clear that the intention of the *Keneset ha-
Gedolah* (Hayyim Benvenisti, who is quoted in the reference)
is that it is permitted to pray in it even regularly, provided the
house was not specifically set aside for the purpose of idolatry.

Nathanson then proceeds to consider the various relevant
talmudic passages, and ends the first responsum by saying:

The law seems to me to be that here, since the building does
not contain any likeness or image, it is permitted to turn this
into a house of study (and prayer) and it is, in fact, a virtue (a
mitzvah) thus to sanctify God's name.

The next responsum is in answer to a further letter by Rabbi
Mittelman in New York.

After writing the above, your second letter of the third of
Sivan reached me in which you say that the building was specifically set aside for (Christian) worship. I do not understand
the relevance of this fact, for, as long as there is no image or
likeness, the building cannot be described as having been set
aside for idolatry. As is explained in the *Shulhan Arukh*, "Yore
Deah" 145 no. 3, the prohibition of a building so set aside, applies
only when idols were brought into it. Here no idols were wor-
shipped at all. As for the fact that they extended the house and
opened new doors in it (which would tend to prove that it
was specifically prepared for Christian worship), all this was for
the purpose of *praying* in it, but not to worship idols there,
that is, likenesses and images. Therefore it is obvious that it is
permitted . . ."

4

---◆◆◆---

WIDESPREAD
DEBATES

THE HISTORIANS who admire
the old Roman Empire generally speak in praise of its religious
tolerance. They contrast Judaism, or Christianity, with its religious exclusiveness, its "jealous God" Who brooks no rival, with
the easy good-nature which led the Romans to permit all sorts of
religions to practice their cults even in the Eternal City itself.
The contrast is largely correct, but it is superficial. The Romans
were not really religious. They had a certain civic piety and con-
formed to an official cult, but there was very little of mysticism
and devotional fervor in the religion of classical Rome. Not being religious, they could not see much difference between one
religion and another. It is easy to be tolerant where one is indifferent.

The responsa literature reveals what some might consider a
deep-rooted intolerance. There is a great deal of bitter controversy to be found in it. There were controversies which
divided communities, spread over whole countries and led to
angry accusations and bans. The disputes were not merely with
the irreligious—as, for example, the denunciations of the false
messiah, Sabbatai Z'vi, and his followers, or of the Karaites who
denied the validity of the rabbinic laws—but also between great
rabbis, each of unquestioned piety and learning. Storms of controversy rage throughout the responsa literature.

The controversies indicate the intense concern which the Jewish people has had for its religion and its laws. The religion of

the Jews touched every aspect of their life and a decision in favor of one side or the other in a controversy might affect the lives of innumerable people. Every Jew was concerned in the matter. Besides, the Law was the Law of God and those who believed that certain scholars were misinterpreting the Law, were bound to believe that they were misrepresenting God's word. Emotion as well as reason was deeply involved.

Such wide-spread controversies could not have arisen frequently in the responsa of the gaonim. Of course, the gaonim, too, had participated in great controversies, but not through the medium of responsa. Since the gaonim had primary authority, their decisions could not be controverted. When the Gaonate faded away, however, and study of the Talmud spread over all the lands of the diaspora and people began to turn with their questions to their local rabbis, these rabbis did not have unquestioned authority and could not settle matters merely by a "yes" or "no." Each community had many scholars who studied the same books that the rabbi studied. A responsum now had to be a learned discussion, more or less among equals. Furthermore, since there generally was a good percentage of scholars in every community, when a dispute arose among the rabbis, the members of the community were competent, or considered themselves competent, to participate in the debate. Consequently, the controversies reached far and deep into every community. They were never "tempests in a teapot," but storms over a large section of Jewry.

Because these controversies indicate the deep concern and the intellectual participation of Jewry in the Law, it is important to see which controversies, as revealed in the responsa, stirred them most.

The Ancona Boycott

The city of Ancona, on the Adriatic coast of Italy, became the pivot around which revolved one of the great disputes recorded in the responsa literature. Ancona, being a port city facing the Balkan mainland and therefore in easy contact with the

Mohammedan world, became one of the favorite cities of refuge for the marranos and the Jews who fled from Spain. The city was in the Papal States, and the popes themselves offered concessions to make the city attractive. The rights of non-Christians were particularly protected, since both Jews and Turks were essential to the commerce of the developing city. Later, even marranos, "New Christians," from Portugal, were given the privilege of sharing this refuge. Pope Paul III, on February 21, 1547, allowed New Christians from Portugal to share the safe-conduct of non-Christians who came to do business in Ancona. Thus there grew up a community of marranos, many of whom returned to their faith and began to live openly as Jews.

When Cardinal Giovanni Caraffa became Pope Paul IV, he turned sharply against the reverts (the ex-marranos) in Ancona. This was part of his general repressiveness which established the ghettos, enforced the wearing of the yellow badge, and the like. He sent a stern representative to Ancona to prosecute those Portuguese who had abandoned Christianity and had returned to Judaism. Before the persecutions ended, a number had been burned at the stake after a trial by the Inquisition. Others fled to the neighboring duchy of Urbino. It seemed to them that the seaport of Pesaro in that duchy could be developed into a port for trade with the Ottoman Empire. The Duke of Urbino encouraged them and offered them protection.[1]

It was in connection with Ancona, where the ex-marranos were so brutally done to death, and with Pesaro, their refuge, that the controversy arose. It centered around the personality of one of the greatest Jewish women of all history, Doña Gracia, of the House of Nasi. This refugee from Portugal, with her son-in-law who later became Duke of Naxos in the Turkish Empire, had settled in Constantinople from which city her business enterprises spread over many countries. She was the guardian mother of marranos everywhere, helping them escape, protecting them, aiding them to re-establish themselves in new homes. In Constantinople, she and her son-in-law, who was also her nephew, maintained a great *yeshiba* whose chief teacher was the famous author of responsa, Joseph ibn Leb.

When Doña Gracia heard of the murder of the Jews in Ancona, she resolved to help the survivors. Since the refugees in Pesaro promised the Duke of Urbino that they would make Pesaro a great port, as Ancona had been, she urged (at the instance of the marranos in Pesaro) that all the Jews of the Turkish Empire organize a boycott against trading with the port of Ancona, thus punishing the papal authorities and encouraging the Duke of Urbino in his hospitality. This was the first time since their scattering over the world, that the Jews attempted to use concerted, united action in self-defense. The suggested boycott created the great controversy which is recorded for us in the responsa literature.

The first questions that trickled into the responsa literature concerned business disputes resulting from the confiscation of marrano goods: specifically, who, in these complicated international transactions, should bear the loss involved. Here we obtain detailed descriptions of what had occurred in Ancona, and we are told of the gathering of rabbis in Constantinople. There the more fundamental disputes arose as to whether such a boycott, pronounced in the synagogues, must be unanimous or not. If it is not unanimous, may it be disregarded, or has it the force of Jewish law? Then we have the record of the disagreements and the debates which led some enthusiastically to advocate the boycott, others to be cautious, and at least one scholar strongly to oppose it.

A special case, a lawsuit involving restitution of confiscated money, reveals clearly the original persecution of the ex-marranos in Ancona. The case must have been a famous one, because it appears in the works of three of the great respondents of the time. Evidently the question was sent far and wide for decision. Joseph ibn Leb of Constantinople has it; [2] Samuel di Medina, the head of the school in Salonika; [3] it is found also in the responsa of Isaac Adarbi who was a contemporary of Samuel di Medina in Salonika. [4] The statement of the case is clear in the works of all three respondents. The following is an outline of the facts as given by Joseph ibn Leb:

It happened in Ancona. "Reuben" owed a sum of money to a Gentile and this Gentile owed a similar sum to "Simon." The three of them came together and the Gentile said to Simon, "Collect the money which I owe you from Reuben who owes it to me." Reuben agreed to pay the debt to Simon (instead of to the Gentile) and the Gentile tore up the note of debt which he had against Reuben; and Reuben now owed Simon the money secured by a note which he executed in Simon's favor.

About eight days before the payment date of the money which Reuben now owed to Simon, the pope decreed that anyone who has any money of Simon's, or money owing to him, should let him (the pope) know of it and turn the money over to his servants, the judges of the land, under the penalty of death and confiscation of property. Thereupon Reuben went and confessed to the authorities that he had money which was payable to Simon; and they warned him that, when the time of payment comes, he should not pay it to Simon but to the officers of the pope, because all the property of Simon was now confiscated by the government. Soon thereafter, the plague (of persecution) spread against all the Portuguese Jews who had been marranos, and all their property was confiscated by the government, including the property of Reuben; besides the fact that many were burned at the stake for the sanctification of the Divine Name. Reuben and Simon were saved, but now Simon demands from Reuben the sum that was owed to him (because of the draft of the money originally owed to the Gentile). But Reuben argues that they had forced him to confess he had money which was due to Simon and that he was forbidden by the pope's officers to pay it to Simon, but to the officers of the State, etc. Does Reuben still owe that money (to Simon)?

Joseph ibn Leb decides that Reuben does not owe anything to Simon, since the money had been confiscated and was no longer under his control even while he still retained it in his physical possession. When, furthermore, the pope's officers had confiscated Reuben's money, they confiscated Simon's money, too, which was in Reuben's possession.

Samuel di Medina, in dealing with the same case, also decides that Reuben does not have to pay Simon, "since Reuben was compelled many days before to inform the pope's officers of

Simon's money; so, from that time on, Simon's claim on that money was gone."

Isaac Adarbi, in dealing with this case, agrees in general that Reuben is no longer liable to pay anything to Simon for the confiscated money. Nevertheless, he has some doubts, and the doubts revolve around the question whether the action of the pope's officers has any legality as government law (*dina d'malkhuta*) which must be accepted, or whether it is sheer robbery, in which case Reuben must make some restitution (since it was his responsibility to protect Simon's money against robbery). He cites the law with regard to what is a valid decree by a government and what is not, quoting Maimonides who says that such decrees which are consistent with past laws are valid government decrees, but whatever the king does wilfully or because of a passing whim is not to be accepted as a government decree. Adarbi continues:

> Since, in our case, we had never before heard of such a decree in the city of Ancona, where Jews had lived for many years in the past, neither in the time of this pope or his predecessors, etc., it is, therefore, questionable whether this is a legal decree. It may be considered, not as legal confiscation, but as sheer robbery; and Reuben is then liable to make restitution to Simon.

Another business matter which came up for settlement, because of the persecution in Ancona, is given by Samuel di Medina.[5] It is sufficient to describe the problem to obtain a clear picture of the commerce between the Turkish Empire and the Italian cities which went through the hands of Jewish merchants:

> "Reuben," who lives in Turkey in the city of Adrianople, sent to Ancona twenty-four hides by the hand of "Simon," who was one of the marranos who had come from Portugal. Simon was to sell them there and send to Reuben in Turkey the equal value in *turpines* (a type of garment). Before the hides could come into the hands of Simon in Ancona, Simon sent to Reuben other goods from Ancona to Turkey that he might sell them in his behalf. After the hides sent by Reuben arrived in Ancona

and were sold, the transaction was recorded in the municipal books, as is the custom there, credited to the name of Simon. Before Simon had time to acquire *turpines* to send to Reuben in payment for the hides, the pope arose and issued his decree against the marrano Jews of Ancona, to destroy them in money and body. Simon was compelled to flee to Rome. While he was in Rome, his property was confiscated and also the moneys due him as recorded in the municipal books.

Now Reuben and Simon are suing one another, Simon for payment for the goods he had sent to Reuben in Turkey before the hides had arrived, and Reuben for the payment of money for the hides.

Following the decrees against the marranos in Ancona, those of them who fled to Pesaro began their agitation for a boycott against Ancona. This development of the case is described in a responsum of Moses di Trani, who was rabbi in Safed at this time. His discussion [6] deals with the actual validity of the agreement to boycott.

The grief in the heart of a man leads him to tell it to others, namely, what happened in Ancona and how from there they went forth to Pesaro and the duke received them gladly, for he saw that it would be of benefit to him if all those who had formerly traded in Ancona would now trade through his city; and they (the marranos), in order to favor the duke, agreed to this attempt to transfer the trade. They sent messengers to Turkey, to the great congregations, that they should agree to this so that no merchant should go to Ancona, but only to Pesaro. The first to agree to this sacred matter were the congregations in Salonika; and their sages decided that all merchants who had hitherto traveled to Ancona should now go to Pesaro. But they made a condition to their *haskama* (their agreement), namely, that this would be valid only if the congregations of Constantinople and Adrianople and Brusa consented. The two first-mentioned communities did consent, although some merchants there demurred. But the congregations in Brusa did not agree at all, saying that their merchants would lose money if they went to Pesaro, because of lack of docking facilities there. Thus, because of this lack of agreement, some merchants went to Pesaro and some continued to go to Ancona, and the agreement lapsed. Thereupon, the great lady, famous in all the kingdoms, saw that the agreement was not being maintained. She wrote again to the sages of the great cities that they should have mercy upon the unfortunate poor who are left in Pesaro, for if these do not fulfill their vow to the duke (namely, to arrange a boycott against Ancona and in favor of Pesaro), their lives will be in danger.

Moses di Trani then goes into a discussion of the validity of such an agreement. Does it require unanimity, or can the leaders or the majority of the communities decide for the entire city even though it involves a loss for some? Especially does he question the validity of such a decree if, at its original promulgation, certain members objected. They surely cannot be compelled to accept a decree which they opposed even though it *is* valid for those who agreed to it. He then concludes with a compromise counsel—that those merchants who still go to Ancona should help in the work of rescue there, and that the business agents of the great lady who go to Pesaro would naturally increase the business of that port and thus mollify the duke.

The chief opponent of Doña Gracia and her son-in-law, the Duke of Naxos, in this boycott was Joshua Soncino, the Italian-born rabbi of one of the congregations in Constantinople. In two of his responsa [7] he gives the fullest account in all the relevant responsa of the struggle in Constantinople itself for and against the establishment of the boycott. On the side of the boycott were Doña Gracia, the Duke of Naxos and Joseph ibn Leb, who was the head of the *yeshiba* which she maintained. Against the boycott were he, Joshua Soncino himself, certain of the congregations and a number of merchants. It took great courage on the part of this rabbi to oppose the tremendous influence of the great benefactors of the community, but he felt compelled to do so.

He tells [8] how, when first the messenger came from Pesaro telling them of the duke's request that they make an agreement with the Jews of the Turkish Empire to boycott the rival port of Ancona, a meeting of the rabbis of Constantinople was convened and he himself was so deeply moved that he wanted such an agreement to be made at once and to be enforced by the full authority of the community. Later he changed his mind. He wondered whether the Jews who had fled to Pesaro would really be in danger if there were no boycott. Also, letters were being received from the original Jewish settlers in Ancona. It was only the late-comers (these letters said), the marranos from Portugal, who were persecuted by the papal officers, but the Italian Jews and other older settlers in Ancona would not only be financially ruined by such a boycott; their very lives would be endangered by the indignation of the pope. Are not they to be considered? All these doubts came into his mind and he decided to oppose the boycott; and his decision was endorsed by Moses di Segovia and Moses ibn Jamil.

In his other responsum,[9] the matter is taken up again and a detailed description is given of the tremendous efforts exerted by the Nasi family and by Joseph ibn Leb to persuade the congregations of Constantinople to agree to the boycott, that is, to its renewal; how Joshua Soncino opposed it at considerable risk; how it was nevertheless proclaimed without unanimity having been attained; how the congregations of the city of Constantinople were now divided against each other. Finally, Joshua Soncino suggests that letters be sent to the great rabbis of Italy to discover how great the danger is to the communities of Pesaro and Ancona if one line of action or the other is followed, and that action then be taken according to the information received.

The whole controversy has great interest, first because of its clear revelation, in first-hand reports, of the life of the marranos in Italy; secondly, also, because of its description of the international trade in which the Jews and marranos participated, and how the principles of Jewish Law were applied to the sixteenth-century trading conditions; and, finally, because of the discussion of the problem of the community's authority over its individual members. Above all, it gives a description of a bold attempt made by scattered Jewish communities to organize themselves in an effort to fight back by the economic means at their disposal against those who persecuted their brethren. The plan failed, as it was bound to fail, since there was no over-all authority available to discipline the self-interest of so scattered and disorganized a people. But the attempt reveals at least the tremendous influence and self-sacrificing devotion of the family of Doña Gracia and, at the same time, the courage of an individual teacher to resist that influence even when it was armed with just indignation in behalf of a noble cause.

The Divorce in Cleves

While divorce is comparatively easy in Jewish Law, nevertheless, great care is exercised in the preparation of the divorce document (the *Get*), the precise spelling of the names and the wording of the formula. This extra care is needed in order to guard against any possible objection to the divorce after it was written and given to the woman. For if the woman marries again and the original divorce which freed her from her first husband proves faulty, her second marriage is adulterous and the children born of that marriage are illegitimate. Hence the large place which divorce laws occupy in Jewish Law.

One of the matters discussed in the divorce law is insanity. Both the husband and the wife must be sane at the time the divorce is given: he, because the divorce is written at his conscious command and he must therefore know what he is doing; and she, because she must be able to receive it from his hand, since, were she not sane, it would be equivalent to a divorce by force, which is contrary to Jewish Law. With regard to the divorcing of an insane woman, however, the law provides certain mitigations of the general prohibition. If a man makes proper provision for the protection of his insane wife, he may divorce her, provided he obtained the agreement of no less than one hundred rabbis residing in three different provinces. The law also provides some mitigation of the general prohibition against an insane man divorcing a sane woman.

The law as codified in the *Shulhan Arukh* [10] is as follows: If a man is at times insane and at times sane, he is to be considered normal when he is in his lucid periods. If he gives a divorce at such a time, the divorce is valid.

The charge that an insane man was permitted to divorce his wife and the defense that at the time of divorce he seemed quite sane (that is, it was during a lucid interval) was the basis of one of the most vehement disputes in the responsa literature. It concerned a divorce given in Cleves in 1766. Scores of responsa were written on this dispute. They are collected in two volumes, one *Or ha-Yashar*, published originally in Amsterdam in the year 1769, and *Or Yisrael*, published in Cleves in the year 1770. Together they contain about one hundred and thirty responsa from the greatest rabbis of that day, all about this *cause célèbre* of the eighteenth century.

The events that led to the divorce are described at the beginning of *Or ha-Yashar*. The peculiar actions of the bridegroom are detailed almost as if from a page in a psychiatrist's notebook.

Isaac Neuburg of Mannheim wished to marry the daughter of Jacob Gunzhausen of Bonn. After the customary negotiations, the marriage was arranged for the eighth of Elul 1766, in the city of Mannheim. On the morning after the marriage, the groom walked around gloomily and, on the Sabbath following, he ran away, hiding himself in a nearby village where he was found after a search. He had taken some ninety-four gold coins in his flight. He now returned them. Then the couple agreed to live together if a home would be found for them near Bonn, the girl's native city. This was done; but very soon the young man said that his wife disliked him, that he was surrounded by enemies, and that he must flee for his life. He was going to leave the continent and settle in London. After discussion between the families, it was agreed that the best thing would be to let him give her a divorce. Thereupon, they journeyed to the city of Cleves, where the rabbi, Israel Lipschutz, discussed the whole matter with all concerned and, agreeing to the request of the groom (who seemed sane in every way), arranged the divorce.

Then the controversy began. The rabbi of Mannheim, Tevele Hess, and a group of other scholars of that city, protested against the divorce. They sent a letter to Frankfort-on-the-Main, asking the rabbinical court there to compel the rabbi of Cleves to admit that the divorce had been given in error and to forbid the young woman (who was therefore still married) to marry anyone else. Their first objection was that the divorce had been obtained under suspicious circumstances. Why should the families have gone to Cleves to get the divorce when they could have gotten it in the nearby city of Coblenz? Secondly, there was also suspicious haste about the divorce; and, third, the young husband showed every evidence of insanity. Thereupon the Jewish court of Frankfort-on-the-Main declared that the groom, Isaac Neuburg of Mannheim, had not been sane at the time, as proved by the fact that on a Sabbath he had run away beyond the distance of a Sabbath journey and that he had asked to be smuggled over to England, etc. The court ordered that the young woman should be advised at once not to rely upon this divorce and not to remarry.

Then Israel Lipschutz, rabbi of Cleves, began his defense. He cited the old Jewish laws of the Rhineland to prove that each rabbinical court is independent of any other and that therefore the court in Frankfort-on-the-Main had no authority over him. He then went carefully into the facts of the case and enclosed statements from others who were present, the scribe and other scholars. These testified that they had talked at length to the young husband and that he was undoubtedly sane. Thereupon the rabbis of Mannheim, who had objected to the divorce, wrote letters to many communities and soon nearly all the great rabbis of the time were drawn into the debate. Among them, Joseph Steinhart of Fuerth asserted in his responsum that, if the man was sane at the time of divorce, it was quite sufficient. The fact that he had made over so much money to his divorced wife was not in itself evidence of insanity. A number of additional responsa from Joseph Steinhart follow in continuation of his arguments. The court in Frankfort now again declared the divorce invalid. Jacob Emden of Altona gave his opinion that, no superior court being in existence, each court, in this case the court of Cleves, had a right to independent action. There was an opinion from the famous Aryeh-Lev of Metz, who argued that the woman should wait three months before she remarried. Ezekiel Landau of Prague also supported the divorce, but suggested that the woman wait a year.

So the debate went on, bringing in all the great teachers of the age. This was frequently the case with any doubtful divorce case. The Jews were sensitive on the subject of the legality— and therefore the purity—of the marriage bond. Should the divorce prove illegal and the woman had meanwhile remarried, the marriage would have been adulterous. This is what the opponents of the divorce feared. On the other hand, if a divorce be declared unfairly illegal, the poor woman remains an *agunah*, unable to remarry, for the husband may actually become completely insane. Although this case concerned only one couple, so much was involved that the greatest rabbis of the day did not hesitate to devote to it a great deal of time, writing long treatises on the subject, until the responsa on this one case add up to one of the most extensive discussions in Jewish Law.

The Sturgeon Controversy

There is not a single area in Jewish Law which has been worked out and clarified so minutely that there can no longer be room for further controversy. Widespread controversies can still arise in almost any field: business contracts, community regulations, divorce, the status of returning converts (marranos), and permitted or forbidden foods. Disagreements can most easily arise when, with the changes of the times, new situations are met or new inventions or newly discovered foods need to be identified and analyzed in relation to the law. There have been, for example, considerable discussions on the question of the various new types of bird brought in recent centuries from one region to another. Whether such birds are kasher or not must be determined by comparison with the types described in Scripture, since there is no local tradition or habit to accept them as kasher.

There is much more room for controversy over fish than over poultry, because of a curious situation in the original laws in the Bible. In Leviticus 11, which describes the forbidden and the permitted animals, the forbidden fish are included under a general definition—namely, those that lack scales and fins—while the forbidden birds are listed in detail and many species are actually named. Indeed, nowhere in the Bible is there to be found a single mention of any species of fish (Jonah's "whale" is spoken of merely as "a large fish"). There is only the rule that fish lacking scales and fins are not kasher and those having them are.

The Talmud, however, does mention various types of fish, particularly in the tractate Abodah Zara. The kashrut [11] of a number of species of fish is discussed there, and the question is settled on the basis whether scales can be seen or discovered on them. Thus we are told that Rab Ami was asked concerning a fish (one that resembled an eel). He held it up towards the sunlight and detected scales; whereupon he declared the fish kasher. Then he was asked about another fish, and he rubbed it on a white dish and some scales came off. He declared that fish kasher, too. There is hardly another test mentioned in the literature that followed, until the thirteenth century, when Nahmanides, in his Bible commentary to the pertinent passage in Leviticus, adds a new element. He describes the shape of the scales [12] and says that the scales must be fixed in the skin yet be removable by hand or by knife, otherwise the fish is not kasher. This new test suggested by Nahmanides was embodied in the later codes. So in *Shulhan Arukh*, "Yoreh Deah" 83 no. 1, where Joseph Caro speaks of the fact that a fish must have fins and scales to be kasher, Isserles adds that they are kasher only if their scales can be removed by hand or with an instrument. While there are other tests—such as the existence of a tradition that certain fish are kasher, and also the problem of the backbone, etc.—the removability of the scales is the crucial test; and it is around this test that the great controversy arose concerning the sterlet, a small variety of sturgeon.

The first opinion with regard to the sturgeon was given in the late eighteenth century by Ezekiel Landau, Chief Rabbi of Prague. He had received an inquiry from Rabbi Hirsch, the rabbi of Temesvar in southern Hungary, with regard to a fish which, he said, some local (Jewish) people testified they had eaten in their native place. Judging by a later discussion of this question, these people were probably Sephardim from further south in the Balkans. The fish was a sturgeon, or sterlet, whose scales, if any, are not readily discernible. Rabbi Hirsch, aware that this fish was unknown in Western Europe, and that Ezekiel Landau had probably never seen it before, sent a specimen of the fish with his message. Ezekiel Landau [13] first says that those who testified that the fish was kasher where they came from are to be considered reliable witnesses as to the existence of a tradition on the permissibility of that fish. As for the objective tests, Landau says he observed two rows of scales, one on the right and one on the left. It is true that these scales could not be removed by hand or with an instrument, but he soaked the fish in a lye-solution and the scales came off. It makes no difference, he says, whether or not the scales are removable specifically by hand or by knife; if they are removable at all, by whatever means, the fish is kasher.

The decision remained unquestioned for a period of years. Then the Chief Rabbi of Moravia, Mordecai Benet, issued an opinion exactly the reverse of Ezekiel Landau's.[14] He rests his decision on the fact that the scales, such as they are, are almost impossible to remove and therefore, according to the test given by Nahmanides, the fish cannot be kasher. He maintains that soaking the fish is no test, unless it is in cool water. If hot water removes the scales, that would hardly be a test. In his scathing closing remarks, he evidently refers to the fact that the followers of Ezekiel Landau had confirmed their teacher's lenient opinion. He says:

> I have already now overstepped the line as a pupil who disagrees with his teacher for the purpose of preventing people from sin; but I see that already the truth has become weakened and is vanishing; flattery has increased through the desire for victory. Since it is not my duty to finish this work, I now seal my lips until God will look down upon the poor estate of the Law and place it again in the radiant light.

This was a challenge to debate. The debate spread to Hungary. Aaron Chorin, a rather modernist rabbi, in the small Hungarian community of Arad, wrote two booklets defending the decision of Ezekiel Landau, entitled *Words of Pleasantness* (1798) and *Coat of Mail* (1799).

It was evidently in reference to Aaron Chorin that Mordecai Benet wrote his other responsum on this matter in *Parashat Mordecai*, "Yoreh Deah" no. 4. Speaking in still bitterer language, he says:

> Woe to the generation! For in our day they have purified that which is forbidden by the Torah, and none protests. Furthermore, they wrongly ascribe such a decision to my great teacher, Ezekiel Landau. Far be it from him or the humblest of his pupils, who walk in his footsteps, to make such a decision. For those fisn, the sterlet, are known by many, and I myself have investigated them in the presence of scholars and I have found their bones so cleaving to the skin on all sides that it is impossible to scale them either by hand or by instruments.

He ends with these words, evidently referring to Aaron Chorin:

> And let not that teacher of poison and wormwood deceive you, for he deserves excommunication. He is doing as Jeroboam and his fellows did (namely, making Israel sin).

Since Aaron Chorin was beginning to be suspected of reformist tendencies, his opinions aroused and intensified the opposition. Isaac Kriegshaber, rabbi of Pacs in Hungary, not satisfied with writing a responsum refuting the view that the fish was kasher, gathered the opinions of many rabbis who declared that the fish was not kasher and published them under the title *Makkel No'am* ("Staff of Pleasantness").[15]

How bitter the controversy became is seen from the fact that soon charges of wilful forgery were hurled. Isaac Kriegshaber claimed that Ezekiel Landau, whose liberal opinion was the foundation for calling the fish kasher, had changed his mind about his decision and, in fact, had asked him, Isaac Kriegshaber, to inform the original inquirer, the rabbi of the congregation of

Temesvar, in his name, that the fish may not be eaten. Ezekiel Landau was dead by this time, but the statement by Kriegshaber elicited an indignant reply from Ezekiel Landau's son, Samuel Landau. The latter takes up the question at issue in two responsa which are published in his father's work, *Noda bi-Yehuda*, II, immediately following his father's opinion cited above.[16]

Samuel Landau's answer to a letter from Isaac Kriegshaber says:

> Your letter has reached me; but I dislike to involve myself in the dispute in a matter which has already become a quarrel and has reached the stage of a war (not for truth but) for victory. Yet I cannot refrain from answering you. Enclosed is a copy of my father's responsum on the question, from which you can see that my father permitted the eating of the fish concerning which he was asked from Temesvar. I am astonished that you have written that my father retreated from this decision and had asked you to send his letter of retraction to the rabbi of Temesvar. Please forgive me, sir, if I say that this is an absolute falsehood. It is known to all that my father was an active correspondent. Why then, if he *had* changed his mind, would he not himself have written to the rabbi of Temesvar, whom he knew well and who had eaten at my father's table for many years? He would have sent such a letter by the swiftest post to keep people from eating that which he would have considered forbidden food. Furthermore, why is there not found here a copy of such a letter which he is alleged to have written to you, sir? How would he have possibly allowed his original decision to go into his book (of responsa) without making a note that he had changed his mind about it? You are not a true witness in this matter, since you do not possess such a letter, and you say that the letter is lost.

Thereafter, the rabbinate of Prague decided officially to renew and reaffirm the decision of the late Ezekiel Landau. And Elazar Fleckeles, a rabbi of Prague, informed Isaac Kriegshaber of Pacs to this effect.[17] This answer is dated the 18th of Shevat, 1819. Isaac Kriegshaber had evidently sent him his pamphlet. Elazar Fleckeles begins as follows:

I have received your scroll and, while it looks like a scroll animated by zeal for the Lord of Hosts, yet it is clear that it really is a scroll animated by that jealousy of scribes which increaseth not wisdom.

Then he cites the proof that the sturgeon is kasher.

All in all, the dispute seems a rather surprising one. While certain other disputes touched many lives—for example, the dispute as to the *etrogim* of Corfu—or were of widespread concern to many families—for example, the disputes over the status of the marranos in marriage—the dispute over the sterlet was really not on a practical matter, since the sterlet actually was hardly seen in the countries where the dispute raged: Ezekiel Landau had to have a specimen of the fish sent to him before he could decide. The inquiry came from southern Hungary where some of the Balkan Jews knew of the sterlet from the Mediterranean lands. In fact, Kriegshaber says that those who ate it must be suspected of being followers of the false Messiah, Sabbatai Z'vi, who had misled so many of the Jews in the Turkish Empire. Why then did the dispute arouse so much heat, including accusations of flattery and forged letters and the like? Such disputes about the *kashrut* of fish had occurred in earlier times. In the time of Rashi and his grandson there had been a disagreement about the "burbot" [18] yet there is no evidence that that dispute created such bitterness. The outburst in connection with the later dispute must have been due to the fact that the time was one of emotional tension. The bitterness engendered by the heresies of Sabbatai Z'vi and his successors had just ended. The raging arguments over Reform were soon to begin. It was a time of fierce polemics, and an almost theoretical question about a rarely seen fish became the occasion for blazing controversy.

The Controversy Over Reform Judaism

Some Conservative congregations in America frequently institute changes in the forms of Jewish worship. The inherited prayerbook is often abbreviated and new prayers in English are added to the service. No Conservative synagogue is now built with a separate women's gallery. Men and women worship in family pews or at least on the same floor level. Almost no new synagogue has the *bima* (*almemor*) in the center of the floor; the worship is now conducted from the pulpit in front of the ark.

All these changes are instituted against very little opposition, except occasionally from some of the older members of the congregation. Beyond these sporadic local protests, almost no notice is taken of the modifications by the Orthodox rabbinate and no public statements or responsa appear with regard to them.

Yet these very changes aroused a tremendous storm when they were introduced over a hundred years ago by the Reform movement in Germany and in Hungary. Reform Judaism was the first modernist movement in the synagogue. The changes in the procedures of worship which it instituted were advocated against a background which was entirely Orthodox. They came, therefore, as a shock and aroused an understandably violent reaction. Reform, coming at the time that it did, was in the nature of a religious revolution.

It was inevitable, therefore, that a flood of questions by individuals and congregations concerning these changes should be directed to leading rabbis and that many responsa should be written on the subject. The advocates of change endeavored to defend their proposal by interpretation of the traditional laws. They wrote pro-Reform responsa. The responsa, pro and con, were not confined to one city or even to one country. Well-known rabbis in Germany, Poland, Austria, Hungary and Italy were drawn into the controversy which soon became a widespread debate.

The first well-known Reformer, Israel Jacobson of Westphalia, founded a modern school in Seesen in 1801 and, primarily as part of the school, built a Temple with an organ in 1810. This event did not occasion much protest, perhaps because it was an isolated experiment and because it was in connection with a new school and was not a modification of an existing Orthodox institution; possibly also because Jacobson was not a rabbi but a business man who had served loyally in defending the rights of Jewry. Zvi-Hirsch Chayes (1805–1855) the well-known rabbi of Zolkiew, in his *Minhat Kenaot,* a volume directed against Reform, speaks almost reverently of Jacobson. He says: [19]

> Then there came to Berlin, Jacobson, the honored sage, the mighty man, a prince in Israel, inner-councillor to the duke of Brunswick and to the king of Westphalia. This perfect man, upright in his qualities and his virtues, who strove with all his might to do good to his people in every way, had conducted himself all his days by the advice of the rabbis and according to the Torah; but in Berlin he changed his mind and was misled by Friedländer and his group.

Jacobson did not move to Berlin till 1815, five years after the dedication of the Temple in Seesen. Yet Zvi-Hirsch Chayes considers him entirely praiseworthy until he came to Berlin. Possibly he had not heard of the Temple in Seesen which Jacobson had built. Evidently that early attempt at Reform was not widely known.

The real rabbinic controversies over Reform do not begin till the founding of the Reform Temple in Hamburg and the publication of its prayerbook in 1818.

The first collection of responsa, *Nogah ha-Zedek* (Dessau, 1818) was in favor of the Reformers. It contained responsa by two Italian and two Hungarian rabbis (Shem-Tov of Leghorn, Jacob Hai Recanati of Verona, Aaron Chorin of Arad and Moses Kunitz of Budapest).

Shem-Tov of Leghorn confines his discussion to the permissibility of using the organ and other musical instruments in Synagogue worship. He says:

> I have been asked by my brethren from a distant land to give my inexpert (that is, unworthy) opinion as to whether it is permitted to use in the Synagogue the instrument known as the organ. Those who favor it say that it is the same instrument as the *Ugav* mentioned in the Psalms (92.4). Those who oppose it say that it is a Christian custom, for they use that instrument in their houses of worship. Besides, the use of music has been abolished (by talmudic law). What then is the law in this matter?

I answer and say that I do not understand how this can be questioned at all, for it seems obvious, in my humble opinion, that it is permitted and the matter does not require further debate. For the rabbis (in the Talmud) who forbade instrumental music, forbade it only in connection with wine, in hilarity and levity; as it is stated in the Mishna: [20] "When the Sanhedrin was abolished, they abolished song in the tavern, as it is said: 'They shall not drink wine with a song (Isaiah 24.9)' " . . . From this it is clear that they did not prohibit (singing to instrumental music) except when it is done in levity and hilarity or drinking. But in cases where levity and hilarity are not involved, as in our case (that is, in the case of worship), but on the contrary the music is for a good purpose (a *mitzvah*), to gladden the hearts of men, women and children who come to hear, causing them to rejoice in the commandments of God—which is the essence of worship since Scripture says: Serve the Lord with gladness (Psalm 100.2), then it is clear that it is beautiful and good to use music both vocal and instrumental.

Rabbi Shem-Tov goes on to discuss other aspects of the use of instrumental music and to show that there is no objection at all to its use in the Synagogue. This decision is endorsed by two Palestinian rabbis who were present at the time in Leghorn, Chaim Judah Ayyes (the grandson of Judah Ayyes, a famous author of responsa) and Judah Aaron Takli.

The second Italian responsum is by Jacob Hai Recanati of Verona.[21] He also speaks of the use of the organ in the Synagogue. He discusses the fact that some find it objectionable because it is used in churches. He analyzes the various types of prohibition due to idolatry and shows that they do not apply in this case.

The two Hungarian rabbis provide much more elaborate responsa. Aaron Chorin of Arad, who had already disputed with many rabbis in Bohemia and Hungary on the question of whether the sturgeon was kasher,[22] now comes to the defense of Reform. He takes up all the relevant questions: (a) prayer in any language other than Hebrew and changing the text of traditional prayers; (b) the use of musical instruments in the service; (c) splitting the community by forming a new congregation;

(d) abolishing the silent recitation of the *tefilla;* (e) changing from the German pronunciation of Hebrew to the Sephardic.

His discussion on the question of prayer in any language other than Hebrew makes use of almost all the relevant sources. He begins as follows:

> Our great teacher (Yehuda ha-Nasi) laid down a great rule in the Mishna [23] —that prayer may be uttered in any language. To which the Talmud adds: Prayer is a plea for mercy; therefore one may voice it in any way he wishes. . . .[24] And where have we greater among the decisors (*poskim*), famous for his piety and scrupulousness in the observances of our customs, than the author of *Magen Abraham,*[25] who quotes (to "Orah Hayyim" 101, no. 5) the words of the *Sefer Hasidim* ("Book of the Pious") no. 788: It is better for a man to read the *Shema* and the (accompanying) blessings in the language which he understands than to pray in Hebrew if he does not understand it . . . for he who does not understand should not pray, since prayer depends upon the heart (that is, upon the understanding and not merely upon the recitation of the words).

Chorin then cites other great authorities to the same effect.

The responsum of Moses Kunitz, rabbi of Ofen, defends the use of the organ in worship. He says:

> The use of the organ is for the glory of God, for it will serve to bring back to the Synagogue those who for a long time have kept themselves away from the "Courts of God." Thus they will be sanctifying the name of God among the multitudes. There can be no greater *mitzvah* than this . . .

The responsum of Moses Kunitz, favoring the use of organ music, created quite a stir. Aaron Chorin was, after all, suspected of modernist tendencies and his opinions were not taken too seriously by the Orthodox; but Moses Kunitz, rabbi of Ofen and member of the rabbinical court (*dayyan*) in Budapest, was a teacher of known piety, having defended the authenticity of the cabalistic classic, the *Zohar* (in his *Ben Yohai*) against the attacks of Jacob Emden.

The following year a collection of anti-Reform responsa appeared. The book was entitled, *These Are the Words of the Covenant*,[26] and included responsa from the most famous Orthodox rabbis of the time. Among them were Moses Sofer of Pressburg, Mordecai Benet of Nikolsburg, the rabbinate of Prague (Elazar Fleckeles, Samuel son of Ezekiel Landau and Lev Melish), Abraham Tiktin, Akiba Eger of Posen, and others.

Moses Sofer first discusses the proposal of the Reformers in Hamburg to hold public services only on the Sabbath and holidays. He stresses the duty to have services three times a day. Then he moves on to the question of music in the Synagogue:

> And as to the question whether it is permitted to have instrumental music in the Synogague, we must draw our conclusion from the fact that our ancestors, who arranged the prayers in the Synagogue, did not ordain music with the prayers. (This was done with purpose, for) although the custom of music with worship originated with us in the Temple (in Jerusalem), nevertheless, our fathers (consciously) abandoned it. This fact proves that they were opposed to it, because since the Temple was destroyed we do not rejoice. . . . We have no right to make innovations which our fathers did not intend. It is a long-accepted commandment with us to pray before God without instrumental music. How dare we now permit that which the rabbis have prohibited? God forbid! Such a thing must not be done in Israel.

Mordecai Benet places special weight upon the use of Hebrew in prayer. He says:

> Now let us get to the root of the law as to whether we must pray in Hebrew or may pray in any other language. Rabbi Jonah (to Alfasi) says that, if the worshipper does not know Hebrew, he can fulfill his duty (of prayer, by praying in the language with which he is familiar). From Rabbi Jonah's statement it is clear that if he *does* know Hebrew, he does not fulfill his duty when he prays in any other language. . . . But we do know the familiar Hebrew prayers, which are in pure and clear Hebrew. If so, there is no advantage in praying in any other language. Besides, one must pay special attention during prayer to the letters and accents of the words, etc.; this one cannot do in German which one speaks daily in automatic habit . . .

The rabbinate of Prague, in a joint letter, denounces the book of pro-Reform responsa, *Nogah Zedek,* and says that those who wilfully change the accepted prayers are neither Jews nor Christians.

Akiba Eger of Posen, speaking also of prayer in any language other than Hebrew, says:

> Even though it is, indeed, the law that one may pray in any language, that law refers only to occasional or incidental prayers. But to fix the regular congregational worship in any other language but Hebrew, God forbid!

The controversy then died down for about twenty-five years. It was revived in 1840 in Breslau. The struggle between Reform and Orthodoxy in Breslau was complicated by the personal dispute between the two rabbis of the community, Abraham Geiger, the Reformer, and Solomon Tiktin (son of the Abraham Tiktin who had contributed to the volume of responsa against the Hamburg reforms). Both parties gathered responsa from various rabbis and published them in German. The Tiktin pamphlet was entitled, *Statement of the facts, etc.,*[27] and the Geiger pamphlet, *Rabbinical Responsa, etc.*[28] When the second edition of the Hamburg prayerbook was issued, in 1841, another collection of responsa was published in German.

The fact that these later responsa for and against Reform were no longer written or published in Hebrew is evidence that the controversy was moving out of the main stream of responsa debate. It is, of course, true that in previous centuries, too, responsa had been written in languages other than Hebrew—many of the responsa of Alfasi and Maimonides, for example were written in Arabic—but only those responsa which were translated into Hebrew passed into the purview of Jewish scholars the world over. It was the reverse with the controversy over Reform. At its beginning, all Jewish scholars were concerned with the debate; the responsa were, therefore, written in Hebrew to appeal to the entire rabbinic world. But after the first set of responsa, there was nothing new to add. The fact simply was that the Orthodox rabbis prohibited the changes and the modernizing congregations disregarded the prohibition. During the middle of the nineteenth century, when attempts at Reform were made in Hungary, there were many responsa directed against the Reformers; but they and the Reformers elsewhere no longer defended themselves by means of rabbinic responsa. They made changes in ritual because they felt these changes to be necessary or desirable, but they were not concerned with whether the changes were legally permissible or not. Debates in the responsa could have continued only if both sides had held to the premise that the law is authoritative. But when one side abandoned the premise, the debate died down. There continued to be *denunciations* of Reform, but no genuine and classic type of responsa debate.

The Etrogim of Corfu

Perhaps the most famous debate in the responsa in the nineteenth and early twentieth centuries concerned the citrons (*etrogim*) used in the ritual of the festival of Succot. The Torah (Leviticus 23.40) speaks of the four plants which must be used in the festival worship. The first of the four is described merely as "the fruit of a beautiful tree." This rather vague description is specifically identified in the Aramaic translation (the *Targum*) as the citron (*etrog*). It is thus not a specific command of Scripture, but an ancient tradition, whose first mention is in the *Targum*, that the "fruit of the beautiful tree" means the citron.

The citrons grow in many countries and islands around the Mediterranean. The Jews of Northern Europe, during the last two centuries, got their citrons chiefly from the Greek Island of Corfu (through the merchants of the port of Trieste) and from the island of Corsica (through Genoa). In 1846, Ziskind Minz of Brody [29] distributed in Galicia *etrogim* from Parga (on the Greek mainland opposite Corfu). But other *etrogim* were being brought from Rapisa and Iyya, two new localities in Corfu. The rabbis of Poland declared that only those citrons which came from Parga (through Ziskind Minz) were kasher. The new ones were suspected of being hybrids, which is contrary to the biblical law against hybridization (Leviticus 19.19). These prohibitory opinions of the Polish rabbis were collected in a volume of responsa entitled (*Peri Etz Hadar* "Fruit of the Beautiful Tree"). Among the rabbis, who prohibited the citrons from the new localities in Corfu, were the famous Solomon Kluger of Brody and Z'vi-Hirsch Chayes of Zolkiev. Their opinions were disputed by Ephraim Zalman Margolis of Brody.[30] The debate spread, scores of authorities in many lands participating.

Among the authorities who wrote responsa on this question were Elazar Horwitz, rabbi of Vienna; [31] Solomon Quetsch, rabbi of Nikolsburg; [32] Moses Schick; [33] Joseph Saul Nathanson; [34] and the great authority among the Habad hasidim, Menahem Mendel of Lubavitch; [35] the other leading authorities of this group were Nehemiah of Dubrovna; [36] Abraham Teomin of Zbarov in the responsa of his grandfather, Jacob Lissa,[37] and many more recent scholars.

During the past generation a new turn was given to this wide-spread debate. In 1891, the Greek population of Corfu was stirred up against the Jews because of a ritual-murder charge. The antisemitic outrages which followed awakened world-wide protest against the use of the *etrogim* of Corfu.[38]

A group of new colonists in Palestine organized for the purpose of raising citrons for the world Jewish market. They gave their organization the biblical name "Fruit of the Beautiful Tree." The late Rabbi Abraham Isaac Kuk took them under his supervision and wrote a book in advocacy of the enterprise.[39] The society was pledged to raise citrons free from any danger of hybridization. Nevertheless, even with regard to the Palestinian *etrogim*, a question was asked of Eliezar David Greenwald.[40] This question could not have been asked except about Palestinian *etrogim*; it could have no bearing on any others. The laws of the Sabbatical year (Lev. 25.1-7) require that all agricultural work in Palestine cease in the seventh year. The year on which the question was asked was a Sabbatical year. Can, therefore, *etrogim* grown in Palestine that year be used for the Succot ceremony? Eliezar Greenwald answers in the negative. On this special question, whether the modern colonists in Palestine must observe the ancient laws of the Sabbatical year, the best-known responsa are by Naftali-Z'vi Berlin of Volozhin.[41]

The debate as it developed is illustrative of the progress of many of the great disputes in the responsa literature. At first a definite decision as to a present problem is based upon past authorities. As opposing opinions develop, the past authorities which had been quoted are re-examined as to the basis for their decisions. The grounds are then shifted entirely; either other authorities are found in the older literature, or the opinions of the authorities hitherto cited are declared irrelevant to the present issue and entirely new premises are found for the debate. If the debate lasts long enough, many different principles of Law come up for analysis and application. Thus this long-lasting debate on the *etrogim* presents a long procession of many sections of Jewish Law. It may be of interest to observe the various types of argument and precedent cited.

The hybridization of *etrogim* was a widespread practice, since the citron tree is delicate and difficult to mature unless it is grafted either on or with a lemon tree or twig. Yet in "Orah Hayyim" 648 (where the *Shulhan Arukh* gives all the various characteristics of the kasher *etrog*) no definite mention is made of any prohibition of a hybrid *etrog*. The commentary *Magen Abraham* does speak of such a prohibition, but not the *Shulhan Arukh* itself. Therefore the respondents who sought to prohibit the Corfu *etrogim*, on the ground of hybridization, went back to another code, the *Lebush*, by Mordecai Jaffe.

This authority is cited, re-analyzed and by some declared irrelevant, in almost every responsum in this long debate. Mordecai Jaffe says that, since hybridization of plants is forbidden, and since plants or animals or anything else with which some sin has been committed may not be used for sacred purposes, therefore, the hybrid *etrog* is forbidden for religious use.

But those who declare the Corfu *etrogim* kasher doubt whether a sin is here committed. Does a Christian or a Moslem gardener commit a sin if he grafts plants? Christians and Moslems are not idolators in the eyes of Jewish Law: they are "Sons of Noah." Sons of Noah are expected to obey seven basic commandments (avoid idolatry and immorality, establish courts of justice, etc.). Surely the prohibition of hybridization is not one of the seven commandments assigned to the Sons of Noah (although Maimonides seems to think they *are* expected to obey this law). If then the authorities (except Maimonides) agree that it is not a sin for a Christian or Moslem to hybridize plants, no sin has been committed with these Corfu *etrogim*, the gardeners being all Gentile. In that case, on Mordecai Jaffe's own grounds, the Corfu *etrogim* are not prohibited. Abraham Gumbiner (*Magen Abraham*) then seeks another basis for the alleged prohibition of hybridized *etrogim*, namely, that a hybrid is not an *etrog*, and some respondents follow *his* reasoning.

The defenders of the *etrogim* thereupon go more deeply into the technique of hybridizing. Basing themselves upon the Talmud, they discuss whether a twig attached to a tree (a "daughter tied to a mother") produces its own fruit or the fruit of the larger tree which dominates it? Whatever the answer, the objection to hybrids can only apply if the fruit is harvested from this grafted twig while it is still attached to the other tree. If, after a while, the twig is removed from the tree to which it had been attached and planted separately, it is now an independent plant and there is no objection to its fruit.[42]

The debate then shifts to the problem of the trustworthiness of the rabbis of Corfu who have declared all these *etrogim* kasher. The prohibitors say that the guarantee of these rabbis cannot be relied upon because the process of growth and harvesting is complex and the situation may change from year to year.[43] But the permitting respondents cite the principle that one (rabbinical) court cannot challenge the decisions of another (unless, of course, it be greater in authority than the original one).[44]

Another stage of the argument deals with the visible characteristics of the grafted and the ungrafted *etrog*: the smooth versus the rough skin, the vertical versus the inclined stalk, and the like. May we judge by these outer signs? How many of these characteristics must be present before the *etrog* is acceptable? If it looks and smells like a proper *etrog,* is that not sufficient without further investigation?

The last stage of the argument moves on to purely formal grounds, the relation between a commandment to be fulfilled (*mitzvah*) and a commandment violated (*'aberah*). Suppose hybridizing *is* a sin and the sin has been committed, is not the commandment (to use the *etrog* on Succot) nevertheless fulfilled even though it began with a sin (*Mitzvah habaah b'aberah*)? Thus the long argument fades off into purely formal debate.[45]

In recent years the entire controversy over *etrogim* has died away, after having lasted for more than a century.

The Shohet of Berdichev

The problems of kasher food touch every traditional household in Jewry. Almost all of the questions which a pious woman would bring to a rabbi for decision dealt with these matters; while on the level of communal organization, the problems of providing kasher food is one which engages much of the attention of the authorities, rabbinical and non-rabbinical. At the very top level of Jewish life, this is likewise true. The problems of *kashrut* occupy a large part of the codes and constitute perhaps the largest single subject in the responsa literature.

The theme is varied. It deals with the mixture of meat and milk, with the problems involved in the newer types of bird and fish, and it concerns also the reliability of those who are entrusted with providing kasher food—the bakers, the milk dealers and, especially, the meat merchants. A great deal of attention centers upon the ritual slaughterers, the *shohetim*.

The *shohet* is a religious functionary. His work begins with the prelude of a benediction. His technique of slaughtering is described in detail in the law. He is under the supervision of a rabbi who examines him as to knowledge and skill and gives him formal documentary permission to perform his function. When he fails, or there is suspicion or accusation of his failure, in any one of his relationships to the law, he creates a problem for which a solution must be promptly found. Questions are frequently asked in the responsa about a *shohet* who refuses to submit his instruments to the rabbi for examination, about a *shohet* whose own life is not of exemplary piety, even about one whose children are not as religious as they should be. The most painful questions are those about *shohetim* who are accused of wilfully deceiving the community and passing on to the people non-kasher or imperfectly slaughtered or imperfectly examined meat.

Many of these questions concern the *shohet's* conscientiousness in examining the lungs of the animal. A considerable section of the law deals with the problems occasioned by various adhesions or abnormal appendages that appear on the lungs. However the various diseases of the lungs in animals might be described in modern terminology, the law was concerned with certain physical manifestations of disease and these were generally judged by growths, appendages, adhesions on the lungs (*sirkhot*). If, for example, the appendage is from the upper part of the lung, the animal is likely to be non-kasher, *trefa*. If blood is seen coursing through the appendage, this argues a perforation of the lung and the animal is *trefa*. If, when the lung is blown up, the appendage likewise inflates, this indicates that it has grown around the perforation and the animal is *trefa*. And so through many tests. Certain shapes and locations of the growths or adhesions must be referred to a rabbi for decision; many of them are left to the knowledge and the conscience of the *shohet*.

A famous case occurred in the early decades of the nineteenth century involving a *shohet* of the large Jewish community of Berdichev in Russia. The case involved the good name of one of the greatest rabbis of the day, Solomon Kluger of Brody, in Galicia, on the Russian border. A judgment of his as to an accused *shohet* in Berdichev resulted in one of the most interesting, vehement and pathetic disputes in the entire responsa literature.

The events leading to the dispute were described by Solomon Kluger himself. In a pamphlet which he sent to many rabbis (and of which one of those who disagreed with him gives the full text as a preliminary to his rejoinder),[46] Solomon Kluger relates that a number of leading members of the community of Berdichev became suspicious of their veteran *shohet*, Abraham.

They noticed that more and more of the cattle which he slaughtered were sold as kasher, twice as large a percentage being
kasher as compared with the number declared kasher before his
time. They wondered whether or not Abraham was passing as
kasher such cattle as should have been declared *trefa*. The rabbis
of Berdichev, taking notice of this complaint, assigned some of
their number to watch him slaughter, and they found his
slaughtering quite according to the law and unobjectionable.

But the protesters were not content. They sent to Brody in
Galicia for Solomon Kluger to come to Russia and investigate
their *shohet*. Rabbi Kluger came to Berdichev and for two weeks
watched the slaughtering without saying a word. What he observed during these two weeks astonished him. The *shohet* Abraham worked with great speed (examining as many as thirty-six
cattle in half an hour), much faster than did the *shohetim* in
Brody; and very few *sirkhot* (adhesions) were found when the
animals were opened. Kluger was convinced that the *shohet*
manipulated these adhesions, tore at them and did not apply, in
doubtful cases, the full tests of inflation by immersing the lung
completely in water. Still he said nothing. He explained his
silence later by saying that in Russia he did not feel safe to talk
out, lest someone denounce him to the government. He waited
until he returned safely to Galicia and then issued his statement,
which he sent broadcast, saying that this *shohet* Abraham did
not perform the proper tests and undoubtedly has been passing
as kasher meat which was not kasher at all. He decided that the
shohet should be discharged from his post and not be allowed
to serve as *shohet* any more anywhere.

In the responsa of Yekuthiel of Enzil there follow (after the
quotation of Solomon Kluger's own pamphlet) two statements
from rabbis: one of Berdichev, declaring that the *shohet* Abraham is conscientious, that his meat is kasher and that he should
be permitted to continue as *shohet*. A similar statement is then
cited from Joseph Hayyim, rabbi of Ivnitza, who wants to know
why Solomon Kluger so stubbornly insists on preventing the
shohet from slaughtering in the future. Does he not give him
any opportunity to repent? But, he says, this stubbornness is

typical of Solomon Kluger. Once he had a disagreement with Kluger about a divorce suit and, even though he showed Solomon Kluger that he was wrong, Kluger nevertheless persisted in his former attitude.

Yekuthiel Enzil [47] then follows with a long refutation of Kluger's action. First, he says, Kluger had no right to serve as sole judge; there should have been three judges. Furthermore, if he was the judge, he cannot be a witness: here is a judge who presumes to take his own testimony. Enzil denies any reality to the alleged facts of the case, namely, that the number of *sirkhot* (adhesions) were suspiciously fewer in Berdichev than in Brody. Frequently, he says, "in the great and small cities in our province," many cattle are found without adhesions at all. He ends with a plea to all the rabbis, to whom he sends his rejoinder, to undo the injustice done to the *shohet* of Berdichev.

Meir Eisenstaedter of Ungvar takes up the question after having received both pamphlets. He discusses the basic question, whether Solomon Kluger had the right to act as a judge in such matters without co-opting two others as judges. Moreover, Kluger had no right to forbid the community to eat from this *shohet*'s slaughtering because he cannot proclaim a permanent prohibition. But, since Kluger has made this decision, let the *shohet* come to Rabbi Solomon Kluger, admit that perhaps he has been too hasty in his handling of the lungs of the animals, let him promise to work more deliberately and let him be restored to his place.

Aaron Moses Taubes of Jassy, Roumania, in his responsum to Yekuthiel Enzil, also attacks Solomon Kluger for having judged alone and for his silence while he was in Berdichev.[48] A similar judgment against Solomon Kluger is made by Moses Solomon of Partzva.[49]

Abraham Teomin, grandson of Jacob of Lissa, wrote a number of responsa which are published at the end of Jacob of Lissa's book, *Nahalat Yaakob*. One of these responsa, a very long one,[50] deals with this painful debate. He argues that Solomon Kluger greatly erred in his decision and makes a great deal of the fact that Kluger cannot be a witness in the case.

One responsum defending Kluger is by Abraham Wolf Frankel of Reishe.[51] He writes to the leaders in Berdichev in defense of Solomon Kluger and calls upon the people of the city to obey his decision.

It seems strange that so famous a rabbinic author as Solomon Kluger should have met with so much opposition in his decision, that he should be accused of not acting in accordance with the Law, that he should be denounced for keeping silent during the time when he was in Berdichev, for allowing the people to eat what he already considered *trefa* meat, that he should also be charged with cruelty against an innocent man, and much more. This was due in part to the fact that Solomon Kluger was caught up in a bitter communal quarrel. Berdichev was the center of power for Hasidism and, as is hinted in one of the responsa, Hasidism and anti-Hasidism played a part in the local dispute that led to the accusations against the *shohet*. The basic fact is that all matters dealing with kasher food, particularly with the trustworthiness of a *shohet*, were always likely to arouse angry words and bitter feelings, so that even as great a scholar as Solomon Kluger, who indeed was a great specialist in such matters and who did what he thought was his clear duty, found himself the target of attack and abuse. The debate over the *shohet* Abraham of Berdichev remains in the responsa literature as an evidence of the deep convictions and the violent emotions which could divide a community, almost in an instant, into two warring camps.

Machine-made Matzot

Modern invention has had a tremendous impact upon the Law. The reaction to various discoveries, such as illuminating gas, the steam engine, electricity, and the like, occupies a considerable proportion of modern responsa literature.[52] Some of these inventions created situations which required immediate analysis; and, after some discussions, a fair consensus was arrived at. But at least one, namely, the invention of a machine for the preparation and the baking of matzot for Passover, created one of the most acrimonious discussions in the history of the responsa literature.

The first such machine seems to have been invented in Austria in 1857, and the use of it quickly spread to various countries, especially to Germany. There was an immediate and violent reaction on the part of the rabbis to its use. It was not difficult to find grounds for debate on the matter, since the laws on the preparation of matzot for Passover have been developed in great detail since ancient times. Even in modern times especially pious people exercise watchful care from the very harvesting of the grain to the completed baking of the matzah (*matzah sh'murah*, "watched matzah"). Furthermore, a distinction was made, not only for the especially pious, but for the average man, between the matzah which he eats all during Passover and the matzah over which he recites the blessing at the *seder*. For the rest of the Passover, after the *seder*, he is not required to eat matzah at all; he is merely required to keep from eating leavened bread and other such foods. But the matzah over which the blessing is recited at the *seder* is the mandatory matzah (*matzah mitzvah*). With regard to this mandatory matzah, special care must be exercised to prepare it according to law.

The baking of matzot by hand, which was of course the method followed all through the ages and upon which all the past laws were based, has resulted in certain definite requirements which were crucial in the discussion over the machine matzot. The kneading of the dough had to be virtually continuous, lest, should the kneading stop, the leavening process might begin. Also, the dough had to be kept away from too much sudden heat until the baking process could actually begin. Great care had to be exercised that wisps of dough should not get caught in cracks of the table, lest these bits of dough become leaven and affect the rest of the matzah dough. Also, while the dough was being kneaded, the workman was expected to watch out for any stray kernels of wheat that had not been crushed in the milling process, for these might leaven. Therefore workers at the matzot had to be adults. The work may not be done by the immature or the unintelligent ("deaf-mute, insane and minors").

All these requirements necessarily came up for consideration when the new method of baking matzah by machine was introduced. The machine had already been used in various cities in Germany when it was brought to the Galician city of Cracow. Solomon Kluger wrote a letter to Rabbi Hayyim Nathan and to Rabbi Lebush Horowitz of Cracow, declaring that the matzot baked on such a machine were contrary to the law and could not be used for Passover, particularly for the mandatory matzot, the *matzot mitzvah*. Kluger's letter, together with a number of other opinions from well-known rabbis agreeing with him, he published under the title *Moda'ah l'Bet Yisrael* ("Announcement to the House of Israel"). This was published in Breslau in 1859. In the same year, the famous rabbi of Lemberg, Joseph Saul Nathanson, gathered the contrary opinions, which declared that the machine was certainly usable and the matzot baked by it kasher. These he published the same year in Lemberg and entitled the pamphlet *Bittul Moda'ah* ("Annulment of the Announcement").

The arguments which were used by Solomon Kluger of Brody became the basic arguments for all opponents of machine-matzot. First, he said, the fact that the machine is used in cities in Germany is of no relevance at all, because nowadays what is done in Germany should not be a guide for more observant communities. Precisely what he means is made clear in responsum no. 7 (in the same book) written by Isaac Nathan Lifshitz of Santov, who declares that he is moved to prohibit the machine in order to circumvent those who desire "new things," and goes on to describe such people as "evil, sinful men who seek new ideas and build palaces out of their own thoughts, but know not God."

Solomon Kluger continues with the following argument, namely, that just as the Talmud never permits the shifting of the reading of the *Megilla* to the Sabbath because the poor count on receiving Purim gifts and would not receive them on the Sabbath if that day were celebrated as Purim, so it is with the baking of matzot. The poor people of the community are given a chance to participate in the baking (that is, because the matzot must be baked hastily so that the dough will not be given a chance to leaven, and many hands therefore are needed); the machine would prevent the poor from receiving an annually-expected income. Secondly, the mandatory matzah, which must be eaten on the first day and the blessing recited over it, must be baked under the supervision of an adult, intelligent Israelite; and, if the people doing the work are deaf-mute or insane or minors, even the supervision of an adult Israelite is not sufficient to make the matzah kasher. But the machine has not even the intelligence of a child; certainly, therefore, matzah baked by an object without intelligence cannot be used. Thirdly, the dough requires continuous kneading, lest it leaven before it is baked. The machine kneads the dough and lays it out for a while on the cutting-table and near the fire, where leavening, because of the heat, is all the more probable. Solomon Kluger concludes with an appeal as follows: "Therefore change not the custom of your fathers. Let the Germans do as their heart desires, but we will go in the footsteps of our fathers."

The second attack on machine-matzot was by Mordecai Zev Ettinger, a brother-in-law of Joseph Saul Nathanson who defended the machine-matzot. One of the earliest works of these two brothers-in-law was a group of responsa, *Mefarshe ha-Yam*.[53] In fact, they wrote a number of books together. But in this controversy they were on the opposite sides. Ettinger said that he saw the machine in actual use, and he forbade it because, when the round matzot were being stamped, the extra dough between one circle and the next was used over again. Clearly this created the danger of leavening. Among the other opponents of machine-matzah were Hayyim Halberstam of Sanz, Isaac Nathan Lifschitz of Santov, and Meir Auerbach of Calisch. Solomon Kluger himself subsequently reiterated his opposition in two more opinions.

The pamphlet, *Annulment of the Announcement*, published by Joseph Saul Nathanson and others, takes up Kluger's arguments one by one. The general answer is that the machine is not to be considered as lesser in intelligence than an "insane person, etc.," because the machine is guided by an intelligent person.

Furthermore, the machine works so rapidly that the danger of leavening is much reduced. As for the poor, the purpose for baking matzah is not to provide for the poor, but for use on Passover. Some of the other opinions add that, having observed the matzah baked in the old-fashioned way, they are convinced that it is impossible adequately to guarantee proper procedure while a mob of untrained helpers dash about the place. The men who stand by the side of Nathanson, defending the machine-baked matzot, include many illustrious names: for example, Israel Lifschitz of Danzig, famous author of the Mishna commentary, *Tiferet Yisrael*, ("Glory of Israel"); Abraham Benjamin Sofer of Pressburg; the rabbinate of Cracow jointly; Jacob Ettinger of Altona; Wolf Hamburg of Fűrth; and Isaac Halevi Bamberger of Wűrtzburg.

The dispute soon grew bitter and the tone of debate sharp. This can be observed from the repetition of his arguments by Solomon Kluger.[54] He repeats the arguments that he gave in his pamphlet and adds, referring to his great contemporary: [55]

> Look and see the words of him who permits this (that is, the use of the machine): how his words are vanity of vanities; how he even prints his words in order to mislead the people. Woe to us that such has happened in our day, that there should be such leaders. For we know his habit: he is always lenient and he always looks for a way of being permissive, knowing that in this generation only he who is lenient is revered as a great teacher.

In the pamphlet in favor of the machine, Z'ev-Wolf says, "Our people is divided into two camps, and the fire of controversy blazes, and our Torah is divided into two conflicting Torahs."

Hayyim Halberstam of Sanz, expressing his opposition to machine-matzot, admits that he has never seen the machine, but his motive for prohibiting it is an interesting one. The responsum which he contributes to Kluger's pamphlet, and which he republishes in his responsa,[56] says:

> With regard to the question of whether it is permitted to make matzot by machine, behold, I have seen the responsa of

the sages of our time (this responsum was written in 1855) who
agreed to prohibit, and they are quite right, even though some
of their arguments can be refuted. It is sufficient ground for the
prohibition to rely upon the statement of Mordecai Zev Ettinger who with his own eyes saw that it was impossible to scrape
the machine clean after each use. In my opinion, there are many
reasons to prohibit, but I keep these reasons to myself, for thus
have I received in tradition from my father-in-law and teacher
(that is, Baruch Teomin Fraenkel of Leipnik, Moravia) that in
matters such as these one should not reveal the reasons, but simply decide the law outright and let him, who will, obey.

Hayyim Halberstam, who objected thus to the matzot made
by machine, likewise objects to *tzitzit* (the fringes) made by
machine.[57] His objections are almost identical with the objections
that he raised against machine-made matzot. He says that he had
not seen the machine, but he relies on the opinion of a rabbi who
had seen it. The objections are that the work is done mechani-
cally and not by the hands of man. The wool used has to be
watched against the danger of being mixed up with other fabrics
(mixed fabrics, *sha'atnez*, being forbidden). He says that, if we
permit it here, it will be accepted in other countries, and the
machine will be made larger and more mechanical, just as
matches are now made. In some countries they will have Christian workmen make the *tzitzit*. So, in general, he decides that it
is safer to forbid it because, he says, "I know the nature of
machines. They are changed every day, and who knows what
they will be like tomorrow." He ends this paragraph by saying,
"And I am confident that I will soon see the overthrow of the
machine." At the end of that responsum, the editor says, "A few
days later, the whole factory, with the machine, burned down;
and that was a sign!"

Rabbi Halberstam was also asked whether it was permitted to
mill flour for the matzot in a steam-mill rather than in a water-
mill as theretofore. His son, who was rabbi of Karshanov, had
the flour for the matzot milled in a Prussian city in a steam-mill
and reported that the mill did not moisten or heat up the grain
and was therefore unobjectionable. Therefore, Hayyim Halber-

stam permitted the use of the steam-mill; but, before giving the reasons for this permission, he expressed his automatic reaction to the suggestion. He said,[58] I have never seen a steam-mill in my life, but I say it is better not to use it. Let us not do anything that we have not received by tradition from our ancestors. I would never permit the use of this machine.

A rather violent letter was written by Moses Jerusalemski.[59] He says that it is the duty of all the chiefs of the generation to stand in the breach of the wall.

I do not deny that I have not seen the machine myself; but from what is explained in the books of the great (I know that it must be prohibited).

Later on in his letter he says that this is part of all the novelties which are destroying Judaism. "For the innovators come to destroy Israel at this time."

Soon the negative opinions mounted up, and the later rabbis no longer cared to go into the reasons for the prohibition which had begun with Solomon Kluger; they merely answered briefly, as did, for example, Abraham of Sarchov, the author of *Abnei Nezer* in 1902.[60]

Your letter about the machine-matzot has reached me, and, although I have never seen the machine, still the words of the Gaon of Kutna are valid, namely, that, since the great ones who preceded us have prohibited it and stormed against those who permitted it, for whatever reason it may be, they must have had good reasons for doing so.

In spite of all the strong opposition to the innovation, the use of the machine spread, chiefly in Western Europe [61] and in other lands, especially in America. While a large number of rabbis, moved by their understandable fear of innovation, especially in regard to such an important ritual as matzah, opposed the use of the machine, nevertheless, the machine had certain great advantages. Aside from all the legal arguments in its favor by Nathanson and his followers, in actual practice, baking matzah by hand, with all the helpers crowding in the bakery, led to inevitable carelessness and often to much more delay in the baking of the matzah than would be required by machines—and the more delay, the more likelihood of leavening.[62] Besides, the spirit of the times was on the side of Joseph Saul Nathanson and, by now, hand-baked matzah, in each village by itself, is almost unheard of. Most of the matzah eaten on Passover all over the world is baked by machine.

In fact, the leading Galician authority of the last generation, Sholom Mordecai Schwadron, seems to feel that it is no longer necessary to go into the debate.[63] A question came to him from Zachariah Joseph Rosenfeld, rabbi in St. Louis, Missouri, about the matzah-baking machine used in his city. Rabbi Rosenfeld no longer asks whether the machine should be used—he seems to take that for granted—he asks merely whether he should not continue to object, as he did in the past, to too large a batch of dough being put through the machine at one time. The danger involved is that, if the batch is too large, the mechanical kneading does not penetrate the whole mass, and there is danger of leavening in the center of the mass. Schwadron discusses this question; but only in the last paragraph of his response does he feel it necessary to revert to the basic question which had created so much excitement for two generations. He says:

> As for the fundamental question of using the machine, the dispute is well-known; it took place in the days of Joseph Saul Nathanson, rabbi of Lemberg; when Solomon Kluger and Mordecai Zev Ettinger, and others, stepped forth to prohibit these matzot. Their chief argument was that making the matzot requires the exertion of a human being, whereas by machine it is done automatically. Yet some other rabbis permitted it, since the machine is started by a man. See if that is so in your case (in the St. Louis machine) and observe that everything is done properly. Then you may permit its use as you did last year.

Although the controversy thus has virtually faded away, it sometimes flares up in different forms. In 1946, a collection of responsa was published in Budapest, written by various rabbis, nearly all of whom had been martyred by the Nazis. This collection of responsa, which had been in preparation for a number of years before the Hitlerite conquest began, by the Talmud

Studies Society of Budapest for its fiftieth jubilee, is entitled
Yerushat ha-Peletah ("The Inheritance of the Remnant") and
many of the responsa in it deal with a variation of the old controversy. The discussion centers around the fact that the machine-matzot now are made by a belt-line system of continuous
baking, and each matzah, as it comes out of the oven on the endless belt, breaks off. The question is whether such a matzah can
be considered a complete unit or merely a fragment of a matzah.

It is evident from these great controversies how deeply Jewry
could be aroused by disputes involving its religious life. It was
never a community which received a mandate from its chiefs
and docilely accepted what was decided for it. The leaders of
the community among themselves had a greater sense of duty
than of discipline. The Law made them all equal and, at any
disagreement dealing with the observances of Jewish life, they
leaped fearlessly to the fray and the people joined them. Questions of the ritual reliability of food, of the trustworthiness of
the *shohet*, of the usability of *etrogim* from Corfu—all these were
matters of major importance. Jewish ritual was observed at great
sacrifice and the people could not tolerate the thought that,
through some one's deception, they had sacrificed in vain.

There is, perhaps, some difference between the disputes in the
Sephardic communities and those in the Ashkenazic. The former
shared the deep concern of the Ashkenazim over ritual matters,
but some types of dispute arose among the Sephardim which
rarely arose among the Ashkenazim, at least, not in recent centuries. The Sephardim, under Mohammedan Law, retained a
much larger communal autonomy than did the Ashkenazim
under the constantly modernizing laws of the West. Therefore,
business law, contracts, sales, and the like (chiefly the *Shulhan Arukh* section, "Hoshen Mishpat"), play a larger role in the
life of the Sephardim than in the life of the Ashkenazim who, to
an increasing extent, had been bringing their civil lawsuits before the courts of the country in which they lived. Such business
disputes had, of course, occurred also among the Ashkenazim
centuries ago when the Jewish communities were independent

units and were compelled to discipline their members that the taxes might be paid. But this financial, communal organization faded away in the Ashkenazic lands. It continued for a long time under Moslem Law in the Sephardic lands. Hence we find in Sephardic responsa constant controversies of the type no longer to be seen in Ashkenazic responsa. The great dispute over the boycott of Ancona is an example of it. This was a dispute among Sephardim. It concerned a financial question, trade and boycott, and involved the right of the community to compel its members to conform. Similarly, we find among the Sephardic responsa many far-flung disputes about wills, as, for example, the will of Nissim Shamama [64] and that of Jacob Gallico.[65] Such questions could not have become controversial among the Ashkenazim in recent centuries. But all Jewry, whatever the social conditions in which they lived, could be affected by their ritual observances. They never could be tolerant because they never were indifferent.

5

---◆---

HISTORY
IN THE
RESPONSA

THE WRITER of Jewish history must always cope with certain special disadvantages. Although Jewish history is both extensive and enduring, it has astonishingly few records. The history of most civilizations records itself in mountains of official archives, the decrees of kings, minutes of their councils, decisions of the courts-of-law, lists of captives, inventories of possessions, records of taxation, and the like. There are very few official archives upon which the historian of Jewish history can draw. Even the Bible has very few records of the decisions of kings and their councils. The one clear case of such official archives in the Bible, in the books of Nehemiah and Ezra, are quotations from the archives of the Persian Empire.

In the long, post-Palestinian history of the Jews, the small and shaky Jewish communities could not have left records like those to be found in the archives of firmly established Gentile municipalities. For that reason Jewish history has to depend upon external sources, records in Church and in governmental enactments, which are usually hostile; or else upon the few travellers' diaries, the handful of chronicles of persecutions written by refugees and survivors, and the few lists of resolutions passed by the occasional organizations of Jews, for example, the Council of the Four Lands in Eastern Europe. Except for these scanty, usually indirect sources, most Jewish records are secondary in nature. They may be poems, dirges bemoaning the destruction

of a community, from whose poetic language one may derive
the actual prosaic facts. They may be changes in law or in the
management of communities, which reflect the troubles of the
times. One of the most valuable secondary sources in which
Jewish history is reflected is the responsa literature.

As a source for history, the responsa literature has grave de-
fects. Many of the most important events never found their way
into this literature. No questions happened to have been asked
of the leading rabbis involving those events, or, if they were
asked, neither question nor answer was preserved. Also, certain
literary habits in certain periods of the responsa literature have
made them a very poor historical source. For example, the considerable responsa literature of the gaonim has the characteristic (at least in our present transcript of it) of omitting the
name and the place of almost every questioner. This is unfortunate for the writers of Jewish history. For centuries questions had been sent to the gaonim in Babylonia from all over
the Jewish world. If only the gaonim had preserved the name
and the habitation of the questioner, we would have had by now
a vivid picture of exactly where the Jews were scattered over
the world during those centuries, and which problems concerned
which particular localities and therefore what their special circumstances of life were in those places.

On the other hand, there is one reason why the responsa are
an exceptionally good source of historical information. The
questions that come up in this literature were submitted for
legal decision; it was necessary therefore for their facts to be
precise and their circumstances sharply delineated. Very often,
in times of persecution, for example, when a decision had to be
made whether a man was to be presumed dead or not, the circumstances of the riot or the attack upon a certain community
were carefully looked into. If, therefore, there is any record at
all in the responsa of an event of this nature, it can be trusted
as factual and need never fall under the suspicion of being
literary embellishment, forgivably exaggerated under the stress
of the emotions of some orphaned refugee. It is, of course, a pity
that more of the great events in Jewish history did not happen

to find their way into the responsa, but the many that did are precisely recorded.

Polish Jewry

One of the turning points in European Jewish history was the Cossack rebellion in 1648, known in Jewish literature by its Hebrew date as *Gezerat TaH*, TaH representing the number 408, which is the equivalent of 1648. This revolt against their Polish overlords by the Cossacks of the Ukraine, under Chmel-nitzki, and their Tartar allies, annihilated a large proportion of the Jewish population in the lands of Poland. It destroyed the prosperity of the whole community and scattered Polish Jewry over the West. Many historians are of the opinion that Polish Jewry never fully recovered from that catastrophe. It was the equivalent in Northern European Jewish history of the year 1492 in the history of the Jews of Spain. Just as in 1492 the Spanish Jews became fugitives, scattered north and east, so in 1648 Polish Jewry was broken and scattered and never regained its communal health.

Among the many rabbis who escaped from Poland, was Mena-hem-Mendel Krochmahl, who became rabbi in Nikolsburg where he died in 1661 (he had been born in Cracow, Poland, about 1600). In his book of responsa [1] he dealt with one of the tragic yet typical cases which perennially come up in the responsa, especially in times of persecution. A woman testified that her husband had been killed in the Chmelnitzki uprisings in Poland. She asked the rabbinical court to declare her a widow, so that she might be free to marry again. If the court failed to do so, she would be in the status of *agunah*, "chained" to a husband who is presumably alive, since there was no evidence of his death. In the outline of events which she and her sister gave to Rabbi Krochmahl, there is a clear picture of the persecutions in Poland. The picture had to be detailed and vivid, because it was the duty of the rabbi to investigate and inquire. The case is given as follows:

There came before me a woman named Sarah, daughter of Reb Mordecai of Tchortria, weeping and mourning over the slaughter, during the persecution of the community of Polni, of her husband, R. Joel, in her presence and in the presence of her sister who stood right at her side. She consulted me about freeing her (from the status of *aguna*), that she may be permitted to marry. . . . In order to test her, I said to her, "There is nothing new in your statement (that is, it contains no details of a personal character). This sort of thing happens often. Many men have come to this country (Moravia), fleeing from the sword. They married here upon their own testimony that their wives were killed. Then it came out that their wives were still alive." But the woman and her sister cried out that this situation (of a woman desiring to avoid remaining an *agunah*) is far different (from the case of a man). Then I was filled with pity for her (continues Rabbi Krochmahl) and I began to search out ways of giving her freedom to remarry. I considered the testimony which these two women had given in Holleschau on the 24th of Elul, 1653, which was as follows:

The woman, Zlata (that is, the wife's sister), testified that she and R. Joel and his wife (her sister, Sarah) and another man and many women had hidden themselves in a small room. Then came the murderers and killed the men. They beat and wounded the women, but did not intend to kill them, saying that it was enough that the women should wander through the world and go begging from door to door. She, the sister, saw that R. Joel, the sister's husband, had fallen to the ground and lay dead. The murderers then began to strip the dead and one said of R. Joel, "Look, this one is not dead yet," and he struck him again. She and her sister did not budge from the spot and saw all this happen. They saw the murderers search the garments of the slain for money, silver and gold. After that the murderers left. Her sister, Sarah, began to shake (the body of) her husband and she called him by name, "Joel, Joel," and she (Zlata) said to her sister, "What are you doing? Don't you see that he is dead?" And she shook him, but there was no sign of life.

Menahem-Mendel Krochmahl's son-in-law, Gershon Ashkenazi, was also one of the refugee rabbis. He later succeeded his father-in-law as rabbi in Nikolsburg and died in 1693 in Metz.

His responsa (*Abodat ha-Gershuni*), without any intention of recording history, give many clear pictures of the tragic events of 1648. For example,[2] he had the problem of a man, whose wife had become lost, asking permission to marry. The description is given in the text of the question:

What happened was this: I have an excellent disciple, named Joel, from the province of the Ukraine, who came, as a refugee from the sword, to this province of Moravia to the community of Holleschau. His wife had been captured by the Tartars (the allies of the Cossacks in the uprising) and witnesses came to testify that, under compulsion, she had converted (to Mohammedanism). Since this fine scholar was modest and attractive, one of the leading citizens of the community took favorable notice of him and desired to marry him to his daughter and to give him a worthy dowry. But the prospective father-in-law hesitated whether he may marry another woman because of the decree of Rabbenu Gershom (tenth century, forbidding polygamy and also forbidding the divorcing of a woman against her will). Then, behold, the eminent scholar, David Halevi (the author of the *Taz*) happened to pass through the community of Holleschau and they asked him if this scholar may marry another woman. He answered that he may marry another woman, and that he does not have to assign a divorce to his first wife through an intermediary. But he did not give any reason for his opinion; he merely answered briefly. Upon this decision the members of the community relied and the marriage was arranged. After that, certain rabbis disputed the decision . . . and since this worthy and pure disciple of mine, Joel, is one of my finest pupils, etc., I, therefore, decided not to rest until I could find a way of justifying him; and I have come to the conclusion that he may assign a divorce to his first wife through an intermediary.

In modern times, since the historical sense is more developed, the slaughter of the Jews by the Nazis will find a more precise and detailed description in permanent records than did the persecutions of 1391 in Spain or 1648 in Poland. The future historian will not need to rely upon chance references that find their way into the Jewish legal literature. Nevertheless, even with regard to this recent event in our history-conscious age, the responsa literature will some day serve the purpose of the future historian, for today again the question of the *agunah*, and her right to remarry, comes up in the legal literature; and once more, the need for precision will leave behind another type of record than that which historians usually preserve.

For example, in the case of the millions slain in the gas chambers, it is almost a vain hope to find alive an actual eye-witness who saw any particular man taken to his death. Most of the witnesses had suffered the same fate. In this case the law must rely upon probability. To what extent may we presume that a man, taken to the extermination camps, is dead? In this regard, a remarkable type of responsum has appeared, and there will undoubtedly be others of the same kind, in which the rabbi, giving his opinion, was himself in the concentration or even in the extermination camps. One such refugee rabbi has relied upon the legal principle that, if the rabbinical court sees a certain event with its own eyes, it does not need witnesses at all. The rabbi himself therefore may judge as to what proportion of those taken away were actually done to death, and he has the right to decide, on the basis of overwhelming probability, that the man in question is dead. Thus, Rabbi Jacob Avigdor, formerly Chief Rabbi of Drohobicz in Galicia, after being released from the concentration camps and while still a refugee in Belgium, before coming to the United States, wrote an opinion on the problem of the *agunah*. Of course, his description is now partly affected by the modern historical interest in detailed delineation of events; yet the events which he delineates are marshalled to support a certain legal investigation and so are in a different mood from those in more conscious historiography.[3]

I have been asked to look into the matter of the *agunot* who have now been freed by the English and American armies but are still in various camps in Germany. Most of them are certain that their husbands are not alive, but there are no witnesses who can actually testify to their death. I know my own humble worth, after having dwelt for many years in darkness and seen the rod of His anger. Naked did I enter into the Jewish quarters, naked I entered thereafter into the walled ghetto. I also was on the road leading to the fiery furnaces, and I too have lain among the dead. Many times have I been rescued by a miracle from all sorts of hideous deaths; and I, with mine own hands, have buried hundreds of the sainted slain and have placed into their graves also bundles of *Sefer Torahs* torn up in the streets. Although unworthy to deal with these difficult matters, especially since for about six years I have not looked into a single book necessary for these laws, nevertheless, I want to say that only those rabbis who were in the siege and in the prison and who drained the bitter cup and whose eyes saw what was done, only they are fit to judge these matters . . .

He proceeds to describe the various steps in the long tragic road of the Jews of Europe toward the gas chambers; and he indicates how small a percentage could possibly have escaped. Thus, on the basis of his own detailed knowledge, he can declare the overwhelming probability to be that any particular missing man may well be presumed dead.

The fact that the problem of the *agunah* recurs throughout the responsa literature is in itself a reflection of an historical situation. It reveals the age-old insecurity, the endless flight and the scattering of families, which was a permanent part of Jewish experience.

There are, of course, many other types of question in the responsa which throw light on Jewish history: business disputes, contracts, debts, communal disputes, taxation, the rights of older settlers in relation to newcomers, and much more. All such disputes reveal social situations which otherwise would not have remained known to us. The history of Jewish life in the Rhineland, in northern France and in Spain, is being ably re-written with the aid of references in the responsa. In this chapter, two segments of Jewish history will be described: the life of the Jews in Poland in its classic period, the sixteenth to the middle of the seventeenth century; and the life of the marranos who, for several centuries, continued to escape from Spain and Portugal. Both of these segments of Jewish history become more specific and vivid as the discussions, and even passing statements, are culled from the literature. "Unconsidered trifles" in the responsa often add up to an important part of history.

The life of the Jews in Poland, Lithuania and in the adjacent Russian lands, in the sixteenth and seventeenth centuries, grows clear to us through these chance statements. Some study has already been made of the responsa from these lands with a view to eliciting the social history revealed in them.[4] Various off-hand remarks in the responsa build up to a picture of the social life of the Jews of Eastern Europe in those centuries.

Having in mind a picture of the wall-enclosed ghettos in Rome and along the Rhine, we usually visualize the Jews in Poland as living in similar isolation. Of course, they lived in a Jewish district and generally had bought the right of residence from the local magnate. But the street was open and there were constant Christian passers-by and customers and merchants. Moses Isserles[5] discusses whether a *mezuzah* should be put on the gates of the Jewish quarter. The questioner wonders why that should not be done. Isserles says:

> In our cities, the whole street belongs to the king and Christians are constantly found in the street, walking to and fro. Therefore it is like a house held in partnership with Gentiles which is free from the need for a *mezuzah*.

Isserles was concerned only with the question whether one should affix a *mezuzah* to the entrance of the Jewish street. He says it is not necessary, but his reason reveals an open street in which Christians are constantly found intermingling with the Jewish residents.[6] In the town of Lubomil, the community insisted that every effort should be made to keep Christians living in the Jewish street, lest, if it became an all-Jewish street, it would be in danger from riots and fire. Hence it was forbidden for a Jew to buy the house of a Christian. If he did so, he had to sell it or rent it to another Christian.

The relationship between Jews and Christians must frequently have developed in neighborly friendliness. Benjamin Aaron Slonik[7] is asked a question with regard to idolatry. A Jew may not, of course, be of assistance to idol-worship. But is the following circumstance deemed assistance to idolatry: Christians borrow from Jews garments and ornaments on the day of their festival (that is, the Christian festival). They put them on when they enter their church and afterwards return them. Is it permitted, for the sake of peace, to lend them such garments and ornaments under these circumstances, or is it forbidden? Incidentally, from the same source,[8] there comes quite an interesting style note, a detailed description of a popular garment. Of course, neither the questioner concerned nor the learned respondent was interested in styles. But the question concerned the tearing of garments (keriah) in case of mourning: Need a tear be made in the outer garment also? During the discussion, a garment is mentioned that is known as a "rock" and another known as a "mantle." The mantle is described purely for the sake of legal precision as follows:

> The garment which is not to be torn, according to Moses Isserles, is not the one which is called "the rock," but the one which they call "mantle," which is a garment whose top surrounds the person around his neck and hangs down below his hips and beyond. It is open in front from top to bottom and it is not provided with sleeves. It is the custom of some of the elders in the city of Cracow to wear it during worship; and when someone dies in the family, they wear it in the cemetery. . . .

The contact which the Jews thus are seen to have had with the Slavic peoples inevitably made them familiar with the Slavic languages, which many Jews used regularly. This is reflected for a special reason in the legal literature. The bill of divorce, the get, is written with great precision, lest any objection be raised later to its validity, especially if the woman remarried. Extraordinary care was exercised in the spelling of names, of people and cities. If a man or a woman had nicknames different from the regular Hebrew names, these had to be recorded, to make identification absolutely sure. Often the nicknames were of Slavic type. Likewise the cities in the Slavic lands, especially in the border lands, were sometimes pronounced in Polish fashion, sometimes in Russian fashion, and sometimes Russianized from Polish when the government changed. How were these names properly to be spelled so that there should be no question about the validity of the divorce document?

This question of names in the divorce document, *Shemot Gittin*, has resulted in hundreds of responsa. From such discussion we get an insight into the language the Jews spoke. Sabbatai Cohen, the famous commentator on the *Shulhan Arukh*, in the responsa at the end of his book, *G'burat Anashim*, discusses the question of the validity of a divorce written in the city of Brest-Litovsk. The city was known among Jews, not as Brest, but as "Brisk," and it was generally so written in the divorce documents. The particular divorce in question was obtained with very great difficulty from an apostate Jew who, according to Jewish law, must give a Jewish divorce to his wife or she is not properly divorced. In the document, however, the city was spoken of as Bresta, instead of Brisk. It would be extremely difficult to get a corrected divorce from this apostate; cannot this divorce be considered valid? The respondent gives a long and complicated answer: [9]

> As for the custom to write, for "Brisk," the name "Brest," this is no proof (in the argument), for this is a custom which is now widespread among our Jews, most of whom speak Russian, and that is why they call it "Brest."

Thus, incidentally, in the course of a long argument, we learn that many Jews already then spoke Russian. So, too, Aryeh ben Shemuel, in answering the same type of question,[10] speaks of the name Hertz which, in those lands, carried the nickname Hertzka. He says it is not necessary to add the nickname Hertzka, because it is only the custom of the province to put *ka* at the end of names, that being the way of "the men of Russia."

The Jews earned their living in many different ways, some of which are, of course, well known. At the top of the economic scale were the merchants who were engaged in what might be called international trade. These were the men who attended the great annual fair of Lublin and some of the minor fairs, such

as that of Yaroslav. References to these great fairs come up incidentally in connection with other legal questions. A question
was asked of the great Moses Isserles [11] about carrying on Shabbat. By means of the *erub*—a legal fiction whereby the whole of
a Jewish neighborhood was proclaimed to be in effect one household—it was possible to carry articles on the street on the Sabbath. There were, of course, doubts: whether, for example, such
an *erub* could be applied in a neighborhood where some of the
houses were owned by Christians. Also, in the question referred
to, it was asked whether an *erub* could be made in the cities
where a fair was in progress and where the visiting Jews lived
but temporarily and in rented quarters. For the sake of legal
precision, in order to answer this question correctly, an exact
description of the circumstance is given us:

> In the city of Lublin, where the great fair takes place, many
> Israelites gather three times a year and dwell there in rooms
> open to the city (that is, in open cubicles); but these rooms be-
> long to Christians and are in the houses of Christians, except
> that the Israelites rent them from the Christians. They are, how-
> ever, reserved for the Jews all year, for (storing) their goods,
> although the Jews do not dwell in them except at the time of the
> fair which is less than thirty days. The Jews also use the house
> of the Gentiles for their minor needs, as cooking their foods,
> and the like. Now they have become accustomed to carrying
> on the street (on the Sabbath) throughout the city. Are they
> acting correctly or not?

Meir of Lublin [12] is asked a question about a *Sefer Torah*
which, in the midst of the Sabbath reading from the Torah, is
found to be imperfect. The question is whether it is permitted
to recite the blessings over an imperfect *Sefer Torah*. But in
introducing the question, the questioner incidentally remarks:

> It happened when we were in the city of Yaroslav, at the fair
> in the year 368 (1608), where it was a regular custom, as at
> every fair, that a place was established as a synagogue to pray
> there every day and also on the Sabbath. Sages and leaders of
> *yeshibot* and many people gathered to read in the Torah.

Then follows the question, namely, that they found the Torah to be imperfect. Thus, incidentally, we learn that the merchants, leaders of the community, provided for the spiritual needs of all the Jews who came and also that the heads of the *yeshibot* attended. We learn from Nathan Hanover [13] that the heads of the *yeshibot* brought their disciples with them and that marriages were arranged at this convenient gathering of many heads of families.

Next to the international merchants in the economic scale were the tax-collectors. The Polish magnates would farm out the right to collect the taxes. Jews usually bought this right and lived on the percentages they received. Such Jewish tax-collectors are mentioned in a question which involves another business of the Jews in those days. Jews would buy the right to handle the produce of an entire district, to buy it from the peasant and to sell it in the market. It happened that these Jewish wholesale produce-dealers were taxed by the Jewish tax-collectors, and the farmer brought the question before Joel Sirkes.[14]

> With regard to Reuben who hired the right from the officers of the king to handle certain cities and villages: He has much produce which he brings in ships to sell to men who come from distant cities. Now there are many Jewish tax-collectors by the authority of the king who ask taxes from all this produce according to the laws of the king. But Reuben argues that he himself is also an agent of the princes and they (the princes) may not really tax themselves. Therefore his business, he being an agent of the prince, should be free from the taxes of the prince. Hence the Jewish tax-collector in this case cannot tax the Jewish wholesaler; or can he? That was the question. . . .

This tax-collecting business did great harm to the Jewish community. Not that it was illegitimate, but it made the Jews the objects of the wrath of those who had to pay the taxes. They were paying taxes to the Jews and they hated them for it. Much of the rebelliousness which resulted in the horrible slaughter in the Chmelnitzki revolt of 1648 was due to the bitterness which the peasants felt against the Jewish tax-collectors. Hence it became necessary for certain Jewish communities to forbid their members to buy the right of collecting certain unpopular taxes.[15]

> It was ordained and decreed, in some of the lands in our kingdom, on pain of many punishments, that no Jew should under any circumstances buy the right to collect the *Chapavi*, because it is the source of great danger due to the outcry of the Gentiles in many places that the Jews dominate and rule them as if they were kings and princes.

The profits from these large tax enterprises must have been considerable and the competition among Jews for the right to conduct this business was very keen. Many cases occur in the responsa of one Jew accusing another of unfairly outbidding him for the right to certain monopolies. Solomon Luria, in two long responses,[16] deals with such a dispute and describes how one man finally got the right away from another by bribing the queen's secretary. One of the men in the dispute says that he did not intend to do anything wrong, but that "This is the custom in our country with regard to taxes (the right to collect taxes) and whiskey (the monopoly for a certain district): that one person acquires it for a certain length of time and then another one outbids him . . ."

The Jews who lived along the Hungarian border of Poland were engaged chiefly in the wine business. This is revealed in a question that came before Meir of Lublin.[17] It was against Jewish Law for a Jew to deal in non-kasher wine; yet, a prohibition from dealing in such wine would have resulted in great hardships.

> Then there came to me the leaders of the congregation of Rimanoff and said to me that it was impossible for them to give up this business since, from days of old, they were engaged in this business with the Hungarians who dwelt at their border. The Hungarians were constantly left in debt to them and the Jews were compelled to take wine from them in payment of their debt. If now they are deprived of this business, they will have no means of livelihood, since those who dwell along the border of Hungary have no other business but this.

The Jews were in the whiskey business, as mentioned above. They either sold it wholesale or they owned taverns. This is revealed in the course of a question about Passover. Since a Jew may not keep leaven over the Passover, he must sell it to a Gentile. The question here involved such a case and the injustice which one Jew did to another.[18]

> I was asked with regard to the following occurrence. One man had wine in his possession in a certain city, while its owners dwelt in another city. When Passover came, the owners asked a Jew in that city (where the wine was stored) to sell this wine before Passover to a Gentile for a small sum. And so he did (a fictitious sale): he sold the wine to a Gentile on the day before Passover. After Passover this Jew took back the wine from the Gentile (of course, repaying him that small sum). Now there is a dispute as to who really owns the wine . . .

The Jews also conducted large-scale business in meat. According to the responsa, it seems that most of the meat consumed by the Gentiles was bought from Jews. The question came up in a curious way. No meat is eaten by Jews from the first day of the month of Ab until after the fast day, the Ninth of Ab. But suppose a Jew was in the business of selling meat to Gentiles to whom, of course, meat was not prohibited during those nine days? May he slaughter meat during this period?

This question was asked of Enoch ben Judah.[19] The question and the beginning of the answer reveal how widespread this meat business was.

> The question concerns permission to slaughter from the beginning of the month of Ab until the Ninth (the fast). He who conducts business in slaughtered meat, may he slaughter and sell to Gentiles on market days or on the day of the fair? Also, may he (the *shohet*) pronounce the blessing of slaughtering if he slaughters only for the purpose of selling to Gentiles, while he himself does not eat of it?

In the second line of the answer, the respondent says, "It is traditional in this land that most of our livelihood comes from this."

A question asked of Samuel ben David Halevi [20] deals with a somewhat different aspect of the problem, namely, whether Jews may do business with meat that is not kasher—meat, for example, that was not slaughtered properly: [21] "In the provinces of Poland and Russia, most people buy their meat from Jews."

A rather unusual mode of earning a livelihood is referred to in Meir Eisenstadt's *Panim Me'irot;* [22]

> When I came to the congregation of Shidlopshi, I was asked a question with regard to the conducting of business on the Sabbath by those who have the concession of blacksmithing (smelting) from the lord of the manor. They acquire the right to mine in the mountains and to find the dust from which iron is made; and they burn and refine that dust in fire continuously, day and night without cessation, and so do those who make glass (use continuous fires). How then shall they conduct their business on the Sabbath?

The matter that interested the questioner and the respondent was the problem of maintaining the continuous furnaces on the Sabbath. But, incidentally, we discover that Jews were engaged in steel, or at least in iron, and in glass manufacturing.

It is, of course, well known that Jews were physicians and had Christian patients. A question which comes up in the Law concerns in what manner and to what extent they may violate the Sabbath in dealing with their Christian patients: [23]

> As for your question with regard to Jewish doctors who violate the Sabbath in going to Christian patients and anoint them and touch their bodies and compound medicine for them, and as for your distinction between whether the treatment began before the Sabbath and continues during the Sabbath, or whether it began on the Sabbath . . .

Among the larger businesses were those of the contractors for army supplies and of some free-lance followers of the army. Some of the responsa describe the merchants who followed the Polish armies towards Moscow in the war at the beginning of the seventeenth century. Of course, this occupation is revealed incidentally in one of the questions which came up frequently

in the responsa, namely, the search for definite evidence that a
man had been killed, so that his wife may be free to remarry.
But in passing, we are told of this business of supplying the
troops and also of a Jewish hero, named Berke, who was killed
in a cavalry charge and whose death caused great grief among
the Cossacks in the Polish Army.[24] The question is phrased as
follows:

> I was asked with regard to the woman, the *agunah*, the wife
> of Daniel, son of Joel, of the congregation of "S'dei Laban,"
> who left his wife and went to the province of Moscow at the
> time of the war, when the king (of Poland) with his army be-
> sieged Moscow, when many Jews went there with whiskey and
> other goods to sell to the others. This Reb Daniel went with two
> wagons of whiskey and other merchandise. He never returned
> home and it was said that he had been killed there as the fol-
> lowing testimony indicates . . .[25]

A curious way of making a living which a number of Jews
followed derived from the specific circumstances of Jewish Law
and Jewish life. Since only a husband could divorce a wife,
while a wife could not divorce her husband, a deserted wife
was in a particularly tragic case. The Jewish communities in
those days made every effort to track down deserting husbands
and apparently certain men earned their livelihood as detectives
of the Jewish court, traveling around to trace down these de-
serters. In the responsa collection of Joshua of Cracow,[26] there
is a responsum from Abraham, rabbi of Brest-Litovsk (Brisk),
where the testimony is given of a man whose job it was to track
down deserting husbands. The testimony, given in Judeo-Ger-
man, is as follows:

> I have been travelling as an agent of the three Lands (the
> three Lithuanian provinces, organized into a central authority),
> for the past four years, to seek those men who deserted their
> wives. For I am an agent for this purpose. I met among the
> south Germans a Jew of Mainz . . .

Then he reports the statement of this Jew concerning the death of a certain person whose death had to be established in order to free his wife to remarry.

A similarly strange occupation is mentioned in the responsum of Meir of Lublin.[27] It also had to do with establishing the death of a husband. The body of a Jew had been found in Constantinople. The body is described, and then, it is said that "this man who was slain used to come often into the Turkish lands to redeem captives, for that was his livelihood." During the Chmielnitzki revolt, the Tartars, who were allies of the Cossacks, captured many Jews and brought them into the Moslem lands. The Polish communities evidently maintained men at the unremitting task of redeeming these captives.

Although the Polish Jews were heavily burdened with such problems as the redemption of captives, they did not fail in their duty to other Jewries. In the responsum of Meir of Lublin,[28] we are told that the Jews of Silesia had been threatened with expulsion from the entire province. However, the government accepted certain gifts and consented to delay the expulsion.

> And to this sum of money the provinces contributed generously, namely, the three provinces of Poland gave one-fifth of the two thousand gold pieces, and so did the provinces of Bohemia and Moravia.

Reading of the piety and the profound Jewish learning which prevailed in those lands, one might forget that the people were just human beings with human weaknesses. Solomon Luria [29] tells of an unfortunate situation in which a father hesitated to let his daughter marry a certain young man who had the reputation of being a drunkard and a gambler. The father went to Cracow, the young man's home town, to try to break off the engagement; but he was persuaded that these were merely the errors of youth and that the young man would outgrow them rapidly. So the father says:

> I was compelled to say Amen, hoping that he would repent and not return to his evil. I bound him by oath not ever again to play any gambling game without my permission. I gave him my daughter in marriage, and he had not been married two

weeks when he went to the drinking places of the Gentiles and he drank and he gambled . . .

The sin which seems to have aroused the strongest indignation in Solomon Luria was the sin of slander. In his responsa, he mentions at least three cases in which he persuaded a slanderer to repent. The ceremony of repentance is of interest. He says that, of course, the man should really undergo whipping; but since that is difficult now, he must stand in the synagogue on Monday or Thursday, before the taking out of the Torah, and, holding in his hands two black candles and wearing black garments, he should speak as follows:— "Hear me, my teachers: I have sinned against the God of Israel, and I have slandered so and so, etc." [30]

Just in passing, we are reminded how marriages were arranged without the prospective bride and groom seeing each other until the time came for the marriage ceremony: [31]

The young man named Abner, the son of Aaron, was engaged to the girl Rachel, daughter of Isaac, of the city of Astia. The time came when the young man came to the city of Astia to see and be seen, as is the custom of the land . . .

These intimate glimpses of the life of the Jews in Poland in the sixteenth and seventeenth centuries were not recorded in the Law for the purpose of imparting information, since the social and economic facts were well known both to questioners and respondents. They are mentioned only incidentally in the course of dealing with certain legal questions. But in this incidental way, an intimate picture of the life of a great, historic community is vividly revealed.

The Marranos

Just as the Jewish community in Poland left its record in the responsa literature, so also did virtually every other large Jewish community. The great Jewish community in Spain, the German community, the North African community, the Turkish communities and, in modern times, the Hungarians and the Galicians have all revealed some of the story of their life in this way. The history of these communities exists to a greater extent in many more direct records, in government archives, histories, chronicles and the like. But an incidental, or an accidental, part of their history shows up in the responsa and is recalled to memory by old lawsuits and old rabbinic decisions.

In the histories of all the Jewish communities mentioned, the responsa are only auxiliary material, but for the history of the marranos of Spain and Portugal, the responsa, for special reasons, constitute the central source. The marranos were not really a community, self-conscious and united by normal inter-group relationships. They were scattered groups of lonely families who lived outwardly in the Christianity which had been forced upon them, but whose real life was in the Judaism which they secretly practiced. When the Inquisition discovered an individual or a family of marranos secretly practicing Judaism, the accused were imprisoned, tortured, tried and, frequently, burnt at the stake.[32] If a family managed to escape from Spain or Portugal, their partial Judaism brought them into contact with Jewish Law. Thus their outer life as Christians left very little record. It was their secret life as Jews which brought them into the literature, either of the persecuting Church or of the welcoming Jewish communities.

Since they fled by secret routes and in many different directions, they came into contact with many different Jewish communities. Thus we find record of their presence and of their problems in the responsa of the rabbis of North Africa, of Egypt, of Palestine, of Turkey and of Holland. The only broad record of this scattered, constantly moving stream of individuals is therefore in the legal literature of the scattered Jewish communities of Europe, Africa and the Near East.

In 1391 a wave of persecutions in Spain swept as many as one hundred thousand Jews into the Church. Some of these, who had no sense of loyalty to their brethren, became mockers and persecutors of the Jews. But the majority of them practiced Judaism secretly and were the first marranos, a term variously interpreted as the "accursed" or the "pigs." These marranos kept in contact with the Jews of Spain and got their teachers and books from them. When the Inquisition was established in Spain in 1481, such contacts became hazardous; and when, in 1492, the Jews were expelled from Spain, the marranos were left alone and began their centuries-long isolation.

In the first generation after 1492, the marranos still had clear memories of Jewish life and worship either from their personal recollection or from contact with their Jewish neighbors. But after the first post-expulsion generations died out, the memories of Judaism grew vague. The influence of the Catholic environment and of their own Catholic life on the surface began to influence their ideas and their customs. Those Jewish ceremonies which were easy for the Inquisitors to detect gradually were altered or dropped away entirely. Thus, in generation after generation of isolation, their secret Jewish life grew ever more strange.

During the passing centuries there was a constant trickle of fugitives from Spain and Portugal. When they came to Jewish communities, their customs and worship created problems of adjustment. The longer the period of a marrano family's residence in Spain and Portugal, the more divergent their customs were. The reaction of Jewish Law to them therefore varied, depending upon the length of their previous isolation from the main body of Jewish life.[33]

The first marrano refugees after 1391 fled to the nearby Balearic Islands (Majorca, Minorca and Iviza) which were still Spanish territory. Many of them remained there as marranos ("Chuetas") and others used the islands as a stage in their flight to Mohammedan North Africa (Tunis, Algiers, Oran, etc.). In the North African cities there was already a vigorous Jewry. Many Spanish Jews, who during the next two centuries were to transform the religious and social life of the native Arabic Jews, settled there. Two famous rabbis were already in North Africa, Isaac b. Sheshet Perfet (born in Valencia, Spain, 1326, died in Algiers, 1408) and Simon b. Zemach Duran (born on the Island of Majorca, 1361, died in North Africa, 1444).[34] Duran's son, Solomon b. Simon (born in Algiers, 1400) succeeded him. His two grandsons, Simon and Zemach, were likewise rabbinical authorities in Algiers. These four rabbis left volumes of responsa, and in these responsa are to be found the first considerable records of the marranos in Jewish Law.

The problems came up in a very natural way. A marrano would suddenly appear in a Jewish community in North Africa and would constitute a problem of status in the Jewish community. This would raise a question of law, involving generally new analyses of situations already described in the Talmud.

In the responsa of Isaac b. Sheshet [35] a question, addressed to Benjamin Amar in the North African town of Bougie, reads as follows:

> You ask concerning a woman, one of those marranos (Hebrew: *anussim*) who came from Majorca with her infant in her arms. She was asked (in Bougie), "What is thy status, that is, are you a Jewess? Married? And what is the status of this son?" She said that a certain marrano from the land of Aragon had asked her hand in marriage according to Jewish Law before the decree (that is, before the persecutions of 1391), but he did not succeed (in persuading her). After the decree, there came a certain Gentile, a friend of the marrano who had wanted to marry her, and pleaded with her to marry him (that is, the marrano). She consented. The marriage took place; but he did not marry her before witnesses and ten men (as the Jewish Law would require), but by Gentiles according to the law of their (Catholic) religion and by the priests of their Church. She dwelt in his house with him as his wife for three months. She became pregnant by him and this (son) is her fruit. Now that man has gone beyond the seas and never returned to her again.
>
> Teach us, O our teacher, what is her status (in our Law) and whether we are to be concerned with her (as married or not).

In his answer, Isaac bar Sheshet makes a careful analysis of the status of this marrano marriage. He decides that it is not valid in Jewish Law, and the woman is therefore free to remarry.

For the history of the marranos, the situation revealed in the question is of especial interest. It portrays almost the initial state of their long history. It speaks of the times "before the decree" and "after the decree." Before the decree (the persecu-

tion of 1391 which swept thousands of Jews into the Church),
the man was going to marry her according to "the Law of Moses
and Israel." After the decree, he married her according to
Christian rites by a priest in the church. The first problem which
the marrano created was the status of their Christian marriage,
often conducted in the presence of Jewish (marrano) witnesses.
Was it the man's intention actually to marry her according to
the basic requirements of Jewish Law (but merely under the
mask of Christian ritual)? Was not the fact itself, that they lived
together as man and wife, to be considered as valid marriage?

Besides the legal question involved, we see something of the
beginning of their flight. Marranos were to continue to escape
for centuries. Here the husband and wife must have made ar-
rangements to meet in North Africa. For safety's sake, they
could not flee together, but went secretly by different routes.
Evidently he perished on his journey: "The man went over the
seas, and never returned to her again." While this unhappy
woman's description of her courtship and marriage makes no
specific mention of any discussion between her and her husband-
to-be as to plans for flight after their marriage, yet such plans
must have been frequently discussed among the marranos. This
is evident from a responsum of David Cohen of Corfu (in the
early sixteenth century). He is asked concerning [36] a woman who
came to Corfu and married there. A rumor arose, however, that
she had previously been married in Apulia (Italy). A traveller
from Corfu was going to Apulia and he was asked to inquire
about her. He learned that she had been married to one of the
marranos there. The question of law is the same essentially as
that in the responsum of Isaac b. Sheshet, that is, the validity in
Jewish Law of a marriage performed by a Christian priest. It is
the condition made previous to the marriage which throws light
on the inner mood of the marranos of Spain and Apulia. The
testimony taken in Apulia reads as follows:

A proposal of marriage was made to the young woman by a
shadkhan who was an *anus* (a marrano) in behalf of a young
man, also a marrano, of the above-mentioned congregation (Is-

trogolo), and the *shadkhan* vowed to get her out of this region and to bring her to Turkey where she could serve God again as in the past.

These marranos clearly meant their marriages to be Jewish marriages, even though they were compelled to have them solemnized in the church by priests. In the responsa by the two grandsons of Simon b. Zemach Duran [37] the question asked reveals the methods used by the marranos in Spain to make their marriage as Jewish as they possibly could. This responsum was written before the final expulsion of the avowed Jews from Spain in 1492:

> Written to the enlightened and understanding Joseph Zarapa while he was in Valencia: You ask about these marranos whose custom in marriage is as follows: Before they go to the church (to be married) they bring two Jews to their house, and in their presence the marriage is performed and the blessings recited. Then they go to the church and the marriage is performed by the priests. Now it happens that one of these women, the wife of a marrano, left her husband and child, escaped through the window and fled to a place where she is now a Jewess . . .

The question is the usual one discussed in those early days of marrano history, as to how valid the marriage is. This particular responsum reveals, not only the fact that the marranos tried to make their marriages as Jewishly valid as possible, but as long as there were Jews still in Spain (that is, before 1492), they kept in contact with them. The answer given to the question is that the marriage is valid. This is based upon the talmudic dictum that a Jew, even if he has sinned, is still a Jew.[38] Here too there were Jewish witnesses. His marriage to a Jewess is valid and, if he divorces her, it is a valid divorce.

The statement as to the validity of their divorces was not merely a general or theoretical one. For, just as the marranos endeavored to make their marriages Jewish, so they tried to make their divorces as valid as possible. This is revealed in a responsum of Isaac b. Sheshet: [39]

As for your question concerning a marrano woman who was divorced from her marrano husband and the witness to the writing and the delivery of the divorce were all marranos; and the woman, through the grace and help of God, escaped from the land of persecution and came to the land of Ishmael (that is, to a Mohammedan country) where she can serve God calmly and without fear; and you state that the witnesses are considered trustworthy among the people of God and the reverse among the Gentiles, and some of them are unable to escape for many reasons (that is, they do not wilfully remain in Spain)—your question is whether these are to be considered wicked men who are unfit to testify (as witnesses to the divorce).

To which Isaac bar Sheshet answers that whoever violates the Torah *under compulsion* retains his eligibility as a witness under Jewish Law. Of course, this applies only to one who in private observes all the commandments of the Torah that he can observe. If he does not observe the commandments (in private), but eats *trefa* food, he is not eligible as witness. As for those marranos who have remained (in Spain) for a long time and have not escaped, a distinction must also be made in this matter (as with the eating of *trefa* food). For some of them, although at first compelled to apostatize, are now willing to remain thus, and, even more, some of them persecute the Jews and try to destroy them utterly, and they also betray those marranos who in heart are loyal to God and are trying to escape. We must, therefore, investigate what type of marrano those witnesses were, before we decide whether the bill of divorce is valid.

There is another responsum by Isaac bar Sheshet [40] dealing with marrano divorce. This responsum likewise throws light on the activity of some treacherous marranos against their fellows. A divorce written by a marrano gave his Christian name first and then (as a by-name) his Jewish name. But Jewish Law requires that the Hebrew name be given first, as the principal and true name, and that all other by-names and nicknames follow for the purpose of additional identification. Is this divorce valid?

To this Bar Sheshet answers, near the end of the responsum:

Since the Spanish government forbids and punishes the use of the Hebrew name and since there are traitors who secretly betray them, the scribe and the witnesses fear for their lives to use their Hebrew names. In that case we may well consider the Christian name as the essential name and it is sufficient to refer to the Hebrew name under the general phase "and whatever other name I may be called by."

The divorce is therefore valid.

Bar Sheshet's contemporary in Algiers, Simon b. Zemach Duran, comes to the same conclusions. He tends to doubt the validity of most marrano marriages,[41] but to uphold the validity of their divorces. While both men followed the law conscientiously, there were enough varieties of situation for them to have come to somewhat differing conclusions. Yet their general agreement reveals the human situation, that marranos escaped singly and that humane considerations led the rabbis to decide, if possible, in favor of granting freedom to the escaped marrano and an opportunity to begin life anew.

Jacob Berab was one of the Jewish exiles from Spain. Although he was only eighteen when he fled to North Africa, he was already learned enough to be selected, in spite of his youth, as rabbi in Tlemcen, North Africa. His knowledge of the situation of the marranos was undoubtedly exact. In one of his responsa [42] he gives a vivid picture of their life.

The question which was asked of him itself reveals some of the wanderings of the marranos:

Reuben, who was in Portugal at the time of the persecution and was forced to become a marrano along with the others, went to Flanders and lived with a Gentile woman who bore him a son. Then, because she did not wish to convert to Judaism, he left her and came to Turkey and brought this child with him to be converted. Then Reuben married a Jewess and she bore him sons and daughters. Later, the son of the Gentile woman died and left daughters from a Jewess whom he (the son) had married (in Turkey). Then Reuben died and the daughters of the son (grandchildren of the Gentile woman) demanded a share of

Reuben's estate. This is disputed by the children of Reuben's Jewish wife.

Jacob Berab, in discussing this question of the rights of the grandchildren of the Gentile woman (who never converted and whom Reuben did not actually marry), goes into the whole question of the status of the marranos in his day. By this time, four or five generations had passed since they first became marranos. Their status is now in dispute. The rabbis who fled from Spain (after 1492) say that by now they have been assimilated among the Gentiles and are themselves Gentiles; but the household of Simon b. Zemah Duran insist that, as far as marriage and divorce are concerned, they are still Jews. In discussing these two lines of opinion, Jacob Berab says that the later opinion (that they are Jews as to marriage and divorce) is based upon the fact "that the earlier marranos did not intermarry with the Gentiles, and that, if some of them did so intermarry, the fact was well known among the rest of them and they kept away from such a person." He concludes that the descendants of this unconverted Gentile woman in Flanders are not part of this Jewish family and may not share in the estate.

The marriage problems of the marranos involved other and more personal problems than the question of inheritance. Joseph Trani (sixteenth century) discusses a tragic situation which frequently arose due to the fact that one brother escaped while another remained. In his responsum [43] he deals with the following problem: A marrano and his wife had escaped. Then he died without children. His widow, according to Jewish Law, could not remarry until her husband's brother released her through the ceremony of *halitza*. Unfortunately this brother was still in Portugal. He was unable to escape. Can this woman ever be released to remarry?

Joseph Trani reviews the entire series of opinions, by now accumulated, which discuss whether such a marrano, still in the land of persecution, can be considered "a brother." If not, the woman need not wait for any release from him and may remarry. The entire long and complicated responsum indicates that the status of the marranos was still in dispute. He says: [44]

Having been sunk in their alienation there for one hundred and twenty years, the majority of them, although they know that they are Israelites and deny idolatry, nevertheless, feel that all the prohibitions of the Torah are now permitted them, for they consider themselves to be under compulsion (and therefore pardonable). It is not their intention to deny in cowardice the Law of Moses for fear of being fed to the flames; but they have no one from whom to learn, especially concerning such matters as living with Gentile women, which is not explicit in the Bible. I have seen worthy and learned men (among the marranos) who fulfilled only such commandments as they could read for themselves in Scripture. Some of these put themselves in peril by circumcising themselves while still in the land of their enemies. Now they grieve over their sin of concubinage. They did not know it was forbidden.

Because of all this, Joseph Trani, although sympathizing with the pathetic efforts of the marranos to maintain some degree of Jewishness, nevertheless concludes that there was by his time sufficient doubt of their descent so that the law of *halitza* did not need to be enforced among them. The woman in this case was therefore free to remarry.

The efforts which the marranos made to maintain their Judaism is revealed in a question which was sent early in their history to Solomon b. Simon Duran in Algiers. The marranos placed particular emphasis on the celebration of Passover. Perhaps this was due to the fact that Passover came at the same season as Easter and thus provided a sharp contrast. Outwardly they would be celebrating Easter, but in their homes they would observe their own Passover. Besides, Passover, the feast of Israel's deliverance from Egypt, was a constant symbol of their own hopes. Yet Passover was an especially dangerous festival to observe. Any family which refrained from eating ordinary bread for eight days would be betraying itself to the Inquisition. The inquiry which came to Solomon Duran was as follows: [45]

I was asked concerning the marranos whose heart is directed to heaven and who desire to fulfill the commandments as far as they can. How shall they conduct themselves on Passover with

regard to their food so as not to sin by eating unleavened bread.
. . . Even if they eat only rice, the Gentiles will accuse them
saying: "Ye are still conducting yourselves according to the
laws of your fathers." Therefore, they fear for their safety.
Therefore some of them, sad and sighing, seek to find some
way to ease the prohibition (of leaven).

Duran thereupon suggests ways in which they might hide
the fact that they are confining themselves to unleavened food.
He suggests recipes. One of his suggestions is that a long time
before Passover (when no one will suspect them) they should
bake matzot, then crush them into meal and, during Passover,
bake the meal into ordinary looking bread or boil it in a pot
(evidently as a sort of dumpling).

It was not merely the ritual commandments which were difficult to maintain. Perhaps more important was the fact that
the doctrine and attitudes of Judaism were gradually changed
by the Catholic atmosphere in which the marranos lived. As the
years went by and their contacts with world Jewry became more
tenuous, their sole source of Jewish knowledge, besides their
fading memories, was what they could derive directly from the
reading of Scripture.[46] But the Bible which they had was the
Catholic Bible, which includes the Apocrypha; and it was from
the Apocryphal letter of Baruch that they derived one of their
characteristic religious attitudes. Samuel Aboab (1610–1694,
rabbi in Venice), discussing the religious status of the marranos,[47] says that even those who tell their children about some
of the Jewish ritual commandments, also teach them that the
real sin of idolatry (worshipping of the images in the churches)
is committed only when they are worshiped in the heart, and
that whoever is not sincere about image worship, but only worships them outwardly through fear, is not guilty of sin and is
free from Divine punishment. This they derive from a letter
ascribed among them to Baruch, son of Neriah, which the Christians have placed in the translations of the Sacred Writings.

A contemporary of Samuel Aboab, Jacob Sasportas (born in
Oran, 1610; died in Amsterdam, 1698) gives the most vivid
description in all the responsa literature of the sufferings of the

marranos in their efforts to escape and rejoin the household of Israel. In poetic language he describes the endurance and the loyalty of the marranos and their unflagging efforts to maintain their attachment to the faith of their fathers:

> ... Others offer themselves up to death, endanger themselves to travel on ships, trudge through deserts as fugitives to escape from the pit of destruction. The Gentiles discover them and sentence them to death; they give them over to the flames; but their hearts do not turn aside and they have no fear. They run like the lightning to do the will of their Father in Heaven.

He then speaks of those who *are* afraid, yet must be forgiven. He therefore speaks in defense of Abraham Bueno who, together with his uncle, was captured by the "Idumeans." They imprisoned them for three years and tortured them to compel them to become Christians. Only after they had killed his uncle, did Abraham Bueno consent to be a Christian. Now he seeks to return to Judaism. The legal question involved was whether he should have allowed himself to be killed rather than yield, since idolatry is one of the sins for which one must accept martyrdom rather than yield.[48] Sasportas argues that the repentance and the return of this unfortunate should be accepted.[49]

The marranos were conscious of the fact that their marriages were irregular according to Jewish Law. Moses Benvenisti (rabbi in Constantinople in the seventeenth century) records one of the pathetic methods which they used to regularize their marriages. In his responsa[50] he has to settle one of the marrano inheritance cases. The question comes from Livorno, Italy. The questioner describes the custom of the marrano immigrants as follows:

> Furthermore, they have this fixed custom, that if the husband or the wife is dangerously sick, they confess their sins and make a will. On that day they remarry their wives under the canopy (*huppah*) and spread the prayer shawl (*tallit*) over them, and bring under the *tallit* the sons and daughters who had been born to them in the land of persecution and proclaim them at that hour to be their legitimate children (*legitimos*); for it seems to

them, if they do not do this, the children are illegitimate (*bastardos*) and will not inherit them.

The records of the Inquisition are full of the tragedies of the marranos. The detailed accounts of the trials describe the Jewish practices of these "New Christians." But the Inquisitors' concepts of Jewish worship and ideas were often perverted, malicious and ignorant. A far truer description of their religious life is found in the Jewish legal literature which could compare the marrano observances with the tradition from which they were derived and discuss their deviations. Furthermore, when the marranos succeeded in escaping from the lands of darkness, they were out of the clutches of the Inquisition, unless it caught up with them again in Mexico or in the Papal States. Generally, however, their wanderings at last silenced the Inquisitors' records about them. Only the responsa literature kept up with them in all their wanderings over land and sea and through the centuries.

Since the responsa were primarily case law, they grew out of life and necessarily reflected life. Therefore, in any country where this literature flourished and many thousands of responsa were written, there would be many echoes of social and personal life. It will be noticed that the examples of history in the responsa given in this chapter came from lands in which many responsa were written. The picture of the life of the Jews in Poland was found in the rich responsa literature of Poland in the sixteenth century, and the history of the marranos came from that productive period in responsa writing in North Africa and in Turkey. Similarly, the history of the Jews in northern France and in Germany from the twelfth to the fifteenth centuries, in Spain in the thirteenth century, in Hungary and Galicia in the nineteenth century could be, and to some extent has already been, described. For in all these lands the writing of responsa was widely practiced. But just as the historians of any one of these Jewries could find material in their responsa, so too it might be possible to write about at least an aspect of the whole of Jewish history from the responsa literature as a totality.

The gaonic responsa, with their numerous answers to questions on the meaning of talmudic passages, then the gradual cessation of such questions in the early post-gaonic responsa, reveal the process whereby the Talmud, which was the property and the unbroken intellectual tradition of the Jews of Babylonia, gradually spread to the Jews of West Africa, Italy, Spain, France and the Rhineland. When the Talmud, through schools and commentaries, became the property of the people, the responsa show that fact, too, in the fuller analysis they contain as they develop into debates between learned equals. The mass of communal regulations in the responsa of Solomon ben Adret of Spain in the thirteenth century, or of Meir of Rothenburg in Germany a little later, reveals the independent, communal organization of the Jews, formed under medieval law and yet independent of it, as well as the fiscal burdens which they were compelled to carry. The continuous predominance of business law in the Turkish responsa shows the autonomy of the Jewish community in the Near East. The bitter disputes over the right of certain members of congregations to divide up and form their own synagogue, which appear in the responsa of Eastern Europe, reveal the rise of the hasidic movement and the intercommunal disputes occasioned by its growing power. The vast mass of responsa in the works of Isaac Elhanan Spektor and in those of his contemporaries in the nineteenth century, which deal with the *aguna*, reveal the sudden breakup of old communities by the mass immigration overseas. Even the discussion of the permissibility of sending a divorce through the mail is an evidence of that same historic movement. And now discussions appear to be bringing again to the fore, after an interval of fifteen centuries, the questions of agriculture in Palestine, the Sabbatical year when the land must rest, the milking of cows on the Sabbath, and a host of similar questions. The old homeland where the law had its birth will now be the scene of its newest development.[51]

6

MODERN
INVENTIONS

THE PHRASE "Atomic Age" has achieved a rapid currency in all languages. Obviously, its swift popularity is due to the fact that it represents an instantly appreciated reality, namely, that the unleashing of the forces of the atom has catapulted human history from one age into another.

Yet many have also fallen into the habit of speaking of "the Jet Age," as if the newly developed technique of jet propulsion for airplanes is, like the release of the atom, a transformation of life, a new turn in history. As a matter of fact, this type of phrase is not new. The long established magazine of the railway industry is called *The Railroad Age*, and that of the automobile industry, *The Motor Age*. All such phrases indicate a widely-held conviction that these discoveries, or technical developments, are not merely the products of a new convenience but the beginnings of a profound change in human life, so that their coming carries us from one age into another in the history of man.

While this common anticipation of the future, this too-facile writing of history in advance, is not always justified, nevertheless, it contains a basic truth, at least potentially. Every new invention may bring some changes, some of which are likely to cause basic transformations in the lives of millions of people. A change in transportation facilities may begin merely with the perfecting of a certain type of engine experimented with in the hope of establishing a new business. But it may well end by covering a country with a network of concrete roads and creating a social revolution in the relationship between farm and city; all of which the automobile has undoubtedly done.

Inventions, thus carrying with them the potential of changing the life of society, must inevitably affect its Law. The Law, confronted with new situations, must fit its categories to a new series of events. The Constitution of the United States, written by candlelight, must be re-adjusted to a society which lives in the age of electricity. This adjustment can always be achieved if the legal system remains flexible. It has been achieved by many modern legal systems with a fair degree of success.

Many modern discoveries and inventions have created problems in Jewish Law, for many of them touch Jewish religious life. When tobacco was introduced into Europe, the question was whether it may be smoked on the holidays, or is that prohibited work? Does it require a blessing to be recited before its use as before the taking of food, drink or the smelling of incense? The invention of the railroads raised the question of whether they may be used for travel on the Sabbath, since the railroad is clearly in a different category from a wagon or a coach which is hired specifically by the rider. Nor does it involve in many cases, as one respondent pointed out, travel on the public highway, which is clearly prohibited on the Sabbath; in most cases it is travel on a private right-of-way. An electric dish-washing machine raises problems. The mixture of meat foods and milk foods must be avoided in vessels that are used in the Jewish home. How sure are we that a set of milk dishes will not be washed in water still containing fragments of the previous washing of the meat dishes? Radio brings its problems. May it be used on the Sabbath? May a religious service heard over the radio constitute a fulfillment of our religious duty of participating in worship?

It is much more difficult for Jewish Law to adjust itself to changed conditions than it is for secular Law. Secular Law has two instruments for adjustment. There is, first, the judge's new interpretation of the meaning of existing laws; and, second, there is the power of the legislature or Congress to create an entirely new law if the old laws cannot be adjusted to suit the new conditions. Since the cessation of the old ordination in the fourth century, there has been no true legislative power in Jewish life, because only the ordained can serve in a Sanhedrin, a religious legislature. Except for the occasional emergency synod gathered by some famous rabbi in past centuries to proclaim some special enactment, Jewish Law may be described as solely "judge-made," a re-interpretation of ancient statutes. It is impossible in Jewish Law as it is at present organized to make a new beginning as a congress or a legislature can. Besides, a law deemed divine cannot be easily set aside. This is one of the main motivations for the efforts in recent years to re-establish a Sanhedrin in the land of Israel.

For this reason Jewish Law is confronted with a difficult task every time an important new invention appears which impinges upon religious life. Which of the older laws has some relevance to it? How can this relevance be distilled into a usable principle applicable to the new conditions? Such re-interpretations require great ingenuity. It is, therefore, remarkable how successfully the old Jewish legal system has managed to cope with new and unprecedented conditions brought about by modern inventions. This chapter will make no attempt at a complete description of the reaction of Jewish Law to modern inventions, but will confine itself to a number of important and telling examples.

Printing

The art of printing was perhaps the chief instrumentality which helped create the modern era. It transformed the medieval culture, which had been restricted to the learned few, into a new era of universal literacy with the opportunity for universal culture. It had the same effect, of course, on Jewish life, but not to so marked a degree. True, books were now more readily available and, therefore, learning much more easily accessible; but even before the age of printing, learning in Jewry was not restricted to the chosen few. Literacy was widespread to a degree not found in other peoples. While there were illiterates, in whose behalf the Reader (*hazzan*) chanted the services, the majority surely could pray out of the book. There were vast numbers of Jewish manuscripts, many scrolls in every ark, prayerbooks for holidays and the rest of the year, legal works and commentaries of many types. It is because of these many-sided contacts with the written word that the art of printing made a sharp impact upon the Jewish community and found a wide echo in the responsa literature.

These questions arose: How sacred were these newly printed works? Were they usable for the purposes of worship? If a Scroll of the Law were printed instead of written by a scribe, as heretofore, could that scroll be used in the public reading which is part of the Sabbath and holiday service? May the people who are "called up" to the Torah recite the customary blessings over a *printed* Torah? In other words, if we print a sacred book, have we thereby fulfilled the biblical command, "And thou shalt *write* them." If the printed books are not to be deemed sacred enough for the purposes of worship, have they at least *some* sanctity? Are they sacred enough to require the careful and respectful handling prescribed in the Law for holy writings; or may they, for example, when worn out, just be thrown away? [1] The earlier responsa, particularly those which were written near the time when printing was invented, were inclined to accord sanctity to the printed book.

Samuel di Medina, rabbi in Turkey in the sixteenth century,[2] evidently in response to a question which was asked of him, describes the methods used by bookbinders in Salonika in making book covers. They took discarded or surplus sheets of printed Hebrew books (some of the commentaries, or the *Midrashim*, or the Bible) and glued them together to help form covers to protect books. Such covers were also cut down from covers of larger books. Sometimes they were trimmed and the surplus trimmings were trampled under foot in the shop. Is such action justified in the Law? In his answer, Rabbi Samuel discusses whether printing is really "writing," in the Scriptural sense of the word, and also whether the fact that the printing is on paper, and not on parchment, detracts from its sanctity. He concludes that the

Talmud provides that only heretical books are to be destroyed and that these pages (from which the covers were made) are certainly not heretical. He is, therefore, strongly inclined to forbid the bookbinder to follow the cardboard-making practice as described. But he hesitates to issue a formal prohibition "until I shall see whether my teachers and masters agree with me; and may God guard me against error."

Benjamin Slonik, who lived in Poland (1550–1619) was asked a similar question [3] as to the cutting up of covers glued together from printed Hebrew pages, and in the same inquiry was asked the more general question as to how sacred printed books really are. He answers:

> It seems to me that we cannot make a distinction between written books and printed books. All sanctity that inheres in written books applies to printed books; for what difference does it make whether the books were produced by writing or by engraving (that is, printing)?

Later respondents, however, when printing became commonplace, were inclined to ascribe lesser sanctity to printed books as compared to handwritten ones. Yair Hayyim Bacharach (born in Moravia, 1639; died in Germany, 1702) was asked [4] concerning a poor scholar who lived in one room. His wife and infant occupied this one room together with all his books. It was, therefore, impossible for him to be as reverential in the presence of the sacred books as the Law requires. Bacharach answers that printed books are hardly sacred, for even written scrolls to be sacred must be made by a scribe with conscious, holy intent whenever the Divine Name is inscribed. This surely is not done when books are printed, especially when many of the printers are not Jews at all.

Elazar Fleckeles (born in Prague, 1754; died there, 1826) gives an entirely new reason why *tefillin* and *mezuzahs* are not usable if printed, but must be written by hand.[5] The Law requires that the Scriptural passages in these (especially the Divine Names in them) be written letter by letter in the order in which they appear in Scripture but when they are printed the printer

sets up the letters in exactly the *reverse* order, which is manifestly illegal for sacred use.

An interesting form of these questions came before the rabbis
of Marrakech in Morocco.[6] A group of Jews was about to join
a caravan across the Sahara. There were enough of them to form
a quorum (a *minyan*) for public services. It was impossible for
them to take along a written Scroll of the Law because of its
size. May they use a printed Hebrew Bible during the Sabbath
services in the desert and call up the usual seven men to the
"Torah" reading? The answer was that it would be preferable
not to use a printed Bible at all, but if they do so, the seven men
"called up" may *not* recite the customary Torah blessings, for
over a printed Bible these blessings would be "wasted blessings"
(*berakhah l'battalah*). Almost precisely the same question was
asked by the United States Defense Department (through its
Joint Chaplaincy Board) of the Division of Jewish Activities of
the Jewish Welfare Board, namely, if Jewish chaplains in the
field were provided with a small printed or photographed replica
of the Scroll, would that Scroll serve for all Jewish religious
purposes? The answer given was that, under field conditions, the
printed Scroll could be used, but the customary blessings should
not be recited.

Of course, although printed books have not the same sanctity
as written ones and cannot be used for ritual purposes where
written books or Scrolls are required, they do have enough sanctity to require reverential handling. This is the decision of
Ezekiel Katzenellenbogen (born in Lithuania about 1670; died
in Germany, 1749).[7] The worn out and discarded pages of
printed Hebrew books should be buried (as is required of worn
out Torah Scrolls).

If printed books are to be treated reverentially, what should be
the attitude to newspapers? It is certainly impossible to make
sure that used newspapers are carefully buried. May then the
name of God (in Hebrew or, for that matter, in any language)
be printed in a newspaper? This question was asked of a number of authorities by Rabbi Jacob Rosenheim, president of the
Orthodox world organization, *Agudat Yisrael*. Moses Sofer (son

of Simon Sofer) [8] answers that even in non-Hebrew newspapers the name of God ought not to be written out in full.

A modern variation in the question of the sanctity of printing has resulted from the process of photographic reproduction of printed books. If a Bible is issued in a photographic edition, and especially if the text is so small as to be unreadable without the aid of a microscope, can such a Bible be deemed to possess holiness and need it be handled with the respect due to a regular Bible edition? This question was asked of Shalom Mordecai Schwadron,[9] of Benjamin Aryeh Weiss [10] and of Wolf Leiter.[11] The discussion involves the older question as to how much sacred intention can be put into the printing process as compared with the process of writing by hand. Photographic reproduction seems still more automatic. While, then, considerable sanctity *is* carried over from handwriting to mechanical printing, less sanctity attaches to this process of photographic reproduction. In addition, the fact that the photographed print is so small as to be illegible by the unaided eye tends to lessen the sanctity of the photograph as Scripture. However, the general tendency of the above authors is toward the opinion that the photographs should be handled with the customary reverence.

Photography itself has brought up a number of new questions discussed in the responsa literature, all of them illustrating how the ancient legal material is brought to bear upon a modern situation.

A question asked of Raphael Ezekiel Hochberg [12] reads as follows:

A widow from a village near here has a son who, during the World War, went into combat. She did not hear from him for a long time and was greatly worried. She then made a vow that, if God help her that her son return safely from the war and that she have the joy of seeing his face, she will donate all her jewelry for charity to the poor. Now she has received a letter from him. He has also sent a photograph of himself and asked her to come and live with him. But upon inquiry she discovered that he had been a captive of the Russians and was now one of the

Bolsheviks and lives with a Gentile wife. Her joy was thus turned to sorrow. She now asks whether she is in duty bound to fulfill her vow, that is, whether having seen his photograph, she has "seen his face."

The answer revolves around the question of whether an image, or picture, amounts actually to seeing the person. The author cites the Talmud,[13] where it is related that the portrait of King Nebuchadnezzar was painted on the chariot of his general Nebuzaradan in the siege of Jerusalem. Does it mean that the king was deemed to have been actually present? He quotes also the legend that the image of the patriarch Jacob is on the Throne of Glory and whenever God looks upon it He remembers, in favor of Israel, the merits of their ancestor Jacob. The author finally concludes that the woman's vow may be relaxed. Seeing the photograph was not "seeing his face."

Another case involving photography is discussed in the responsa of Isaac Schmelkes, rabbi of Lemberg.[14] This is a modern variation of the classic and tragic problem of the *agunah*, which involves the attempt to find sufficient evidence of the death of the husband so that the woman might be permitted to remarry. Deborah, wife of Benjamin Kessler, whose husband was in America, received a letter that her husband had been killed in a train accident. His body was badly mutilated, but some friends identified him by a photograph. The photograph was enclosed in the letter to his wife. The question was whether identification in this case, by help of the photograph, was sufficient. The author is dubious about relying *only* on the photograph.

An analagous question was brought before Shalom Mordecai Schwadron.[15] A man committed suicide in a prison in Odessa. His possessions provided contradictory evidence as to his identity. His reputed widow came with a photograph which was recognized by a number of people as the photograph of the deceased. Is the photograph to be accepted as evidence of identity? The author decides that the photograph may be accepted as auxiliary evidence.

In the year 1878, Moses Schick [16] was asked about a new cemetery custom which since his day has become widespread, namely, affixing to the tombstone a photograph of the deceased. The question was asked concerning, first, a statuary bust of the deceased, and also included is the question of the photograph. Moses Schick forbids the use either of statuary or of photographs.[17]

Electricity

Even as the invention of printing achieved changes in the cultural pattern of the world, from limited to widespread literacy, so the discovery of electricity and its uses has created a revolutionary transformation in daily life. Unlimited light and power were available only to the nobility in the Middle Ages, and even to them only in clumsy fashion. The average man had to do all his work laboriously by his own power and he dwelt in darkness after the sun had set. Now cheap light became increasingly available to everyone, thus merging its influence with the use of the printed book, adding hours of reading and making limitless power available on distant farms and in homes, and abolishing much of the drudgery of the past.

Precisely because Jewish Law concerns itself with all of life, electricity, which touched almost every aspect of life, was bound to have a profound impact on Jewish legal literature. As soon as appliances making use of electricity for light and for power became available, it was natural that questions should be asked of rabbis, and that these questions and their answers should find their way quickly into the responsa literature.

Many types of question were asked: first, as to the character of the electric light. Just as the question was asked whether a printed book had the sanctity of a book written by hand, so in the matter of the electric light the question dealt with the sanctity of an old practice. Lights are used ritually for the Sabbath, for holidays and for the festival of Hanukkah. The lights originally used were oil and wicks, and then candles, which change in itself created some legal discussion. But now, can this new light of electricity be deemed sacred enough to be used for the Sabbath, for Hanukkah or for *Yartzeit?*

One of the earliest authorities to deal with the question of the suitability of electricity for the Sabbath lights is Isaac Schmelkes of Lemberg.[19] He says that electric light (and also gas light) are usable for Sabbath light, since any light that has a wick (in this case, the filament) which carries the flame can properly be called *Ner*, "light." Therefore, the electric light may be used and the Sabbath blessing recited over it. But, he adds, it cannot be used for the Hanukkah lights, because olive oil is part of the original Hanukkah miracle and also because electric lights, being used daily, would not add the necessary distinctiveness to the observance of the holiday.

Later authorities tend to disapprove of the use of electricity for the Sabbath lights. Thus the recent book of responsa, *Yerushat ha-Peletah* ("The Inheritance of the Remnant"), a collection started before the Hitlerite persecution and published after the war, contains a responsum by Chaim Isaac Halberstam who forbids the use of electricity for the Sabbath lights. The author first determines that a blessing must accompany the kindling of the Sabbath lights (since there are some opinions that a blessing over the light is unnecessary).[20] He then turns to the explanation of Solomon ben Adret [21] as to why certain commandments (*mitzvot*) are not provided with an accompanying benediction while most of the others are. Adret explains that the act of giving a gift to the poor, although it is a *mitzvah*, need not be preceded by a benediction because the poor man may refuse to accept the gift, in which case any blessing recited over this *mitzvah* by the donor would be a wasted blessing (*berakhah le-batalah*). Hence, Adret declares it to be a general principle that any deed which is not in the full power of the doer to *complete* may not be preceded by a blessing. This principle is now applied by Halberstam to the electric light, as follows: Since the continuous burning of the electric light (for the duration of the Sabbath meal) cannot be guaranteed by the householder, for it may be turned off at the power house, he may not make a blessing over it. Since, therefore, the Sabbath light cannot be kindled without a blessing, the electric light may not be used as the ritual Sabbath light. There are, however, some modern opinions which would permit the use of it.

The chief legal problems involved in the use of electricity go far beyond the question whether the electric light may be used for the ritual Sabbath lamp. The basic questions involving Sabbath work are those which deal with the prohibition of lighting fires, of cooking, and the like. These widely elaborated laws need now to be restudied and applied to this new instrument of light and power.

With regard to the Sabbath, two basic Sabbath laws are involved; the prohibition against kindling fire, and the prohibition against doing certain other types of work. Is the glowing filament, in an electric lamp, fire? Is it not merely a glowing bit of metal which, according to the Talmud,[18] may be extinguished on the Sabbath? May an electric light be turned on or off? May an electric oven be turned on or off? May a telephone receiver be lifted, since that action may cause a spark at some switchboard? May a radio be turned on and off? There are literally hundreds of questions involving electricity. Furthermore, since new electrical devices are constantly being invented, new questions arise every day in the responsa literature as to electric broilers, electric dishwashers, and many other utensils.

In one connection, at least, the law was interpreted more leniently with regard to electric lights than with regard to earlier methods of illumination. The law prohibits using the Sabbath lights for any work requiring concentration, such as studying, lest, absorbed in his study, the student unconsciously adjust the light [22] and thus violate the Sabbath law against "kindling" light by increasing the flame. This unintentional kindling or brightening of light could occur quite easily with the ancient type of illumination, namely, a wick floating in oil. When, however, wax candles came into use, the need for adjustment was much less likely and some authorities permitted studying under such lights on the Sabbath. But electric lights need almost no adjustment to improve their light; hence the respondents began to permit study by electric light on the Sabbath. Thus, Mordecai Winkler [23] explains that earlier authorities, who prohibited study before oil or naphtha lamps, did so because two lamps were needed and, therefore, there was likelihood of adjusting the lights; but electricity gives a clear and adequate light. So, too, Simon Greenberg [24] permits the use of the electric light, but makes a distinction between a swinging lamp (which might be moved) and a fixed electric lamp. The fixed lamp is certainly permitted.

The likelihood is that when the students of the Law will take cognizance of the new three-way electric lamps, there will be responsa about them and they may well be prohibited for use in study on the Sabbath, since manifestly there would be a danger of turning them up for brighter lighting.

The historic Sabbath laws prohibit almost all manner of work (derived primarily from agricultural work, such as plowing, digging, scattering earth, and the like), and also specifically prohibit the lighting of fire. Nevertheless, the use of electric power for work or for light could not be simply declared as prohibited without previous analysis and discussion. For, although the release of power may be very great and a vast amount of work may be done by it, yet the actual human labor involved is very small, often merely the simple turning of a switch.

Considering then the small amount of effort involved in turning the switch, the work done by a person can be considered merely a secondary cause of the final result (*gorma*) and not a real violation of the direct rabbinical laws against Sabbath work. It would be only a violation of the rabbinical, secondary safeguards. Hence it would be permissible to ask a Gentile to turn the switch. This is, indeed, the permissive attitude taken by some of the respondents. On the other hand, when we consider the immense amount of real work accomplished by the electricity so released, surely we might argue that the biblical laws against work and kindling fire are flagrantly violated and it is, therefore, forbidden even to ask a Gentile to do it.

Thus, for example, Shalom Mordecai Schwadron [25] is asked concerning the use of an electric light in the synagogue on Sabbath and also the use of it immediately at the close of the Sabbath, since the furnaces (in the power house) which created the electricity were burning during the Sabbath. His answer is, generally, permissive. He first discusses the fact that the work is done by Gentiles for a community of which the majority is Gentile and where the Jew does not specifically order this work done for him. He ends by saying:

> I will not withhold the fact that I doubt whether the kindling or the extinguishing of electric lights is really work forbidden by the Torah, since there was no light comparable with this in the Tabernacle (from which, by analogy, the prohibition is derived). This light is no fire that consumes. It does not burn up the filament. (In other words, the prohibition could not be considered biblical, but merely a rabbinical safeguard and, therefore, a Gentile may do it for a Jew.)
>
> Therefore, it is possible to be lenient in this matter, especially since, in this case, the light is to be used for the honor and need of the synagogue, and the failure to extinguish it (by a Gentile, after the services) would involve the waste of money dedicated to holy purposes.

So, too, Abraham Steinberg [26] inclines to the conclusion that the turning on or off of the switch is not really the activating power of the electricity. The power is already there, waiting for release. Turning on the switch is merely removing a hindrance to a power already present (like turning on a faucet with the water pressure already in the pipes). Hence, turning the switch is merely a secondary cause and it is permissible to have a Gentile do it.

In another responsum,[27] however, he himself leans toward the prohibition of electric light on the Sabbath. In this responsum he directly controverts the permissive attitude of Shalom Mordecai Schwadron (mentioned above) and says that Schwadron's argument, that there was no light comparable to this in the Tabernacle, is not a decisive argument because the Bible specifically prohibits the kindling of "fire" and that means any kind of fire, whether there was such a fire in the Tabernacle or not.

The more recent authorities are increasingly strict in the matter, and by now a sequence of prohibitory decisions has accumulated. Isaac Schmelkes of Lemberg [28] says that, while it is true that the law permits the extinguishing of a glowing metal [29] (and therefore one would think that the extinguishing of the filament of a lamp would likewise be permitted), yet the flame of electricity is really fire and it is prohibited to kindle or to extinguish it on the Sabbath.

In this strict interpretation he is followed by Chaim Ozer Grodzinski of Vilna.[30] After refuting a permissive opinion, he concludes that turning the switch is a uniting of the two wires by hand and, therefore, is the prohibited work of kindling fire by hand. These two leading authorities are followed by other respondents who decide in a similar vein.

Thus the weight of opinion in the responsa is by now prohibitory and has bearing upon other electrical devices, in which the electricity does not create heat for warmth or cooking, nor a glow to give light. Touching the button of an electric doorbell lights a spark. Lifting the receiver of a telephone kindles a light on a switchboard. Talking into the microphone of a loudspeaker amplifies power (although some deny this and permit the use of the microphone on the Sabbath). Opening the door of an electric refrigerator kindles a light and also activates electric power. However, the responsa discussion on the use of these new instruments on the Sabbath, while inclined to be prohibitory, is still far from constituting a decisive weight of opinion.

As new electrical and electronic devices are invented, many of them come up quickly for consideration in the responsa literature. Not all of them concern the laws of Sabbath-work as do those mentioned above. Some of them concern the laws of permitted and forbidden food and the handling of dishes. Others concern religious worship. Thus, the electric broiler brings up a discussion whether a glowing grid of wires *above* the meat actually draws out the forbidden blood as does a wood or coal fire underneath the meat.

Radio and television have given rise to a host of questions as to religious worship. If a man, on the New Year, hears the *shofar* blown over the radio, has he thereby fulfilled his duty of "listening to the voice of the *Shofar*"? If he hears a benediction over the radio or television, must he say "Amen"? Among the well-known respondents who have discussed this question are Ben-Zion Uziel, Sephardic Chief Rabbi of Israel,[31] and the martyred Jehudah Leib Zirelsohn.[32] Besides dealing with other considerations, both authorities are concerned with the character of the broadcaster. Only a worthy person can serve as cantor or leader for the prayers of others. Unless one know, therefore, whose voice it is he has heard, he may not respond "Amen"; to which problem Jehudah Leib Zirelsohn makes an interesting comment, namely, that some day, with television, when people will be able to *see* the cantor or reader and recognize him as a worthy person, such services may well be acceptable.

An interesting variation of the problem of the use of electricity was asked in 1946 by Rabbi Isaac Heller, the *shohet* in the Israeli town of Nathania. The question was asked of Eliezer Judah Waldenberg of Jerusalem.[33] It is as follows: Is it permitted to prepare food on the Sabbath (that is, to cook food on the Sabbath) by the following method: placing the dish with the uncooked food upon an electric stove and, before the Sabbath, setting an electric clock that will turn on the power, begin the cooking and turn it off when the cooking is over? The entire action is automatic. Rabbi Waldenberg answers that, as to setting an electric clock before the Sabbath to light electricity and to extinguish it on the Sabbath, this has by now been permitted by the great rabbis of the past generation, namely, Joseph Saul Nathanson and Moses Schick and others, and he refers to his own book, *Responsa Tzitz Eliezer*.[34] While it is permitted to arrange thus for the automatic kindling and extinguishing of electricity by a clock set before the Sabbath, it is forbidden to cook food on the Sabbath by any method at all. He ends by saying that there is no question that it is forbidden to place uncooked food there before the Sabbath (to cook during the Sabbath). It is even forbidden to put cooked food to re-heat it.

Later, in volume II of his book of responsa, he answers a variation of the same question,[35] asked him by the rabbi of Afula in Israel. "May one use hot water from an electrically heated water tank which is lit before the Sabbath?" He says that it is permitted to heat water this way because no work is being done thereby by the person, nor is likely to be done. This is different from the case of the cooking mentioned above, where there is a temptation to stir the pot in which the food is cooking; but the boiling of the water requires no effort and is therefore permitted. However, when the faucet is opened to get some hot water, cold water automatically takes the place of the hot water which is thus drawn off. Is it, therefore, permitted to turn on the faucet on the Sabbath? He gives a number of possible reasons why it should be permitted—because the man who draws off the water does not actually pour in the cold water to be boiled and, therefore, it is only a secondary action on his part. Nevertheless, he comes to the conclusion that it is not permitted to turn on the faucet.

The vast number of new responsa which deal with modern inventions is, in itself, an indication of how the Law touches almost every angle of life. There are decisions on printing and photography, canning of food, dentistry, modern city water systems, modern bathrooms, railroads, railroad tank-cars, airplanes, soilless agriculture (hydroponics), refrigeration of meats, electric iceboxes, television, and much more. The Jewish legal system, ancient though it is, reveals itself in these modern responsa as admirably flexible and adjustable.

7

CURIOUS
RESPONSA

THE FAMOUS SATIRIST, Isaac Erter, in his *Ha-Zofeh l'Bet Yisrael*,[1] mocks the learning of the rabbis. He described Satan as saying to him:

> If thou dost not believe, O man of little faith (the folly that exists in the rabbinical writings), incline thine ear and hear the words of thy sages—those who seem like sages to thee—what they do say in their books. These are their words literally in their books. Then (Erter continues), like a stream of mighty waters, his (Satan's) lips poured forth quotations of follies and idle talk. It was unbelievable that the like should be found in the books of our sages and our lawgivers; men of fame, honored by the congregations, I will now place before my brothers, the House of Israel, some of the words which I have heard.

Then follows a footnote citing what seems to the satirist to be foolish matter discussed in the rabbinical writings.

In so extensive a literature as the responsa, to which such a large variety of human beings have contributed, there are bound to be some discussions that are trivial, some that smack of the superstitious, and other that seem to be downright foolish. But, of course, this applies only to a small proportion of an immense literature. Also it must be said that some of these statements were not intended seriously, but were simply playful. And some of them are more important than appears on the surface.

In volume II of the responsa of Hayyim ben Mordecai Sofer, the first responsum deals with the question of whether a pious and learned Jew may make his living conducting a modern lending-library.[2] One may be sure that to Isaac Erter this would seem to be a trivial matter, unworthy of serious discussion. Yet when one considers how the old-fashioned Hungarian rabbis worried over the new enthusiasm of Jewish students for modern literature and the consequent neglect of the classic talmudic studies, one can understand why that incident was deemed worthy of a serious responsum and why the rabbi answered the question so vehemently and indignantly in the negative. The changes brought about by modern life seemed to him to present so dire a menace to the old Talmud-absorbed way of life, that the question of the lending library, which would seem trivial and even ludicrous to some of us, was vital and significant to him.

So it is with many themes in the responsa which to us seem rather bizarre. They were not as strange to the respondent as they may appear; or, even if the respondent himself did not deem them too important *per se*, he respected the earnest desire of the pious questioner for an answer; and he was perhaps concerned, too, with demonstrating that there was hardly *any* question with which the sharp instrument of the Law could not successfully cope.

This chapter is devoted to citing a number of responsa which may well be described as curious ones. Some were serious in their import to the respondent. Sometimes, as in the case of the responsum on the mechanical robot, the matter was important to the respondent for reasons of family tradition. Some of them may merely have been playful and a demonstration of the ability of the Law to handle the matter.

The Robot and the Minyan

Among the strangest of the responsa are two by father and son dealing with the theme of the mechanical robot. The idea of a human-like machine which, in some mysterious way, is given the power of motion and labor, has been widely current in world literature. In modern times, the creation of a mechanical monster was given currency by Mrs. Shelley in her famous story,

Frankenstein; and by the Czech dramatist, Capek, who, through his play, *RUR*, gave the modern world the term "robot." The modern form of the story is a combination of an old legend with modern scientific ideas. In earlier days, the source of the energy was not some new scientific technique, but magical power.

The Talmud [3] tells of the Babylonian scholar, Raba, who created such a "man" and sent him to his colleague, Zeira. Zeira spoke to him, but the "man" did not answer. Zeira then said, "Art thou then made by magic?" And he destroyed him.

Rashi (eleventh century), in his commentary to this passage, reveals the medieval European concept of this marvelous creation. He says that Raba made this "man" by means of the magic letters in the *Sefer Yetzirah* (the "Book of Creation"). This cabalistic book has much to say about combining the letters of the Hebrew alphabet and putting them to magical use. Of course, this goes still farther back to the midrashic conception of how God Himself, in the creation of the world, used the letters of the alphabet as instruments in His creative work. Combined with this concept was the biblical picture of Adam being made out of the dust of the earth and his life given to him by the infusion of the spirit of God. It was, therefore, a rather short leap for the mystic imagination to believe that a very righteous man could repeat God's process (as indeed, Raba in the Talmud is said to have done). The medieval legend takes the following shape: Certain famous rabbis formed the shape of a human being out of clay and, by a mystic combination of the Divine Name, (from the *Sefer Yetzirah*) gave this creature life or half-life. This sort of machine, known in modern times as a "robot" created through "science," is known in medieval Jewish literature as a *Golam* created through cabalistic magic.

It was almost inevitable that an idea so widespread should find its way into the responsa literature. The law with which it came to be connected was one that is discussed frequently in the legal literature, namely, the question of the quorum of ten (the *minyan*) needed for public worship. In villages, especially for weekday services, when men are at their work, the problem of gathering ten men is frequently a troubling one. Suppose there are only nine? The Talmud discusses the question. Rab Huna says [4] that he would count the Ark and nine worshippers as equivalent to a quorum of ten. Also the question is frequently asked, "Can a child under thirteen (therefore, religiously a minor) be counted into the quorum of ten?" The law, as given in the *Shulhan Arukh*,[5] says that there is a custom in times of emergency to count as the tenth a boy holding a Bible in his hand. Another form of question in this matter is whether a man who is asleep in the synagogue can be counted as one of the ten.[6] From these questions it seemed an easy transition to the strange question whether a mechanical man, a *Golam*, may be counted into the quorum of ten.

This curious question is the theme of a responsum by Zevi Ashkenazi (1658–1719).[7] In answer to this question he refers, of course, to the talmudic statement of Raba having created such a robot; and he finally concludes that, since Rabbi Zeira did not hesitate to destroy the creature which Raba had made, it was not human (otherwise Zeira would have been a murderer) and cannot be counted in the *minyan*.

The same question is taken up by Zevi Ashkenazi's son, Jacob Emden,[8] and is also decided in the sense that they are not to be counted, since even deaf-mutes, who are clearly human and have some intelligence, are not counted.

The fact that father and son, both keen-minded scholars, dealt with the same curious theme, indicates that there was a family reason behind the discussion; as indeed there was, since the first medieval *Golam* is said to have been made by their ancestor, Elijah of Chelm, in the sixteenth century; and both of them refer to it. To what extent these fine scholars believed in the possibility of making the *Golam* is hard to say. Ideas of magic were as current in those days as ideas of science are today, and just as it would not be too difficult at least to half-persuade many modern people that an animated robot can be made by science, so it would not have been difficult to half-persuade keen minds of the past that an animated *Golam* could be made by magical combinations of the Divine Name. At all events, Jacob Emden, strong-minded opponent though he was of the amulets and charms alleged to have been made by his rabbinical opponent, Jonathan Eibeschuetz, nevertheless does not hesitate, at the end of his responsum on this curious subject, to record that his ancestor suddenly became afraid that the robot would destroy the world. He succeeded in averting this danger by snatching off the name of God that was attached to the clay of the creature's forehead, but not before the *Golam* was able to scratch his face.

The Balloon Over the Succah

The *succah*, which every householder should build for the Feast of Tabernacles, must be made according to certain specifications as to dimensions. Also, it must be loosely constructed so as to be a "temporary dwelling place," and the covering of foliage must not be either too thick or too thin. These laws are all detailed in a separate tractate in the Mishna (Succah) and in a tractate in the Talmud. Among the requirements are that a *succah* shall not be built under the roof of a house, because it must be in the open air; nor, for that matter, may it be built under the branches of a tree.

These requirements, forbidding the cover of any sheltering layer over the loose foliage of the *succah* roof, have given rise in recent years to a rather strange responsum. Moses Perelmuter, rabbi of Lodz, Poland,[9] asked of the famous Rabbi Shalom Mordecai Schwadron (Maharsham) the following questions:

If a balloon, which can be steered at will by the pilot, hovers over a *succah*, whether close to the ground or high up, is not that *succah* unfit, since it is thereby "covered"? Moreover, if the balloon (or dirigible) was hovering over the *succah* at the time that it was built and then departed, is not the *succah* still unfit, since it had been built under forbidden circumstances (that is, it was built, as it were, under a roof)?

Shalom Mordecai Schwadron gives a careful and a learned answer which is published in Perelmuter's book, following his own opinions which are cited first. He calls attention to the fact that the Talmud makes a careful analogy [10] between the construction of a *succah* and a "tent" in the laws of uncleanness. This analogy to which Schwadron refers is a natural one. The Bible (Num. 19.14) states that, if a dead body is found in a tent, all the people within the tent are ritually unclean and so are the open vessels within the tent. This leads to a great deal of technical discussion in the Mishna, which has a whole tractate devoted to the subject (Oholot) as to what constitutes a tent. Suppose it were loosely built, with only a mere suggestion of a latticed roof, would that be a "tent" which makes all people in it unclean if a body is in it? Hence, it is a natural thing for the rabbis in the Talmud, in discussing the proper construction of a *succah*, to compare it by analogy with the construction of a "tent" of uncleanness.

Schwadron, answering the question of Moses Perelmuter about the balloon over the *succah*, says that in the laws of uncleanness there is a discussion of the effect of a movable cover, as to whether such a covering makes a "tent" and spreads the uncleanness of the body to everything under it. Thus the Mishna [11] says that, if a large sheet is blown by the wind, it is not to be considered a "tent" with regard to the objects over which it hovers, unless one corner of it is anchored down by a stone and thus made fixed. So, too, a ship (if it carries a dead body) is not considered a tent (making all who are on the ship unclean) until it is anchored and fixed in one place. Therefore, he says, as long as the balloon is moving, it is not a disqualifying covering over the *succah*.

As to the *succah* having been built at the time when the balloon was hovering over it, and Perelmuter's concern that then, even if the balloon departs, the *succah*, having been made under prohibited conditions, is now unusable, he says that this is not so. He discusses by analogy the question of a man building a *succah* under a hinged or removable roof. Of course, he should first remove the roof before putting the foliage on the *succah*. But, suppose he builds the *succah* while the roof is still on, then removes the roof after the *succah* is finished, shall we say that the *succah* was made under forbidden conditions and therefore is forever unusable? Schwadron cites authorities which permit the use of the *succah* made under these conditions.[12]

It is hardly likely that Perelmuter, who raised the question first, or Schwadron who gave it such careful consideration, was really concerned with the possibility that such circumstances might become frequent. The fact is that the question was asked by Perelmuter one day before Succot in that year and was answered by Schwadron a few days later during the half-holiday of Succot. In all likelihood, Perelmuter saw a balloon or a dirigible sail over the city of Lodz and the question merely struck him as an interesting and reasonable one. At all events, his learned curiosity produced the responsum so ingeniously worked out.

The Self-winding Watch

The laws concerning work on the Sabbath occupy a large proportion of Jewish legal literature; and, in spite of the fact that these laws have been studied for centuries, and the Sabbath has been observed all this time with comparatively little violation by all Jews everywhere, it is always a little startling to discover that many of the basic principles underlying the laws still are unclarified. Even in the latest discussions involving the laws of the Sabbath there seems to be a need for re-analyzing or delimiting certain basic concepts. In responsa written in our day concerning Sabbath work, the basic principles are still re-discussed, as, for example, which type of work is forbidden most strictly (being of direct biblical source) and which type of work is less strictly forbidden (being merely rabbinic amplification of the biblical laws); and what of work done on the Sabbath by secondary causation, that is, if a man does one thing which may or may not be prohibited, but what he does results in something that is prohibited (*psic reshei*); or, what of work the results of which are something he does not want or which is of no use to him, and, therefore, could not have been intended by him? Which type of work may one ask a Gentile to do for us and which may one not ask? All these and many more principles, which one would imagine to have been definitely defined and delimited long ago, nevertheless still come up for re-analysis and re-definition.

A recent responsum which goes deeply into a re-discussion of some of these principles is a curious one written in Zurich, Switzerland, in 1939, and appropriately concerns the new type of watch made nowadays in that country. Rabbi Mordecai Jacob Breisch, of Zurich, Switzerland, was asked in behalf of Rabbi Solomon Baumgarten, formerly of Vienna and now in London, whether one may wear on the Sabbath a wristwatch of the new type which winds itself automatically by the mere natural and unintended motions of the hands. One can easily see that this question could well be used as a starting point for a reconsideration of many of the principles of Sabbath work; and, indeed, Rabbi Breisch has four full pages of careful re-analysis of some of them.

In talmudic times, they naturally had no spring-watches and, therefore, an analogy to the type of work involved must be found in some other kind of labor mentioned in the Talmud. The Mishna [13] states that, if a string of the harp used by a Levite in the Temple service should break, it may be tied together even though this occurs on the Sabbath. The Talmud [14] describes the process of tying the strings and concludes that a knot would prevent the string from giving its clear tone and thus make it unusable for the Temple services. Therefore, another method of repair is suggested, which is more fully described by Rashi's commentary to this passage. He says that, in the Temple on the Sabbath, the Levite whose harp string broke may unwind the upper peg until a new length of string reaches the lower peg and then start winding up the lower peg until the string is tightened. The procedure is a sufficiently close approximation to the winding up of a watch. But while this sort of work is permitted in the Temple, outside of the Temple (that is, not for the purpose of maintaining the Temple service) such work is not permitted on the Sabbath.

On this basis, it becomes clear that winding a watch is not permitted on the Sabbath. This is definitely stated (on the basis of Rashi's comment) in the code *Hayyei Adam*.[15] Rabbi

Breisch, beginning with this clear prohibition against winding a clock or a watch on the Sabbath, goes into the question of whether a Christian may be asked to wind the clock. This question depends upon the nature of the work involved. Is it a Torah-based prohibition and, therefore, to be observed undeviatingly; or is it a rabbinically-based safeguard and, therefore, susceptible to more lenient interpretation. He finally indicates, on the basis of previous authorities, that a Gentile may be asked to wind up a watch that is still going but not one that has run down, because the latter would involve much more work and is in the stricter category.

Now as to the modern self-winding wristwatch: the work of winding is not consciously done and, therefore, that too can be looked upon with some leniency. Although he does not quite put it in these words, what he says seems to amount to this: that what may be consciously told to the Gentile to do, with regard to a clock or a watch on the Sabbath, may without conscious attention be done, as it were incidentally, by a Jew himself on the Sabbath. Therefore, he comes to the conclusion, after his long and learned analysis, that it is permitted to wear that self-winding watch if it is still going (when put on); but if it had run down, it should not be put on on the Sabbath day.

The Fore-edged Book

Among the luxurious ornamentations produced by the bookbinder's art is the skillful painting of pictures on the front edge of the book or on the top or bottom edge. These pictures are visible when the book is closed and invisible when the book is open, just as the gilt on the top edge of a book is visible when the book is closed and not visible when the book is open. Sometimes such pictures are so cunningly made that they appear when the front edge is spread first in one and then in the opposite direction.

Apparently such fore-edged paintings used to be made also on Hebrew books, because Moses Sofer, the son of Simon Sofer, has a responsum about them.[16] He asks whether it is permitted on the Sabbath to open such a book. Does not opening the book destroy or disperse the picture or the writing, while closing the book restores the picture or the writing? He considers this question not only important enough to deserve his own careful consideration, but puts it to the famous Shalom Mordecai Schwadron.

The question was not without precedent. In fact, Moses Isserles, in the sixteenth century, had a responsum on this subject, or, at least, on a subject closely analagous to it.[17] Apparently, Moses Isserles did not have such luxury-books with landscapes painted on the fore-edge, but it *was* the custom for people to write words, possibly the title or their names, on the top edge of the book or on the front—words which would be legible when the book was tightly closed and disappeared when the book was opened. Isserles was asked whether such a book may be opened or closed on the Sabbath, because that would certainly seem equivalent to erasing and writing words. The question has left a considerable record in legal literature. There is a full discussion of it by two of the classic commentators on the *Shulhan Arukh*, *Magen David* and *Magen Abraham*,[18] and also a decision in the later code, *Hayyei Adam*.

Moses Sofer, who raises the question in modern times with regard to the pictures painted on the fore-edges and top of a book, makes use of the arguments of his predecessors and comes to a conclusion in which the permissiveness of law is balanced by punctillious piety.

The law goes back to the Mishna,[19] as to whether it is permitted to write with the finger in dust on the Sabbath. This is non-enduring writing and the Mishna considers one free from punishment if he does so. But this is understood to mean that, while he is free from punishment, he still should not do it. The *Shulhan Arukh* therefore [20] puts the law on evanescent writing cautiously: "One must take care not to write in the dust on the Sabbath." The commentator, *Magen Abraham* is careful to add that if, however, one does so, he is free from punishment.

The writing or the picture on a fore-edged book can be described as temporary writing, since it disappears and returns when the book is opened or closed. But, after noting that fact, both Isserles and the commentator, *Magen David*, say that the "erasing" or the "writing" involved in the opening or the closing of a book should be judged even more leniently than the writing in dust (which is non-punishable), because the man writing in the dust *intends* to write in the dust, but the man who opens and closes the book has no intention at all with regard to destroying or forming the letters. He merely is concerned with using the book. Besides, Isserles adds, the letters are not actually being erased or written when the book is opened or closed. They are always there; opening or closing the book merely brings together separate parts.

The code, *Hayyei Adam*, is also quoted by Moses (b. Simon) Sofer in his responsum, as it is in all these earlier authorities. The *Hayyei Adam*[21] clearly says that there is no erasing or writing involved in opening or closing such a book. Moses Sofer, in summing up the situation, says that, while it is clear to him that there is no prohibition in opening or closing a fore-edged book, still, out of piety, he would prefer people to be strict in the matter; and he expresses the well-known maxim, "He who is stricter, blessing cometh upon him." He ends by suggesting that it would be better to suggest to the bookbinder to avoid the letters or decorations on the ends or the fore-edges of books, but to use solid colors.

Thumb-Prints on the Sabbath

The practice of taking thumb-prints from recruits in the European army appears in the responsa literature about 1935. The European armies were not concerned with what day of the week the recruits were registered; and so it often happened that pious Jewish young men were registered on the Sabbath. Therefore, the question came up as to whether the thumb-prints which each recruit was required to make do not constitute a violation of the Sabbath. This question was answered by Aaron Walkin of Pinsk-Carlin in 1935.[22] It was also answered in 1937 by Nachum Weidenfeld of Dombrova.[23]

The problem involved is whether the law which prohibits writing on the Sabbath prohibits also the making of illegible marks
and smudges. The law goes back, as many of the laws of Sabbath
work do, to the work done in setting up and taking down the
Tabernacle in the wilderness. The beams by which the Tabernacle was held together had to be marked when the Tabernacle
was taken apart. How were they marked so that each beam could
be re-joined at the next encampment with the one to which it
fitted? One opinion holds that Hebrew letters were used: thus
aleph and *aleph*, etc., to mark the two that belonged together.
Others (Rabbi Jose) believed that mere marks were made,
strokes, and the like. These marks were permitted in the Tabernacle, but not permitted outside on the Sabbath. Therefore, the
rabbis who believed that letters were used, argued that the writing of even two letters was specifically prohibited, while the
mere making of marks was only secondarily prohibited. Rabbi
Jose would say that the making of marks on the Sabbath was a
primary prohibition. This is expressed in the law in the Mishna [24]
as follows: He who writes two letters on the Sabbath violates the
Law; and Rabbi Jose says he who makes marks on the Sabbath
violates the Law.

Maimonides [25] follows the majority of the rabbis and says
that it is legible writing which is primarily prohibited. However,
even making a smudge is prohibited, though only secondarily, by
derivation from writing.

Aaron Walkin then says that thumb-prints are certainly prohibited, because they are more than mere smudges. A man makes
many lines and patterns with his thumb-print. It is a complete
picture and, as a matter of fact, since it has become a widespread
means of identification, the thumb-print can be looked upon as
actual writing and certainly is prohibited on the Sabbath.

In spite of the fact that Walkin makes it clear that a thumb-
print is prohibited on the Sabbath, he nevertheless concludes that
thumb-printing, as it is actually carried out during the induction
of a recruit, does not violate the Sabbath for the Jewish recruit.
He bases this opinion on the statement in Maimonides [26] that, if
a man holds the pen and a child guides the man's hand, the man

is innocent of violating the Sabbath by the sin of writing because it is the guiding of the hand that counts. In the thumb-printing at the induction, the Christian officer holds the thumb of the Jewish recruit and presses it into the dye and then onto the paper. Hence, the Jewish recruit does not violate the Sabbath.

Nahum Weidenfeld deals with the question in virtually the same way as Aaron Walkin, but finds some additional grounds for leniency, namely, that the recruit does not make this mark willingly, but out of fear of punishment; and the material used to make the mark is not really ink, but a species of dye or paint; but finally the permission is based upon the fact that the Christian officer guides the hand of the Jewish soldier.

Pouring Out the Soda Water

Sometimes in the legal literature, an issue comes up which would hardly be considered a legal question in other systems of law. It would be rather a question of taste or spiritual attitude. But such questions do come up often in the responsa because the talmudic literature, upon which Jewish Law is based, is in itself a mixture of the legal, the spiritual and folkloristic. When the folkloristic questions arise, the arguments or proofs are generally based upon the midrashic or aggadic parts of the older literature. The same careful analysis which is applied to the strictly legal questions is applied to these matters as well.

The *Shulhan Arukh* [27] says that it is customary, when a person dies in the house, to pour out all the drawn water. Upon this custom was based a curious inquiry by Joseph Schwartz, which led to a strange discussion on the part of scores of his colleagues. In his rabbinic magazine, *Va-Yelaket Yosef*,[28] he says that the *Shulhan Arukh*, recording our customs, speaks of pouring out *all* water in a house when someone dies there. Should not this custom be extended in modern times to pouring out the glasses of soda water that may have been on the table at the time of the death? He himself makes a preliminary analysis of the matter. He says that the answer to this question depends upon what is the purpose behind the custom of pouring out the water. The commentator to the *Shulhan Arukh*, Sabbatai Cohen,[29] gives two reasons, one that might be described as social and the other as folkloristic. The first is that pouring out the water was the method of informing the neighbors that a person had died. This avoids the necessity of going around and spreading the sad news. If that is the reason, then pouring out the ordinary water is quite sufficient to spread the information (and the soda water need not be wasted). The second reason, somewhat magical in nature, was the folk belief that the Angel of Death washed his sword in the water and therefore all the water is dangerous and must be poured out for safety's sake. Schwartz first concludes that only the first reason applies, namely, informing the neighbors. This he derives (quoting his father) from some of the aggadic material in the Talmud. The Talmud says [30] that Miriam— like Moses, her brother, later—was one of the privileged people who die "by the kiss of God," that is, without the intervention of the Angel of Death. Now the Bible says (Numbers 20, 1-2) that, when Miriam died, the people lacked water. This was evidently due to the fact that they poured it out at her death, as was the custom. Since, then, the Angel of Death was not involved in her case, for she died by the Divine Kiss, then the pouring out of the water could only have been to inform everybody of her death. Therefore, the pouring out of a certain amount of water is sufficient and the soda water need not be poured out.

However, towards the end of the discussion, he reverts to the belief that the second reason (the Angel leaving blood) is also important and therefore ends uncertainly. He asks other scholars to give their judgment.

In later numbers of this magazine,[31] two famous scholars take up this question. Shalom Mordecai Schwadron, the Galician authority, says that there is no real basis for this custom in the works of the earlier authorities; but certainly there is a legal objection to wasting and destroying things unnecessarily (*bal tashhit*). For example, hot water should not be poured out because this involves a waste of the fuel, which went into the heating of the water. Pouring out the soda water would certainly be an unjustified waste and a violation of the prohibition "thou shalt not destroy."

Benjamin Weiss believes that both reasons for the custom (the spreading of information and the sword of the Angel) are correct. But since this is only a traditional custom, we follow in such cases the exact words handed down in the tradition. The words from former times describing this custom speak of "water" and not "soda water," and we should not go beyond that. Therefore it is not necessary to pour out soda water found in a room where a person dies. This rather unimportant discussion of a folk-custom for some reason awakened the interest of many of the scholarly minds and scores of answers were received on it.

The Hypnotized Shohet

One of the discussions which run through the entire legal literature from talmudic times down to our day, is the question of the relation between the inner attitude (*kavvana*) and the outer action in performing the commandments (*mitzvot*) required of each person.

If a person fulfills a commandment automatically—if, for example, he mutters the blessing over the bread without paying any attention to what he is saying—is he truly fulfilling the commandment? In other words, do the commandments require conscious attention and intention (*im mitzvot tzerikhot kavvana*)? This widely discussed subject has been more or less decided as follows: Those commandments that involve words can easily become automatic; therefore, the recital of the more familiar prayers *do* require *kavvana*, intention, in order to keep them from degenerating into a recital by rote. Those commandments, however, which require action, like building the *succah*, do not require conscious and direct intention, because the effort in itself is an expression of intention. However, if the act, though requiring effort, is such as to be ambiguous in its purpose, in other words, if one can perform the act for either one purpose or another, then such an act requires direct attention. Thus, a Scroll may be written for use in the synagogue service or only for school purposes. If it is written for the synagogue, the scribe must consciously declare his intention that the names of God are hereby written as sacred.

With all this past discussion in mind, Joseph Schwartz [32] asks this curious question: If a ritual slaughterer, a *shohet*, is put under hypnosis and, while under hypnosis, is directed to slaughter an animal, is the animal so slaughtered kasher or not? What is, of course, involved is the question whether ritual slaughtering, *shehita*, requires conscious intention or not. If it does, this is not a kasher slaughtering, because it is actually the intention of the hypnotizer, not of the hypnotized *shohet*, which is directing the act.

The *Shulhan Arukh*,[33] however, says that *shehita* does not require conscious intention (*kavvana*), but it does require effort, "the strength of a man." If, for example, a man throws a knife, without the intention of slaughtering the animal, and by accident the knife strikes it and makes the kind of cut required, the slaughtering is kasher since conscious intention is not required. If, however, instead of throwing the knife with strength, the knife falls from his hand and happens to strike an animal standing below him, it is not a kasher slaughtering, because we require the effort, "the strength of the man." Therefore, Joseph Schwartz is inclined to believe that although the *shohet* is under the influence of the hypnotist, still, he is not quite so mechanical an automaton as could be described in terms [34] of "doing merely the imitative act of a monkey." He has at least some awareness (he does not need too much awareness, since *kavvana* is not required) and he certainly is aware of using "the strength of a man."

The question is taken up by Jechiel M. Fried,[35] in the same volume, who says that the man under hypnosis is certainly somewhat dazed and may be compared to a confused, partially insane man who *may* slaughter if watched.[36] Or he may be considered to be like a drunken person. Then it depends how deeply drunk the person is, or, in this case, how deeply he is hypnotized. Furthermore, while it is true that slaughtering itself does not require conscious intention, still the recitation of the blessing over the slaughtering *does* require conscious intention. It is, therefore, a question whether this hypnotized person, like a drunken person, can recite the blessing with sufficient awareness. But even so, only a person who habitually omits or neglects the blessing may not slaughter, and we are not dealing here with a man habitually hypnotized. Jechiel Fried concludes that, as long as the man is not merely "performing the imitative deeds of a monkey," but has *some* consciousness of what he is doing, the slaughtering is kasher.

Selling a Portion of Paradise

May a man sell, here, on earth, a portion of his reward in Paradise? This curious question has come up a number of times in the responsa of the last generation. Aaron ben Mayer Gordon, rabbi in New York, discusses it in his responsa *Eben Meir*.[37] He begins with a reference to the Talmud [38] where there is a debate on the question of how much reward people get for command-ments observed. The conclusion is that there is no such reward on earth, which indicates that the reward will be obtained in Paradise; so that, while we are still on earth, the rewards are not in our possession.

The *Shulhan Arukh* [39] states it as law that a man may not sell something which is not yet in existence. He may not sell or give as a gift, for example, the offspring of a cow that has not yet given birth, or fruit that has not yet appeared on the tree. The author of the responsum continues to analyze the sale of things that do not exist or are not clearly definable as to quantity, and the like. He then goes on to a more directly relevant statement in the Talmud.[40] A discussion is reported there about brothers of whom one is engaged in business, the other in studying Torah. Can the merit attained by the one studying the Torah be trans-ferred to the businessman who does not study Torah? The third case cited is the telling one. Hillel and Shavna were brothers. Hillel studied Torah and Shavna engaged in business. Finally Shavna said to Hillel, "Let's pool our acquisitions and divide the profit," in other words, each will get half of the money and half of the spiritual reward. But this suggestion was countered by the verse in the Song of Songs (8.7): "If a man would offer all the substance of his house for love, he would be utterly contemned" (in other words, Paradise, like love, cannot be purchased). The respondent concludes that "One who mockingly sells his portion in the world to come, thereby shows clearly that he is a wicked man and has no portion of Paradise to sell."

The author knows that he is not discussing a serious question in the Law, and yet he is quite serious about discussing it. The motivation is clear enough. There were many mocking skeptics, eager to demonstrate that they had no faith in the religious promises of life after death. The way they demonstrated it was to offer to sell for very little whatever portions they had. He ends his rather sad responsum with this thesis:

> Although it should not have been necessary to put this question in writing, yet, because purchasers and sellers of Paradise have increased these days, because, God pity us, they despise the Law and say, "There is neither Divine justice nor Judge," and they consequently sell their portion of the world to come; therefore I felt it necessary to tell a man that this is no genuine transaction even if the purchaser is sincere. May God guard us from these light-minded ones and put into our heart the will to serve Him in truth.

The idea of selling one's portion in the world to come has a very ancient background. Esau, who sold his birthright to Jacob, is described in the Midrash [41] as selling, not only his earthly birthright, but also his portion in Paradise. In other words, that wicked man, Esau, the prototype of all the wicked, openly declared that he did not believe in the world to come and therefore sold his eternal birthright.

Insurance for Wages Lost During Seven Days of Mourning

The various benefit lodges that grew up in America, particularly among the immigrants, have left a number of traces in the responsa literature. Among the benefits were those by which a certain amount of money was paid to a member if he lost wages through sickness, or to his family for his funeral expenses, and the like. Some of these lodges offered a strange-sounding benefit to pious Jewish workmen: if one of them lost a close relative and, as a result, had to stay home and mourn for seven days (shiv'a), the lodge provided a benefit payment to reimburse him for the seven days work that he lost. It is on this type of insurance that a question was raised and its answer given in *Eben Meir*," [42] by Aaron ben Mayer Gordon. The specific question was this:

Suppose the death occurs on the day before the holiday. According to the laws of mourning, the need to mourn for seven days is then suspended by the intervention of the holiday. The person then mourns formally for one hour (sits shiv'a) and does not need to mourn for the rest of the seven days. Now, the benefit insurance promised by the lodge was for seven days; the man mourned only one hour. Is the lodge required to pay for the seven days of mourning? In other words, is it the member or the lodge that benefits from the intervention of the Jewish calendar?

In answering this question, the author refers to the *Shulhan Arukh*,[43] where there is a general discussion about a workman hired to water a garden. Nature intervenes: an unexpected rain waters the garden adequately without the workman's effort. Shall we say that the man was hired to water the garden and the garden is now adequately watered and he should be paid? Or, shall we say that he was hired to do the watering and, since he did not do it, he should not be paid? The *Shulhan Arukh* there makes a clear distinction based upon earlier law, that it depends upon the nature of the contract between the two men. If the worker was a hired workman, specifically to be paid for this work, he does not get any wages if the rain did the work. But if he is, for example, a sharecropper (aris) who is paid, or who pays, by a portion of the crop, then he is really a partner and both sides must share in the benefit that nature may bring.

The question in this case, therefore, is whether the lodge members are partners or not? And he concludes that they are partners, because they all share profit and loss. Since the member is a partner, like the sharecropper, he must be paid for the benefit which the calendar brings him.

The well-known maxim, *de minimis non curat lex*, "The Law is not concerned with trifles," may be a true statement of a general principle, but is certainly not a correct description of actual practice. In actual experience, the Law is always concerned with what may appear to be trifles. A legal discussion may begin with broad principles, but soon the application of the principles leads to refined distinctions, careful differentiations and most meticulous attention to details. Most of the literary lampoons against lawyers refer to their excessive concern with definitions and their willingness and tendency to make much ado about matters of little consequence. This is an inevitable development; for the Law is concerned with the organization of actual living, and life itself consists of a multitude of minimals. Disagreements often come down to a word used or omitted or an apparently minor action which may reveal larger intention.

While Jewish Law is based on broad principles, constituting in ultimate meaning the revealed will of God governing human life, in real practice it comes down to sharp definitions, careful limitations and the tiniest of details. The ability of the Law to handle the smallest details is in itself an evidence of its versatility as an instrument, as it is also an inevitable outcome of the endless quest for definiteness and precision.

One does not get a complete picture of the responsa literature, therefore, unless he notes the trivial matter which it discusses. There are, as has been indicated, some very curious and apparently insignificant subjects which are debated in this literature; but precisely in these minimals, in these little, unimportant matters, does the Law reveal its skill and its willingness to deal with every detail of life. They reveal also the mood of the students of the Law, which occupied the mind and developed the intelligence of a good proportion of each community. These legal studies were the expression of their duty, the shield of their social order, the climate of their intellectual growth and also the theme of their mental relaxation.

8

---◆---

PROSPECTIVE
DEVELOPMENT
OF THE
RESPONSA
LITERATURE

THE MIDRASH refers to the patriarch Jacob as "Old Israel." Later rabbinic writers borrowed this phrase and used it as descriptive of the Jewish people which has been aged by harsh experience as well as by the passing of time. But Heinrich Graetz, the classical Jewish historian, thought of Jewry in other terms. In 1864, he wrote an essay entitled, *The Rejuvenescence of the Jewish People*. To him the true glory of Jewish history lies in the fact that Jewry has been able to attain age without senility. Time and again its "youth is renewed like the eagle," so that after centuries of living it is still dynamic and creative.

The rejuvenescence of which Graetz spoke is evident in many fields of Jewish self-expression, particularly in the rabbinic literature which, as an elaboration of the Talmud, has itself endured for fifteen centuries. It is remarkable that talmudic studies, which after all are based upon one specific literature, have been able to endure, proliferate and, even in our day, produce new *hiddushim*—analyses, problems and solutions.

This continuing creativity is evident especially in the responsa literature. The history of this literature shows a constant succession of dimming and brightening, aging and renewal. The Spanish sequence, which included Solomon b. Adret, Isaac b. Sheshet and Simon Duran, slowly faded in North Africa. The Rhineland sequence began in France with Rabbenu Tam, continued with Meir of Rothenburg and Israel Bruna, and faded out in Vienna with Israel Isserlein. The Levantine group, including David ibn Zimra in Cairo, continuing with Levi ibn Habib, Jacob Berab, Joseph Caro in Palestine, and with Elijah Mizrachi, Samuel di Medina and Joseph ibn Leb in Turkey, finally faded into the work of lesser men. The Polish center was bright with such luminaries as Moses Isserles, Solomon Luria and Meir of Lublin. The Hungarian epoch added the names of Meir Eisenstadt, Moses Sofer, Judah Assad, Moses Mintz and Eliezar Deutsch of Bonyhad. The second Galician era included the honored names of Joseph Saul Nathanson, Solomon Kluger, later Isaac Schmelkes and finally Shalom Mordecai Schwadron. Russian Jewry, though greater in other rabbinic fields than in practical responsa, nevertheless contributed the works of Hayyim of Volozhin, Menahem-Mendel of Lubovitz and Isaac Elhanan Spektor.

The production of responsa literature is thus seen never to have been quite steady or continuous. It always faded away in every land after one or two generations of activity. Then followed a period of quiescence, which, however, did not last for more than a generation or two. In some new country, or even in the same land (as in Poland), responsa activity revived and came to a new flowering often as splendid as that of the preceding era.

For the last twenty-five years, the responsa literature has been in a state of comparative quiescence. Some books of responsa have been published, but many of them deal with theoretical questions of talmudic problems, and are in the nature of learned correspondence between specialist scholars rather than practical answers to urgent questions derived from life's experience. Certainly there are no respondents of great stature in our day. There is no one who would be the "court of last resort" (*posek aharon*) as Isaac Elhanan Spektor, or Shalom Mordecai Schwadron, or Meir of Lublin, or Solomon ben Adret were in their day. Can the fading responsa literature come again to a new flowering as it has frequently done in the past?

One cannot safely reason from analogy in this matter. This age is considerably different from preceding ages of change. The succession of two world wars in one generation, the irresistible penetration of the modern spirit into every corner of life even in the remotest parts of the globe, the mass attack on the physical life of world Jewry, the political changes due to the establishment of the State of Israel—all these factors have created unprecedented conditions of life and new moods in world Jewry. One may not predict therefore with any degree of confidence that any branch of Jewish literature, even though it may have revived many times in the past, will necessarily or even probably revive in these revolutionary times. What then are the prospects, if any, for further development or even substantial continuation of the historic responsa literature?

The vigor of the responsa literature depends primarily upon the vitality of Jewish religious life. As long as observant Jewish life continues substantially as it has for centuries, and the people adhere to the inherited laws and customs, then the varied circumstances of a widespread religious society are bound to produce a constant stream of questions. But as soon as religious life retreats from a certain field of experience, that field immediately disappears from practical religious Law and, therefore, from the responsa literature. A listing of the types of questions asked and answered in any generation or in any land would reveal which field in Jewish Law or ritual was the most intensely cultivated in that time and place. Likewise, if we notice the fields in which fewer and fewer questions are asked, we can learn e silentio where Jewish observance is fading away.

For centuries the responsa of all the lands were dominated by questions of civil law—problems concerning partnerships, contracts, etc. But during the last century such questions have virtually disappeared from the literature. This is simply a reflection of the fact that the Jewish communities are no longer self-contained and self-sufficient; that Jews no longer bring their business disputes to their own Jewish courts, but to secular courts. There are no civil law responsa nowadays, because there are virtually no questions of civil law brought to the rabbis. A vast field of Jewish observance has thus died out, and the responsa literature reflects the change.

If there is further modern shrinkage in observance, there will be further narrowing of the field of responsa. In the twelfth-thirteenth centuries, Isaiah di Trani, the Elder, expressed great concern in his unpublished responsa as to the religious situation in Greek Jewry—a powerful and influential Jewry in those days.[1] He denounces the communities and their leaders for the almost complete neglect of the laws of ritual bathing for women (*mikvah*). This neglect was overcome in later times, and for many centuries the ritual bath and the practices involved in ritual bathing occasioned literally thousands of responsa.

There is little doubt that the observance of ritual bathing has again fallen into wide disuse in America. Will it be revived as it was revived in the Greek community seven centuries ago? One cannot predict; it certainly seems to be a harder task to re-establish in the life of modern women this meticulous ancient ritual whose observance or non-observance affects the intimacies of family life. If the ritual bathing is not revived, or until it *is* revived, a section of the responsa literature will have faded away.

So it is with many other fields of religious observances. A modern manufacturer having a government contract, which necessitates work being done on the Sabbath, is not likely to inquire, as his predecessors had inquired, how this contract may be carried out under Jewish law; what sort of arrangement may be made with non-Jewish partners for them to be responsible, or how to avoid profiting from the work on the Sabbath. In business life, Sabbath observance has diminished, and with it a vast area of responsa activity.

The responsa of Isaac Elhanan Spektor and of many of his contemporaries a century ago were filled with questions concerning the *aguna*, the woman "chained" by the fact that her husband has disappeared and there is no adequate evidence of his death. She cannot be divorced or declared to be widowed. The rabbis exerted great efforts either to trace the missing husbands or, by ingenious responsa, to free the "chained" wife. The multiplicity of the responsa in those days was a reflection of the vast immigration to America,[2] thousands of families breaking up as a consequence.

In our times, due to Nazi mass-murder and the war, there has been a greater and more catastrophic break-up of family life because of the disappearance of husbands. Yet there has been no noticeable increase in publication of responsa on the *aguna* question. Evidently fewer questions are now being asked. More and more young women must be accepting the decisions of the civil courts and obtaining their freedom without recourse to the more difficult Jewish law. The appearance of many *aguna* questions a century ago was in essence a sociological fact; but the *disappearance* of the *aguna* question today is a religious fact.

The crucial element in the future of the responsa is the observance of Jewish Law. We are in a period of widespread non-observance and, as a consequence, millions of Jewish men and women are not even aware of such religious questions as would surely have come up for answer if they had been more observant.

There are, of course, many responsa which are not dependent upon the questions which arise from the daily experience of the people. A fair proportion of the responsa are merely exchange of letters between scholars. They have generally nothing to do with practical problems. They are disagreements as to the analysis of classical texts, or over attempts to harmonize the opinions of past scholars; or they constitute discussions of the rules rather than cases of the Law. These technical responsa are written nowadays in fair number. The rabbinical magazines have more of them than of practical responsa. Yet even the continuation of such theoretical responsa depends upon the existence of a large body of men trained in the disciplines of rabbinic literature. The mass-murder of European Jewry meant the destruction of a great human reservoir of learning. The continuity of rabbinic studies which had lasted for centuries has been broken. One cannot know whether efforts now exerted in America and in Israel will succeed in developing a large enough group of rabbinic scholars, out of which may emerge men who can write responsa in the classical manner.

At present, with widespread non-observance, and the shrinkage of rabbinic study, the prospects for substantial continuation of the responsa literature are not promising. For the time being "there is no voice (to ask) and no one answering."

A rabbi will answer all religious questions put to him, but he will not record his answer unless the problem involves some new situation or a new phase of an old situation. If it is an old question, it is already recorded in the codes and he simply refers to the relevant section. It is only when something new comes up, which is therefore not dealt with in the codes, that he feels justified in working up and writing out the answer. The responsa literature is, by intention at least, always original, or a reflection of new circumstances.

It is this insistence upon novelty that carries hope for the further development of the literature. While it may be true that the questioners are few and the responders still fewer, nevertheless the objective conditions for new responsa are definitely better. The whole modern world is new and different; people live an entirely different life from that of their grandparents. Inventions and new types of social organization force new problems to the attention even of the unwilling.[3] Medical science has adopted radically new procedures and these inevitably bring up new problems. The average pious Jew may generally have very few questions to ask, but when a member of his family is now hospitalized questions come up that never arose before. May the patient receive blood from other people? skin? bones? May the cornea taken from the dead be used for the benefit of the living? These and a host of other problems, which never could have arisen before in their present form, almost force a resort to responsa and constitute a spur to new responsa writing. The organization of the younger Orthodox rabbis in America, which normally would leave the writing of responsa to the older, European-born rabbi, feels compelled to have its own responsa committee because of the host of new questions which press for a solution.

Besides the new inventions and methods which impel the writing of responsa, there are new groups who are turning toward the study and to the writing of responsa. The Conservative movement surely did not contemplate at first the need for any responsa coming from their group. The first significant work of the Conservative rabbinate in this field was the keen and warm-hearted essays by Rabbi Louis Epstein on the *aguna* problem. His suggestion was that, at the time of the marriage, the husband appoint the wife to be his agent, so that in case he should disappear, she, as his representative, could appear before a rabbinical court and in his name ask that a divorce be granted. Although this proposal was buttressed by brilliant analyses of the relevant talmudic and post-talmudic texts in the classical responsa style, neither Louis Epstein nor his colleagues meant to put this proposal into effect unless and until the Orthodox rabbinate passed its judgment upon it. They were not at the time ready for independent writing of responsa.

When, however, the Orthodox rabbinate indignantly rejected this suggested solution of the *aguna* problem, the Conservative rabbinate began to move toward independence in the responsa field. A new and growing interest in the literature began to manifest itself among them, and in the last few years an impressive number of books have been written making wide use of the literature. Histories have been written based largely on responsa material. The biographies of a number of the great respondents based upon their responsa appeared. More historical and biographical studies of the literature have appeared in recent years than ever before; and almost all of them by Conservative rabbis.

In addition to writing *about* the responsa, actual responsa are beginning to appear from Conservative Judaism. The mood of these responsa is, of course, different from most of the Orthodox responsa, though the material and the literary method is the same. The spirit of Conservative responsa was indicated some time ago by Boaz Cohen in the introduction to his invaluable *Kuntres ha-Teshubot* ("Index to the Responsa"). They turn to the earlier respondents, whose decisions are not yet hedged about by the cautionary safeguards of the more recent decisors. When they come to deal with the problems of the Sabbath, they will in all likelihood turn to the modern Sephardic respondents (as for example Joseph Messas of Tlemcen, I. M. Toledano formerly of Cairo, and now of Tel Aviv), who are astonishingly liberal as to the use of modern methods of transportation.

Perhaps still more surprising is the rapidly growing interest of the Reform rabbinate in the responsa. The Reform movement, unlike the Conservative, began with an open revolt against the authority of the Orthodox rabbinate and its right to determine every detail of worship and ritual. A movement which rejects the legal authority of the codes and the rabbinical responsa would hardly be expected to move toward a study or use of the legal literature. Yet this is exactly what has happened. The Central Conference of American Rabbis (Reform) has had a Responsa Committee almost from its very beginning in 1889. Its work was rather sporadic until the chairmanship of Jacob Z. Lauterbach, who encouraged the asking of legal questions and who answered with responsa in the classical style. His responsum on the wearing of the hat or on birth control were in the traditional manner, but not, of course, in the Orthodox spirit. The decisions are liberal and permissive with due regard to traditional sentiment. In general, the Reform movement, in turning again to the responsa, is inclined to use them as a general guide rather than as authoritative law. This is the mood of the most recent books by Reform rabbis in the field.[4]

An interesting result of this growing activity on the part of the Conservative and Reform rabbinate is the cooperation in military responsa by Orthodox, Conservative and Reform rabbis. Since the beginning of World War II, the Division of Religious Activities of the National Jewish Welfare Board has succeeded in producing almost one hundred responsa acceptable to all three cooperating groups. Some of these were issued for the use of chaplains, under the title, *Responsa in War Time*. Of course, the fact that these responsa were not meant for civilians, but only for the restricted field of military life, made it somewhat easier to achieve this unusual unanimity in the delicate and difficult field of Jewish Law.

A strong impulse toward the study and the writing of responsa will come from the new State of Israel. It is not that the State is a merger of "Church" and State. It seems certain that the new State will guarantee freedom of religion, not only as between Jews, Moslems and Christians, but as to all varieties of Jewish observance. Yet a great and new activity in responsa is bound to come from the Orthodox leadership in Israel. This activity will revive interest in some sections of the responsa which have fallen into neglect.

The Jewish civil law, which faded in the last century, becomes suddenly of immediate importance. At present the civil law in Israel is, necessarily, a makeshift. The lawyer and the judge must be acquainted with English Law because of influences remaining from the days of the British Mandate; he must know Jewish Law and also some Moslem Law. Yet it is inconceivable that as Israeli Law develops and integrates, the traditional Jewish civil Law as embodied in the codes and developed in the responsa will not exert a deep influence. There are already beginnings of careful scientific study of the traditional Law as to its availability and applicability to modern conditions. What, for example (to cite an actual responsum) has traditional Law to contribute to labor problems and collective bargaining?

The establishment of the State of Israel may also add an entirely new section of laws to the responsa literature. Actually these laws themselves are very old, but they had never become part of the literature. The Bible contains many laws governing agriculture. These were codified in the Mishna. They include laws of the harvest, requiring that harvesting never be quite complete, that gleanings and the corner of the field be left for the poor. There is also the law forbidding any agriculture at all every seventh year, and more of the same. These laws apply only to agriculture in Palestine. Since the responsa literature developed chiefly during the diaspora period, after the Jewish farm population in Palestine had ceased to exist, no questions concerning these Palestinian agricultural laws were asked of the rabbis and, therefore, no responsa appeared.

But now that there are many pious Jewish farmers in Palestine, the old agricultural laws present practical and serious difficulties. In recent years they have begun to appear in the Israeli and other responsa. A recent responsa volume by the Sephardi Chief Rabbi of Israel [5] contains responsa to questions asked by agriculturalists about the prohibition, in the first three years, of fruit from a newly-planted tree (*orlah*). On the troublesome question of letting the land lie fallow on the sabbatical year, he provides an elaborate responsum concerning the new American invention of growing crops in liquid-filled tanks without soil (hydroponics). The question is whether or not such soil-less agriculture may be permitted on the sabbatical year, since the law says "Thou shalt not sow thy field" (Lev. 25.4), and a tank is surely not in the same category as a field. He decides against the use of hydroponics in the sabbatical year. The same volume contains a considerable number of answers to other inquiries from agricultural settlements. Before a decade will have passed there will no doubt be hundreds of agricultural responsa, a subject matter which is entirely new for this literature.

In general, the individualistic mood of the modern personality makes it difficult for a detailed life-controlling legal system to maintain itself extensively. The shrinking area of law observance and of mass study of the ancient literature necessarily results in fewer legal questions being asked and therefore in a diminution of the responsa writing. However, the radical transformation of modernity which, for the present at least, has indeed diminished the old Orthodoxy and has thus shrunk the writing of responsa, is simultaneously bringing about new activity in this field. It is of the essence of responsa to deal with the new and the uncodified. The crowding novelties of inventions and the new situations in the State of Israel are virtually forcing the Jewish rabbinical scholar to deal with practical problems.

The new interest in responsa has in modern times gone beyond the primary purposes of the Law itself. The responsa are now studied with an entirely different end in view than to determine whether or not a certain new food is kasher or whether an electric refrigerator is usable on the Sabbath. Modern scientific research is investigating the responsa as literature for the purpose of adding to history, sociology and other humanistic sciences. The modern interest in history as an outgrowth of social and psychological attitudes, rather than as a sequence of outward events, such as wars and dynastic changes, raises the responsa literature to a position of high importance. Therefore more and more biographies will be written, more of the inner life of Jewish communities will be reconstructed, more of the changing moods of Jewry in various lands will be clearly portrayed, and the course of the majestic stream of Jewish Law will be more accurately charted as it flows through the landscape of general legal thought. This social and psychological knowledge will be found along the banks of the responsa literature which, over the long centuries, has carried with it from its distant sources some of the sacred earth of Sinai, where ultimately it had its origin.

NOTES

INTRODUCTION

1. *Sifron shel Rishonim,* Jerusalem, 1935, p. 60, no. 6.
2. *Entwurf ueber eine Geschichte der Nachtalmudischen Responsen,* Z. Frankel (Jahresbericht Fraenckelscher Stiftung), Breslau, 1865.
3. *L'Korot haYehudim,* Ben Zion Katz, Berlin, 1899.
4. *B'Ohalei Ya'akob,* Simha Assaf, chapter VIII, Jerusalem, 1933. *Die Marranen in der Rabbinischen Literatur,* H. J. Zimmels, Berlin, 1932.
5. *Izvonot.*
6. Samuel Weingarten in *Sinai,* vol. 29, pp. 99 ff.
7. L. Finkelstein, *Jewish Self-Government in the Middle Ages,* New York, 1924. A. A. Neuman, *The Jews in Spain,* Philadelphia, 1942.
8. *The Responsa of Solomon ben Adreth,* Isidore Epstein, London, 1925.
9. *Rabbi Meir of Rothenburg,* Irving A. Agus, Philadelphia, 1942.
10. *Rabbi Isaac ben Sheshet Perfet and His Times,* Abraham M. Hershman, New York, 1943.
11. *The Responsa of Solomon Luria,* Simon Hurwitz, New York, 1938.
12. *Kuntres ha-Teshubot,* Boaz Cohen, Budapest, 1930.

1. ORIGINS AND DEVELOPMENT OF THE RESPONSA
Pp. 21–45

1. See the article, "Roman Law," in *Encyclopedia Brittanica.* For the Mohammedan responsa see Baron, *Social and Religious History of the Jews,* Columbia University Press, first edition, 1938, vol. I, p. 338, and reference in vol. III, p. 81, note 8, especially the bottom of p. 82.
2. b. Temurah 14a to 14b.
3. b. Hullin 95b.
4. b. Baba Bathra 41b.

5. b. Baba Bathra 139a.
6. *Ozar ha-Geonim*, Berakhot, no. 33.
7. *Ozar ha-Geonim*, Berakhot, no. 41.
8. *Ozar ha-Geonim*, Yebamoth, no. 474.
9. *Ozar ha-Geonim*, Berakhot, no. 20.
10. See his biography, Chapter 2, pp. 71 ff., below.
11. See his biography, Chapter 2, pp. 74 ff., below.
12. See his biography, Chapter 2, pp. 76 ff., below.
13. Near the beginning of responsum no. 72.
14. See his biography, Chapter 2, pp. 65 ff., below.
15. See his biography, Chapter 2, pp. 68 ff., below.
16. See Chapter 2, p. 71, below.
17. See pp. 76, 132, below.
18. See his biography, pp. 84 ff., below.
19. See Chapter 2, pp. 87 ff., below.
20. See Chapter 2, pp. 89 ff., below.
21. See Chapter 2, pp. 94 ff., below.
22. See Chapter 2, pp. 96 ff., below.
23. See p. 269, below.

2. THE LEADING RESPONDENTS
Pp. 49–98

1. b. Sanhedrin 5a.
2. Budapest, 1928.
3. *Yad Malachi*, p. 130, no. 40.
4. *Meshib Dabar*, no. 24, end of the responsum.
5. *Zekher Simha*, VIII, end of Introduction. See also Alexander Siskind Kalir about his father, Elazar Kalir, in the introduction to *Heker Halakha*. He says that his father wrote many responsa but did not believe in publishing them.
6. Introduction to "Yore Deah," *Hatam Sofer*, Pressburg, 1841.
7. In the responsa of Isserles, no. 25.
8. *Korei ha-Dorot*, p. 22a, edition Venice, 1746.
9. Responsa, "Yore Deah," nos. 38 and 207.
10. The correspondence which has been published as *Minhat Kenaot*, "The Offering of Jealousy" (or "Zeal").
11. See Chapter 3.
12. Responsum no. 146.
13. *Medieval Jewish Chronicles*, I, 128.
14. See his responsa, no. 388.
15. In his responsa, no. 262, end.
16. *Abkat Rokhel*, no. 73.
17. See his responsa, I, 142, 145; and also his commentary on the Ethics of the Fathers (IV, 5).
18. Cf. Landshuth, *Amudei ha-Abodah*.

19. Meir of Rothenburg's answer is published in the *J.Q.R.*, O.S., VIII, pp. 237 and 527.

20. See Irving A. Agus, *Rabbi Meir of Rothenburg*, Philadelphia, 1947, 2 vols., vol. I, p. 17.

21. Thus, he says (ed. Berlin, p. 165, and Cremona, 192), "It is not my habit to answer the litigants alone nor their relatives."

22. In his responsa "Eben ha-Ezer," no. 155, quoting the opinion of his teacher, Joseph Taitesak (see *Shem ha-Gedolim* under letter "Yod").

23. *Yam shel Shelomo* to Gittin, 4:24.

24. Cf. Responsum no. 161.

25. See Responsum no. 83, and especially Responsum no. 85.

26. See signature to *Abkat Rokhel*, no. 140.

27. See *Responsa of Maharam Lublin*, no. 123 ff.

28. Responsum no. 88.

29. Cf. Emden's *Sefat Emet*.

30. See Chapter 4, below.

31. *The Responsa 'Noda bi-Yehuda' as a Source for Jewish History*, Solomon Windt, New York, 1948.

32. See *Hatam Sofer*, "Yoreh Deah," no. 332.

33. Lemberg, 1827.

34. See *Anshe Shem*, p. 98.

35. See Schwadron's introductory statement to volume I.

36. For Nisan and Iyyar, 5711 (1951).

37. For example, in volume I, no. 120, he says of a certain rabbi: "He did not need to worry quite that much."

3. A SELECTION OF RESPONSA
Pp. 101–146

1. Maimonides' code, the *Mishneh Torah*.

2. *Sefer ha-Yashar*, 48, no. 6.

3. b. Menahos 43b.

4. See Chapter 2, pp. 65 ff., above.

5. Responsa nos. 415 ff.

6. See also Agus, *Rabbi Meir of Rothenburg*, vol. I., p. 279-80. The responsum is found in the Berlin edition of the *Responsa of Meir of Rothenburg*, edited by Moses Bloch, p. 187, no. 80.

7. For a description of the two older types of ordination, see Chapter 7, pp. 25 ff., above.

8. Evidently the emissary who carried the correspondence.

9. See Chapter 5, below.

10. See his Responsa, no. 6.

11. See Chapter 2, above.

12. The responsum is no 47 in volume III of the collection of Duran's responsa (*Tashbetz*).

13. b. Sanhedrin 44a.

14. b. Yebamoth 47b.
15. b. Yebamoth 23a.
16. b. Kiddushin 65b.
17. Baba Bathra, the second chapter, and Kiddushin 59a.
18. See Chapter 2. For Isserlein's letter to Regensburg see his Responsa, vol. II, no. 128.
19. The second chapter of Baba Bathra.
20. See his Responsa, no. 151.
21. See *Hatam Sofer*, "Yoreh Deah," 230.
22. See his biography, Chapter 2, above.
23. b. Baba Metziah 108a.
24. The responsum is no. 4 in his collection (*Maharik*).
25. No. 57 in volume I of the collected responsa of Elijah Mizrahi.
26. b. Abodah Zara 36a.
27. Responsum no. 72.
28. *Terumat ha-Deshen*, no. 10.
29. Chapter 14, no. 12.
30. Leviticus Rabba 27.6.
31. b. Nedarim 30b.
32. b. Sabbath 118b.
33. b. Beza 9a.
34. See Louis Finkelstein, *Jewish Self-Government in the Middle Ages*, N. Y., 1924; A. A. Neumann, *The Jews in Spain*, Philadelphia, 1942; Moses Frank, *Kehillot Ashkenaz u-Battei Dinehem*, Tel Aviv, 1938.
35. See Epstein, *Responsa of R. Solomon b. Adreth*, London, 1925; Epstein, *Responsa of R. Simon ben Zemah Duran*, London, 1930; Hurwitz, *Responsa of Solomon Luria*, N. Y., 1938; Hershman, *Rabbi Isaac Perfet*, N .Y., 1943; I. A. Agus, *Rabbi Meir of Rothenburg*, N. Y., 1948; M. S. Goodblatt, *Jewish Life in Turkey*, N. Y., 1952.
36. Cracow, 16th Century.
37. *Shulhan Arukh*, "Hoshen Mishpat," 281:7, note by Isserles.
38. Responsum no. 3.
39. Responsum no. 49.
40. b. Baba Bathra 158b ff.
41. "Hoshen Mishpat," no. 211.
42. Responsa, Solomon Luria, end of no. 50.
43. m. Gittin I, 1.
44. See pp. 137 ff., 178 ff., below.
45. See article "Judeneide," and the copperplate in *Encyclopedia Judaica*, and "Oath, More Judaico" in the *Jewish Encyclopedia*.
46. See above, Chapter 2, pp. 87 ff.
47. The responsum is in "Yoreh Deah," no. 71 in the first volume of his *Noda bi-Yehudah*.
48. b. Shabbat 115b and 117a.
49. To Babba Kamma IV, in section Boaz.

50. In *Tosafot* to b. Sanhedrin 63b.
51. Chapters 2, pp. 91 ff., and 4, pp. 183 ff.
52. The question is no. 72 and no. 73 in the third section of the first volume of his immense collection of responsa *Sho'el u-Meshib* ("He Asks and Answers").

4. WIDESPREAD DEBATES
Pp. 149–190

1. See the general description of the boycott in *The House of Nasi—Doña Gracia*, by Cecil Roth, Chapter VII.
2. See his responsa, vol. II, no. 54.
3. See Responsa, Rashdam, vol. II, no. 55.
4. *Dibre Ribot*, no. 83.
5. Responsa of Rashdam, vol. II, no. 54.
6. Responsa *Mabit*, vol. I, no. 237.
7. *Nahalah l'Yehoshua*, nos. 39 and 40.
8. In responsum no. 39.
9. No. 40.
10. Eben ha-'Ezer, 121, no. 3.
11. b. Abodah Zarah, 39a.
12. Commentary to Lev. 11. 9.
13. *Noda bi-Yehudah*, vol. II, "Yoreh Deah," no. 28.
14. *Har ha-Mor*, no. 12.
15. See also Chorin's letter in *Kerem Hemed*, II, no. 11.
16. "Yoreh Deah," 29 and 30.
17. See his responsa, *Teshuba meAhabah*, III, no. 329.
18. See *Hagahot Asheri* to Abodah Zara 39 ff.
19. P. 3a, in the note.
20. b. Sota 48a.
21. Author of the responsa *Piske Recanati ha-Aharonim*.
22. Cf. above, p.
23. Sota VII, 1.
24. b. Sota 33a.
25. "The Shield of Abraham," by Abraham Gumbiner 1635–1683, a leading commentator on the *Shulhan Arukh*.
26. *Eleh Dibrei haB'rit*, Altona, 1819.
27. *Darstellung u.s.w.*, Breslau, 1842.
28. *Rabbinische Gutachten u.s.w.*, 1842–3.
29. Cf. *Hokhmat Shelomo* no. 2, by Solomon Quetsch of Nikolsburg; published at the end of *Har ha-Mor*, the responsa of Mordecai Benet.
30. *Bet Ephraim*, "Orah Hayyim" nos. 56, 57.
31. *Yad Elazar* no. 57, p. 33.
32. *Hokhmat Shelomo* no. 2.
33. Responsa of Maharam Schick, no. 326.

34. *Sho'el u-Meshib*, part III, section 1, no. 144 and part IV, section 2, no. 126.
35. *Zemach Zedek*, no. 64.
36. *Dibre Nehemiah*, no. 50.
37. *Nahalat Ya'acob*.
38. Cf. Ephraim Deinard, *The War of the Lord Against Amalek*, Newark, 1892.
39. *Etz Hadar*, Jerusalem, 1907.
40. See his *Keren l'David*, Satmar, 1929, no. 156.
41. *Meshib Dabar*, II, following no. 50.
42. So, Ephraim Margolis, *Bet Ephraim*, no. 56.
43. *Heshek Shelomo*, I, no. 7.
44. Responsum of Yehiel Brody at the end of *Mitzpeh Aryeh*, I.
45. Aryeh-Lev of Brody, *Mitzpeh Aryeh*, I, no. 54.
46. See Yekuthiel Enzil of Stri, in his responsa, no. 52.
47. Responsum no. 54.
48. See *Toafot Re'em*, "Yore Deah," 1 and 2.
49. *Heshek Shelomo*, II, 1.
50. Number 3.
51. See his responsa, *Meshib kaHalakha*, "Yoreh Deah," 1.
52. See Chapter 6, pp. 233 ff.
53. Published at the end of *Yam ha-Talmud*, Lemberg, 1827. See above p. 92.
54. Published at the end of *Ha-Elef Lekho Shelomo*, pages 15 to 20, of the addendum.
55. Page 17, column 1.
56. *Dibre Hayyim*, I, "Orah Hayyim," no. 23.
57. See volume II of his *Dibre Hayyim*, "Orah Hayyim," nos. 1 and 2.
58. "Orah Hayyim," 35, volume II.
59. See his *Be'er Moshe*, no. 27, page 52. The letter is reprinted in the *S'de Hemed*, on page 194, after the laws of Hanukkah.
60. See no. 372 of "Orah Hayyim," part 2.
61. See the description in *S'de Hemed*, "Hometz u-Matzah," p. 98, column 1.
62. See a description of that situation in *S'de Hemed*, *l.c.*, 95, column 1.
63. See responsa of Maharsham, vol. II, no. 17, near the end.
64. See Boaz Cohen, 893, 1047, 1068.
65. *Ibid.*, 891.

5. HISTORY IN THE RESPONSA
Pp. 193–223

1. *Zemah Zedek*, no. 78.
2. In responsum no. 36.
3. See his *Helek Ya'akob*, vol. II, page 67, ff.
4. Ben-Zion Katz, *L'Korot ha-Yehudim*, Berlin, 1899; Simon Hurwitz, *The Responsa of Solomon Luria*, New York, 1938.

5. In his responsa no. 132, section 6.
6. See also the reference given from Joel Sirkes, New Series, no. 4, by Ben-Zion Katz; this is lacking from some editions which are abbreviated. See Katz, no. 7.
7. *Masat Binyamin*, no. 80.
8. Responsum no. 80.
9. Responsa, no. 1, p. 57, edition Warsaw, 1879.
10. *Sha'agat Aryeh v'Kol Shahal*, edition Neuwied, 1736, p. 30b.
11. Responsa, no. 120.
12. Responsa, no. 84.
13. *Yeven Metzula*.
14. *Bach*, Old Series, no. 27.
15. See *Bach*, Old Series, no. 61.
16. Nos. 35 and 36.
17. See his Responsa, no. 50.
18. See responsa, *Masat Binyamin*, no. 43.
19. *Hinukh Bet Yehudah*, no. 20.
20. Responsa, *Nahlat Shibea*, no. 70.
21. See note on page 37, column I (edition Fürth, 1692), in the parentheses.
22. I, no. 38.
23. See Joel Sirkes, *Bach*, New Series, no. 2.
24. Meir of Lublin, Responsa, no. 128.
25. Responsum no. 137.
26. *P'nei Yehoshua*, vol. II, no. 63.
27. No. 89.
28. No. 40.
29. Responsa, no. 69.
30. See also responsum no. 59, where a similar ceremony is described.
31. See *Masat Binyamin*, no. 16.
32. Roth, in *J.Q.R.*, N.S., vol. 22 (1931), pp. 1-36, summarized the religious life of the marranos as reflected in the Christian records.
33. The record of the marranos in the responsa literature has been discussed by H. J. Zimmels, *Die Marranen in der Rabbinischen Literatur*, Berlin, 1932, and by S. Assaf in an essay in his *B'Ohalei Ya'akob*, p. 145 ff.
34. See Chapter 2, above, p. 71.
35. No. 6.
36. Bayit, 24, ed. Constantinople; Bayit, 20, ed. Ostrow.
37. *Yakhin u-Boaz*, II, 19.
38. b. Sanhedrin 44a.
39. No. 11.
40. No. 43.
41. *Tashbez*, III, no. 47 and no. 43.
42. No. 39.
43. *Maharit*, "Eben ha-Ezer," no. 18.
44. P. 23a.

45. *Rashbash*, responsum no. 90.
46. See above, the responsum of Joseph Trani.
47. *Debar Shemuel*, no. 45.
48. b. Sanhedrin 74a.
49. *Ohel Ya'akob*, no. 3.
50. *P'nei Moshe*, I, no. 61.
51. See Chapter 8, below.

6. MODERN INVENTIONS
Pp. 227–242

1. For a discussion of many of these questions, see Berliner, *Ueber den Einfluss d. Hebr. Buchdrucks*, Frankfurt a/M, 1896. I. Z. Cahana, "Ha-Defus ba-Halakha," in *Sinai*, vol. 16, 1.
2. Responsa of Rashdam, "Yoreh Deah," no. 184.
3. *Masat Binyamin*, no. 99.
4. Responsa, *Havot Yair*, no. 184.
5. *Teshubah me-Ahabah*, III, 391.
6. Quoted in Joseph Messas, *Mayyim Hayyim*, no. 79.
7. In his responsa, *Keneset Yehezkel*, no. 37.
8. In his *Yad Sofer*, no. 5.
9. Responsa, *Maharsham*, III, 357.
10. *Eben Yekarah, Tinyana*, no. 33.
11. *Bet David*, no. 8.
12. See *Mar'ei Yehezkel*, no. 9.
13. Sanhedrin 96b.
14. *Bet Yitzhak*, "Eben ha-Ezer," no. 87.
15. *Maharsham*, III, no. 256.
16. Responsa, "Yoreh Deah," no. 170.
17. See, however, Greenwald, *Kol-Bo al Abelut*, p. 380, note 1.
18. b. Shabbat 42a.
19. *Bet Yitzhak*, "Yoreh Deah," I, 120 no. 5 and II, 31 no. 8.
20. *Tur*, "Orah Hayyim," 263.
21. Responsa, no. 18.
22. *Shulhan Arukh*, "Orah Hayyim," 275:1.
23. In his responsa, *Lebushei Mordecai, Tinyana*, "Orah Hayyim," no. 52.
24. In his responsa, *Maharshag*, I, no. 29.
25. In his responsa, *Maharsham*, II, no. 246.
26. In his responsa, *Mahazeh Abraham*, no. 42.
27. No. 51.
28. In his *Bet Yitzhak*, "Yoreh Deah," I, 120 no. 4.
29. b. Shabbat 42a.
30. *Ahiezer*, III, 60.
31. In his *Mishpetei Uziel*, "Orah Hayyim," nos. 5, 13, 21.
32. *Ma'archei Leb*, "Orah Hayyim," no. 5, also addendum no. 1.
33. See his responsa, *Tzitz Eliezer*, part II, no. 6.

34. Part I, no. 20, Chapter 9.
35. Part 2, no. 18.

7. CURIOUS RESPONSA

Pp. 245–264

1. Edition Warsaw, 1809, page 77 and footnote.
2. *Mahanei Hayyim*, II:1.
3. b. Sanhedrin 65b.
4. b. Berachot 47b.
5. "Orah Hayyim" 55:4, in the note of Moses Isserles.
6. *Ibid.*, 55:6.
7. In his responsa, no. 93.
8. *She'elot Yabetz*, no. 82.
9. *Eben Shoham*, no. 30, Pietrikow, 1910.
10. b. Succa 21 ff.
11. Oholot VIII, 4.
12. Such as the gloss to Asher ben Yechiel to the first chapter of the tractate Succot and *Neta' Sha'ashu'im*, by Zvi Hirsch of Buczacz (no. 11).
13. Erubin X, 13.
14. b. Erubin 103a.
15. "Laws on the Sabbath," Rule 44, no. 19.
16. *Yad Sofer*, no. 25; Budapest, 1939.
17. Responsa, no. 119.
18. To "Orah Hayyim," 340 no. 4.
19. Shabbat XII, 3.
20. "Orah Hayyim" 340 no. 4.
21. Rule 38, 5, Laws of the Sabbath.
22. *Z'kan Aharon*, II, no. 13.
23. *Hazon Nahum*, no. 31.
24. Shabbat XII, 3.
25. *Yad*, "Shabbat" XI, 17.
26. *Ibid.*, XI, 14, and based upon the Tosefta XI, 16.
27. "Yoreh Deah," 339:5.
28. I, 7, 1899.
29. The "Shakh."
30. b. Moed Katan 28a.
31. Responsa nos. 15 and 16.
32. *Va-Yelaket Yosef*, VIII, 15.
33. "Yoreh Deah," 3:1.
34. At the beginning of the Tosefta, Hullin.
35. No. 53.
36. "Yoreh Deah," 1. 5.
37. Pietrikoff, 1909, no. 3.
38. *Hullin* 142.
39. "Hoshen Mishpat," 209 no. 4.

40. b. Sota 21a.
41. *Midrash ha-Gadol, ad. loc.*
42. No. 2.
43. "Hoshen Mishpat," 334:3.

8. PROSPECTIVE DEVELOPMENT OF THE RESPONSA LITERATURE
Pp. 267–277

1. See Solomon Schechter, in *J.Q.R.*, O.S., IV (1892), 92.
2. Cf. Chapter 2, above.
3. Cf. Chapter 6, above.
4. See *Reform Jewish Practice*, vols. I and II, by Solomon B. Freehof, 1944 and 1952.
5. Ben-Zion Uziel, in *Mishpetei Uziel, Tinyana,* "Yore Deah," vol. II.

REFERENCE LIST
OF RESPONSA

Only the collections of responsa mentioned in the text and notes of this volume are listed here. The word "Responsa" is used in this list wherever the name of the volume is *She' elot u-Teshubot.*

ABOAB, SAMUEL, Debar Shemuel, Venice, 1702.
ABRAHAM OF SARCHOV, Abnei Nezer, 4 vols., Pietrikow, 1902 ff.
ADARBI, ISAAC, Dibrei Ribot, Sedilkow, 1813.
ARYEH B. SAMUEL, Sha'agat Aryeh v'Kol Shahal, Neuwied, 1736.
ASH, MEIR, Imrei Esh, 2 vols., Lemberg, 1852; Ungvar, 1864.
ASHKENAZI, GERSHON, Abodat ha-Gershuni, Frankfurt am Main, 1699.
ASHKENAZI, ZVI (Hakham Z'vi), Responsa, Lemberg, 1900.
ASSAD, JUDAH, Jehudah Ya'aleh, Lemberg, 1873; Pressberg, 1880.
AYYAS, JUDAH, Bet Yehudah, Leghorn, 1746.
BACHRACH, JAIR CHAIM, Havath Jair, Lemberg, 1894.
BAMBERGER, SELIGMAN BAER and his son SIMHA, Zekher Simha, Frankfurt-am-Main, 1925.
BENET, MORDECAI, Har ha-Mor, Prague, 1862.
BENVENISTI, MOSES, P'nei Moshe, 3 vols., Constantinople, 1669, 1671, 1719.
BERAB, JACOB, Responsa, Venice, 1663.
BERLIN, NAFTALI ZVI, Meshib Dabar, Warsaw, 1894.
BREISCH, MORDECAI JACOB, Helkat Ya'akob, Jerusalem, 1951.
BRODO, ARYEH LEV, Mitzpeh Aryeh, Lemberg, 1880.
CHAYES, ZVI HIRSCH, Minhat Kanaot, Zolkiew, 1840.
CHORIN, AARON, Imre No'am, Prague, 1798.
———, Shiryon Kashkashim, Prague, 1800.
COHEN, DAVID (RADAK), Responsa, Constantinople, 1537.
COHEN, SABBATAH (SHAKH), G'vuros Anashim, Dessau, 1697.
COLON, JOSEPH B. SOLOMON (MAHARIK), Responsa, Lemberg, 1798.
DEUTSCH, ELIEZER, Peri ha-Sadeh, 4 vols., Paks, 1906 ff.
DURAN, SIMON B. ZEMACH, Tashbetz, Amsterdam, 1738.
DURAN, SIMON AND ZEMACH, Yakhin u'Boaz, Leghorn, 1782.
DURAN, SOLOMON B. SIMON (RASHBASH), Responsa, Leghorn, 1742.

EIBESCHUETZ, JONATHAN, B'nei Ahubah, Prague, 1819.

EISENSTADT, MEIR, Panim Meirot, vol. 1, Amsterdam, 1718; vol. 2, Sulzbach, 1733; vol. 3, Sulzbach, 1738.

Eleh Dibrei ha-Berith (a collection), Altona, 1819.

EMDEN, JACOB, She'elat Yabetz, Lemberg, 1884.

ENOCH B. JUDAH, Hinukh bet Yehudah, Frankfurt-am-Main, 1708.

ENZIL, YEKUTHIEL, Responsa, Lemberg, 1882.

ETTINGER, ISAAC AARON, MAHARI Halevi, Lemberg, 1893.

ETTINGER, ISAAC AARON WITH NATHANSON, JOSEPH SAUL, M'farshe ha'Yam, Lemberg, 1827.

FLECKELES, ELAZAR, Teshubah Me'ahabah, 3 vols., Prague, 1809-1821.

FRANKEL, ABRAHAM WOLF, Meshib ka-Halakha, Cracow, 1885.

Gaonim Batrai, Turka, 1764.

GORDON, AARON, Eben Meir, Pietrikow, 1909.

GREENWALD, ELIEZAR DAVID, Keren l'David, Satmar, 1929.

GRODZINSKI, CHAIM OZER, Ahiezer, vol. III, New York, 1946.

HALBERSTAM, CHAIM, Dibre Hayyim, Lemberg, 1875.

HALEVI, SAMUEL B. DAVID, Responsa Nahalat Shive'a, Fuerth, 1692.

HAYYIM OF VOLOZHIN, Hut ha-Meshulash, Vilna, 1882.

HOFMANN, DAVID, Melamed le-Ho'il, Frankfurt am Main, 1926.

HORWITZ, ELAZAR, Yad Elazar, Vienna, 1870.

IBN HABIB, LEVI, Responsa, Lemberg, 1865.

IBN LABI, JOSEPH, Responsa, vols. 1-3, Constantinople, 1560-1573; vol. 4, Amsterdam, 1726.

IBN ZIMRA DAVID B. SOLOMON, (RADBAZ), Responsa, vol. I, II, Venice, 1749; vol. III, Fuerth, 1789; vol. IV, Sedilkow, 1846; vol. V, Leghorn, 1818.

ISAAC BAR SHESHET, Responsa, Lemberg, 1805.

ISSERLES, MOSES (RAMA), Responsa, Sedilkow, 1834.

ISSERLEIN, ISRAEL, Terumat ha-Deshen, Warsaw, 1882.

——, Lekket Yosher, Berlin, 1904.

JACOB B. MEIR (Rabbenu Tam), Sefer ha-Yashar, ed. F. Rosenthal, Berlin, 1898.

JERUSALEMSKI, MOSES, B'er Moshe, Warsaw, 1901.

JOSEPH HAYYIM B. ELIJAH, Rab Pe'alim, Jerusalem, 1901.

JOSHUA OF CRACOW, P'nei Yehoshua, Lemberg, 1860.

KALIR, ELAZAR, Heker Halacha, Muncacz, 1895.

KARO, JOSEPH, Abkat Rokhel, Leipzig, 1849.

KATZENELLENBOGEN, EZEKIEL, Keneset Yehezkel, Altona, 1732.

KLUGER, SOLOMON, Tub Ta'am v'Da'at, Lemberg, 1903; Podgurza, 1900.

——, Ha-Elef l'kha Shelomo, Lemberg, 1910.

——, Mo-da'ah l'Bet Yisrael, Breslau, 1859.

——, Sheyarei Taharah, Zolkiev, 1852.

KRIESHABER, ISAAC, Makel No'am, Vienna, 1798.
KROCHMAHL, MENAHEM MENDEL, Zemach Zedek, Lemberg, 1861.
LANDAU, EZEKIEL, Noda' bi-Yehudah, 2 vols., Stettin, 1861.
LEITER, WOLF, Bet David, Vienna, 1920.
LEVIN, B. M., Otzar ha-Geonim, 12 vols., K Haifa, 1928 ff.
LURIA, SOLOMON (MAHARSHAL), Responsa, Lemberg, 1859.
MARGOLIS, EPHRAIM Z., Bet Ephraim, Warsaw, 1884.
MEDINA, SAMUEL B. MOSES (RASHDAM), Responsa, 3 vols., Salonica, 1797-8.
MEIR B. BARUCH OF ROTHENBURG (MAHARAM m'Rothenburg), Responsa, Cremona, 1557; Sedilkow, 1832; Lemberg, 1860; Berlin, 1891; Budapest, 1895.
MEIR OF LUBLIN (MAHARAM Lublin), Responsa, Metz, 1769.
MENACHEM MENDEL OF LUBOVITCH, Zemach Zedek, New York, 1945.
MESSAS, JOSEPH, Mayyim Hayyim, Fez, 1911.
MIZRACHI, ELIJAH, Responsa, vol. I, Jerusalem, 1938; vol. II, Mayim Amukim, Berlin, 1788.
MOELLIN, JACOB (MAHARIL), Responsa, Cracow, 1881.
MOSES SOLOMON OF NASHALSK, Heshek Shelomo, Warsaw, 1888.
NATHANSON, JOSEPH SAUL, Sho'el u'Meshib, Lemberg, 1868 ff.
———, Bittul Moda'ah, (ed.) Lemberg, 1859.
NEHEMIAH OF DUBROVNA, Dibre Nehemiah, Vilna, 1866.
Nogah ha-Zedek (a collection), Dessau, 1818.
Or ha-Yashar (a collection), Amsterdam, 1769
Or Yisroel (a collection), Cleves, 1770.
PERELMUTTER, MOSES, Eben Shoham, Pietrikowi, 1910.
QUETCH, SOLOMON, Hokmat Shelomoh, published at the end of Har ha-Mor by Mordecai Benet, Prague, 1862.
RAPPAPORT, ABRAHAM, Etan ha-Ezrahi, Ostrow, 1796.
RASHI (SOLOMON B. ISAAC), Sefer ha-Ora, Lemberg, 1905.
———, Siddur Rashi, Berlin, 1911.
———, Mahzor Vitri, Berlin, 1896.
SASPORTAS, JACOB, Ohel Ya'akov, Amsterdam, 1737.
SCHICK, MOSES (MAHARAM Schick), Responsa, Lemberg, 1884; Satmar, 1904.
SCHMELKES, ISAAC, Bet Yitzhak, Pzemszl, 1875 ff.
SCHREIBER, SIMON, Hit-or'rot Teshubah, Budapest, 1928.
SCHWADRON, SHOLOM MORDECAI (MAHARSHAM), Responsa, vol. I, Warsaw, 1903; vol. II, Pietrikow, 1905; vol. IV, Pietrikow, 1917; vol. V, Satmar, 1926; vol. VI, Jerusalem, 1946.
SIRKES, JOEL (BACH), Responsa, 2 parts, Frankfurt-am-Main, 1697; Koretz, 1785.
SLONIK, BENJAMIN, Mas'at Binjamin, Sedilkow, 1833.

SOFER, ABRAHAM SAMUEL, K'tab Sofer, Pressberg, 1873 ff.

SOFER, HAYYIM B. MORDECAI, Mahaney Hayyim, vol. II, Muncacz, 1872.

SOFER MOSES, Hatam Sofer, 2 vols., Pressberg, 1855 ff.

SOFER, MOSES BEN SIMON, Yad Sofer, Budapest, 1939.

SOLOMON B. ADRET, Responsa, vol. I, Vienna, 1812; vol. II, Leghorn, 1657; vol. III, Leghorn, 1778; vol. IV, Vilna, 1881; vol. V, Leghorn, 1825; vol. VI-VII, Warsaw, 1868.

SONCINO, JOSHUA, Nahalah l'Yehoshua, Constantinople, 1731.

SPEKTOR, ISAAC ELHANAN, Be'er Yitzhak, Koenigsberg, 1858.

———, En Yitzhak, Vilna, 1889.

STEINBERG, ABRAHAM, Mahazeh Abraham, Brody, 1927.

STEINHART, JOSEPH, Zikhron Joseph, Fuerth, 1773.

TAUBES, AARON MOSES, To'afot Re'em, Zalkva, 1855.

TEOMIN ABRAHAM, at end of Jacob Lissa's Nahalat Ya'acob, Breslau, 1849.

TRANI, JOSEPH (MAHARIT), Responsa, 2 vols., Fuerth, 1768.

TRANI, MOSES (MABIT), Responsa, Lemberg, 1861.

UZIEL, BENZION, Mishp'te Uziel, Tel Aviv, 1935 ff.

WALDENBERG, ELIEZER JUDAH, Tzitz Eliezer, Jerusalem, 1947-1952.

WALKIN, AARON, Z'kan Aharon, New York, 1951.

WEIDENFELD, NAHUM, Hazon Nahum, New York, 1951.

WEIL, JACOB, Responsa, Hanau, 1610.

WEISS, BENJAMIN ARYEH, Eben Yekarah, Lemberg, 1894; 2nd part, Przemszl, 1902.

WINKLER, MORDECAI, Lebushei Mordecai Tinyana, Budapest, 1922.

Yerushat ha-Peletah (a collection), Budapest, 1946.

ZIRELSOHN, JEHUDA LEIB, Ma'arehei Leb, Kishenev, 1932.

INDEX

299